Women Against the Iron Fist

In Memory

of my father, H. L. Mence, 1902–1965, who refused to strike-break in London in 1926 and was sacked in consequence, and of my teacher the late Professor Winston Rhodes, 1905–1987, of the University of Canterbury, New Zealand.

Women Against the Iron Fist

Alternatives to Militarism 1900–1989

Sybil Oldfield

I don't think there's much point talking about the past unless we also talk about the future.

Dr Adelaide Hautval (former slave-doctor in Auschwitz who refused to carry out Nazi orders)
The Listener, 21 Oct. 1971

Basil Blackwell

First published 1989

Basil Blackwell Ltd
108 Cowley Road, Oxford, OX4 1JF, UK

Basil Blackwell Inc.
3 Cambridge Center
Cambridge, Massachusetts 02142, USA

British Library Cataloguing in Publication Data

A CIP catalogue record for this book is available from The British Library.

Library of Congress Cataloging in Publication Data
Oldfield, Sybil.
Women against the iron fist : alternatives to militarism. 1900 to 1989/Sybil Oldfield.
p. cm.
Includes index.
ISBN 0-631-14878-7 (Hbk) 0-631-14879-5 (Pbk)
1. Women and peace. I. Title.
JX1965.043 1989
327.1'72'082—dc20 89–34962
CIP

Typeset in 11 on 13 pt Imprint
by Photo·graphics, Honiton, Devon
Printed in Great Britain by T.J. Press (Padstow) Ltd.

Contents

Acknowledgements

I am grateful to the following people and institutions who have kindly given permission to reproduce material originally published or owned by them:*

Edition Christian Brandstätter, Vienna, for the German propaganda postcard;

Historia-Photo, Hamburg, for the photograph of German women munitions workers;

Imperial War Museum, London, for the photograph of British munitions workers;

National Portrait Gallery, London, for the photograph of Kate Courtney;

Oorlogsmuseum, Bloemfontein, for the photograph of a child victim at the Bloemfontein concentration camp;

Mary Evans Picture Library for the photograph of Maude Royden;

Mrs Helen Blackstone for permission to quote from Maude Royden's writings, including her unpublished memoir, *Bid Me Discourse*;

Oxford University Press for excerpts from *Simone Weil: Seventy Letters* (ed.) Rees, and *Selected Essays* (ed.) Rees;

Routledge & Kegan Paul for excerpts from Simone Weil's *Oppression and Liberty* and *The Need for Roots*;

*The author and publisher have made every effort to trace the copyright holders of the material quoted in this book. Should the rights of any copyright holder be infringed, we shall be pleased to make all due acknowledgements in future editions.

Professor Quentin Bell for the page from Virginia Woolf's Third Scrapbook for *Three Guineas*, now in the Documents Section, University of Sussex Library;

Professor Quentin Bell and Hogarth Press/Chatto & Windus for the Gisèle Freund portrait of Virginia Woolf taken from Ian Parsons and George Spater, *A Marriage of True Minds* (1977);

Familienarchiv, copyright Inge Aicher-Scholl, for the photograph of Sophie Scholl;

Wesleyan University Press for excerpts from Inge Scholl, *Students Against Tyranny: The Resistance of the White Rose 1942–43* (1970);

Harper & Row for excerpts from Sophie Scholl's diary and letters (ed.) Inge Jones, translated as *At the Heart of the White Rose* (1987);

Virago Press for excerpts from the translation of Christa Wolf, *Cassandra: A Novel and Four Essays*; translation copyright © Farrar, Straus, and Giroux Inc. 1984;

International Creative Management for the poems of Muriel Rukeyser;

New Directions for the poems of Denise Levertov;

Random House for the poems of Sharon Olds;

The poem 'When' by Sharon Olds first appeared in *New England Review* and *Bread Loaf Quarterly*, Middlebury, Vermont (Summer 1983);

Norwegian Embassy for the photograph of the Norwegian Prime Minister, Gro Brundtland.

I am also grateful for the assistance given me by the Fawcett Archive, City of London Polytechnic, Bibliothèque Marguerite Durand, Paris, the interlibrary loan section of the University of Sussex Library, and the Archivist, British Library of Political and Economic Science, London School of Economics. This book was researched with financial assistance from the Norman Angell Research Fund, University of Sussex. Finally, without the capable and committed secretarial assistance of Catherine Beatty and Janet Grundy, and the meticulous editing skills of Caroline Bundy, this book could not have been completed.

Preface

The twentieth century has seen a great tradition of dissident male thinkers – men who have dared to advocate anti-militarism and internationalist humanism; they include Tolstoy, Romain Rolland, Keir Hardie, Norman Angell, Liebknecht, Barbusse, Nansen, Hesse, Gorki, Schweitzer, Ernst Toller, Gandhi, Kraus, Tagore, Einstein, Bertrand Russell, Albert Luthuli and Martin Luther King. All these men have been honoured, even though they have not been heeded. But the many women who have also testified in our century to anti-militaristic, internationalist humanism, sometimes at the risk of their lives, have hardly as yet managed to make themselves heard. This book will attempt to give some of these women their due. What it will not do is to claim that women as a sex have been any more consistently anti-militarist than men. Most women, like most men throughout recorded history, have always accepted, however regretfully, the periodic necessity for war. Only a few men and women have perceived that war itself is, almost always, the ultimate evil.

To be opposed to war might seem to be as banal as to think ill of evil. But war has not always been considered evil in our century – far from it – and still today even a nuclear war is not yet universally acknowledged to be the worst of all evils. The legitimation of 'the iron fist', the myth of war-prevention by war-preparedness, the preferability of death to defeat are still with us. Too many rulers the world over are still thinking like Bismarck. Therefore these essays on some of the outstanding twentieth-century women implacably opposed to the legitimation of war have to begin by illustrating and analysing the potent ideology of Bismarckian militaristic *Realpolitik* before 1914.

Part I

The National Virility Test of War

1

The Dubious Legacy of Bismarck and von Treitschke

'Generally speaking, militarism flourishes more in peacetime than in war.'

Alfred Vagts, *A History of Militarism*

Throughout the 1930s Virginia Woolf pondered the question: 'How are we to prevent war?' She came to the conclusion that war will not be prevented for as long as men in power continue to exclude women's socially constructed, traditional values of the private life – including the value of every irreplaceable individual – from the citadels of national and international decision-making. For as long as the Creons continue to shut the Antigones away, including the Antigone within themselves,[1] there will be 'no alternative' to war. On 2 January 1940 Virginia Woolf wrote to Shena, Lady Simon: 'mustn't our [women's] next task be the emancipation of man? How can we alter the crest and spur of the fighting cock? . . . So many of the young men, could they get prestige and admiration, would give up glory and develop what's now so stunted – I mean the life of natural happiness.'[2]

[1] Virginia Woolf, *Three Guineas*, Hogarth Press, 1938, Part III. Creon, king of Thebes, sentenced his niece Antigone to be immured until she died of hunger and thirst for disobeying his order prohibiting the burial of her traitor brother. She chose death rather than allow the state to forbid compassion. See Sophocles' *Antigone*.

[2] N. Nicolson (ed.), *Leave the Letters Till We're Dead: The Letters of Virginia*

In her 'Thoughts on peace in an air-raid' (written 2 Sept. 1940), Virginia Woolf expanded on her conviction that women in the future must try to help men to emancipate themselves from their need to identify masculinity with aggression and domination: 'We must create more honourable activities for those who try to conquer in themselves their fighting instinct, their subconscious Hitlerism. We must compensate the man for the loss of his gun . . . we must give him access to the creative feelings . . . We must free him from the machine.'[3] Finally, just a few weeks before her suicide, Virginia Woolf wrote again to Lady Simon, but this time in despair: 'No, I don't see what's to be done about war. Its manliness; and manliness breeds womanliness – both so hateful.'[4]

How right was Virginia Woolf to diagnose gender-stereotyping and, above all, the *manliness* of war, as its most stubbornly-rooted trait in our collective psyches? Did men in power before World War I consistently identify their highest good (or God) with the supremacy of their collective masculinity, the state – a supremacy established whenever necessary by killing competition in the name of 'patriotism' or 'Patrie' or 'Fatherland'? And did the mass of men and women not in power before 1914 agree with their leaders in finding warfare manly?

The most important nineteenth-century statesman for whom military might was self-evidently right was Bismarck. Bismarck dominated German and European politics for nearly 30 years between 1860 and 1890 and his legacy was to be fatal both to Germany and to the world in the twentieth century as well. Bismarck's boasted realism (or *Realpolitik*) was simply his often-asserted conviction that the only practical political reality is power and that the sole ultimate source of power is physical force – or, less politely, the capacity to kill. Morality is secondary, a means to be manipulated rather than a guide or a goal for political action. 'To his coldly realistic eye that which existed was neither the patrimonial state nor the state of Laws, but the power-state [*Machtstaat*].'[5] As Bismarck himself wrote: '[In]

Woolf, 1936–1941, Hogarth Press, 1980.

3 Virginia Woolf, 'Thoughts on peace in an air-raid', in *The Death of the Moth*, Hogarth Press, 1942 (published posthumously).

4 Nicolson, *Leave the Letters*.

5 Otto Pflanze, 'Bismarck's *Realpolitik*', *Review of Politics*, Oct. 1958. See also Erich

politics I do not believe it possible to follow principle in such a way that its most extreme implications always take precedence over every other consideration.'[6] In domestic politics, the state – or *Machtstaat* – is controlled by whomsoever has the power of the army, the police and the means of communication behind him or her. In international politics, the militarily strongest state will always be dominant. 'In foreign affairs he also concluded that the final arbiter between states was not a legal instrument, such as the treaties of 1815 or the German confederation, but the possession of superior force.'[7]

Thus Bismarck was one of the very first social Darwinians, declaring: 'It is a principle of creation and of the whole of nature that life consists of strife . . . through the insects to the birds, from birds of prey up to man himself; strife is everywhere. Without struggle there can be no life and, if we wish to continue living, we must also be reconciled to further struggles.'[8] As early as 1850 Bismarck had declared to the Prussian Diet: 'Just show me an objective worth a war, gentlemen, and I will agree with you.'[9] In 1861 he said: 'Hammer the Poles until they wish they were dead . . . if we want to exist we have no choice but to wipe them out.'[10] A year later Bismarck articulated Prussia's claim to dominate a united Germany *because* it was Prussia alone that possessed the necessary war-machine of blood and iron – both the source and the validation of power:

> Germany does not look to Prussia's liberalism, but to its power; Bavaria, Württemberg, and Baden may indulge in liberalism; but no-one will assign them Prussia's role because of that . . . The great questions of the time will not be resolved by speeches

Eyck, *Bismarck after Fifty Years*, George Philip and Son, London, 1948; J. C. G. Röhl, *From Bismarck to Hitler*, Longman, 1970, Introduction; Edward Crankshaw, *Bismarck*, Macmillan, 1981, chs. 11 and 20; and, most important of all, F. Fischer, *From Kaiserreich to Third Reich: Elements of Continuity in German History, 1871–1945*, Allen & Unwin, 1986.

[6] Letter to Gerlach, quoted in Otto Pflanze, *Bismarck and the Development of Germany*, Princeton UP, 1983, ch. 3.

[7] Pflanze, 'Bismarck's *Realpolitik*'.

[8] Pflanze, *Bismarck and Germany*.

[9] ibid.

[10] Peter Vansittart, *Voices 1870–1914*, Cape, 1984.

> and majority decisions – that was the great mistake of 1848 and 1849 – but by iron and blood.[11]

During the 1870 Franco-Prussian War Bismarck called war 'the natural condition of mankind' and five years later he could proudly assert that the whole German nation had now become 'Prussianized':

> We Germans fear God, and nothing else on earth [loud shouts of Bravo!]; and it is the fear of God which makes us love and cherish peace. But whoever violates peace will realise that the *war-like patriotism*, which in 1813 called the whole population of the then tiny, weak and impoverished Prussia to the colours, *is now a common attribute of the whole German nation*, and that he who attacks the German nation in any way will find them armed and united, and every soldier with the firm belief in his heart, 'God will be on our side.' [Loud and long applause, during which Count Moltke goes up to the Chancellor and congratulates him on his speech.][12]

Finally, during his enforced retirement, Bismarck actually claimed a moral as well as a rational justification for war, even invoking the superhuman in his adage: 'War is a moral medicine used by Nature when she has no other way of restoring people to the right path.'[13]

Bismarck's 'right path' was a synthesis of nationalism, militarism and authoritarianism – still a potent brew in politics today. He quelled all opposition during his Chancellorship by his apparent pragmatic success. His grasp of what constitutes reality, both in politics and in life, seemed unassailable. However, twentieth-century enthusiasts for the 'iron-fisted' approach of coercion by threat or coercion by war might reflect that the Hohenzollern dynasty Bismarck made absolute was dethroned 30 years later, that the Prussia he promoted was wiped off the map in 1945 and that the Germany he united and strengthened is now divided and occupied for the foreseeable future.

As Bismarck himself admitted in his old age: 'In politics there is

[11] F. B. M. Hollyday (ed.), *Bismarck*, Prentice-Hall, 1970.
[12] W. N. Medlicott and Dorothy Coveney (eds), *Bismarck and Europe*, Arnold, 1971; my emphasis.
[13] Vansittart, *Voices 1870–1914*.

no such thing as complete certainty and definitive results.'[14]

But if one can never be sure of the end, how can one justify dubious (or downright evil) means?

To Bismarck's disciple Heinrich von Treitschke, however, war was neither dubious nor evil. Treitschke was Bismarck's most effective publicist and his pamphlets and articles had already stimulated expansionist German nationalism in the 1860s. In 1864 Treitschke had backed the annexation of Schleswig-Holstein and in 1870 that of Alsace-Lorraine: 'These lands are ours by the right of the sword and by virtue of a higher right, the right of the German nation . . . We Germans . . . understand better what is good for the Alsaciens than those unfortunate people themselves . . . Against their own will we wish to give them back their true selves.'[15]

From 1874 until his death in 1896 Treitschke held the Chair of History at Berlin University and for each of those 22 years he repeated his series of lectures on politics, *Die Politik*, in which he did not argue but simply asserted (as Bismarck himself had also done) the self-evident rightness of power rooted in military supremacy. Treitschke lectured each new academic generation of young German males on the *vir*tus, that is, the essential *virility* of war. Time and again he hammered home his equations: war = manliness, peace = effeminacy, and in doing so he presented himself as one who was now revealing a truth too long forgotten:

> [After internal law and order] the next essential function of the State is the conduct of war. The long oblivion into which this principle has fallen is a proof of how effeminate the science of government has become in civilian hands. Without war no State could be . . . every sovereign State has proved that it is war which turns a people into a nation . . . The men of action are the real heroes of history . . . The features of history are virile, unsuited to sentimental or feminine natures . . . the weak and cowardly perish and perish justly . . . The grandeur of war lies in the utter annihilation of puny man in the great conception of the State . . . the chaff is winnowed from the wheat. To Aryan races, who are before all things courageous, the foolish

[14] Pflanze, *Bismarck and Germany*, ch. 4.

[15] *Preussische Jahrbücher*, 26 (1870), quoted in Pflanze, *Bismarck and Germany*, ch. 20.

The harvest of Bismarckism – militarism identified with virility. German postcard *c.*1915.

> preaching of everlasting peace has always been vain. They have always been men enough to maintain with the sword what they have attained through the spirit.[16]

And so forth and so forth. The sexism and racism of Treitschke's admiration for manly Aryans had already been anticipated by Bismarck in his ruminations on 'the Teutons' in 1868:

> As in nature itself, some nations are masculine and others feminine. The Teutons are so masculine that, taken individually, they are quite ungovernable. Each conducts his life as he pleases. But when they are rallied together they are irresistible, like a torrent which destroys everything in its path. Feminine, on the other hand, are the Slavs and the Celts. Of their own accord they can do nothing, they are not productive . . . Among the Prussians there is a strong mixture of Slavic and Teutonic

[16] Heinrich von Treitschke, *Politics*, Bk I, *The Idea of the State* (translated and published in London in 1916 as British anti-German war propaganda).

elements. That is one main cause of their usefulness to the State. They have something of the subordinate character of the Slavs and yet something of the strength and manliness of the Teutons.[17]

'Femininity', for Bismarck, thus meant passivity and the inability to be productive; its only useful quality was its penchant for subordination. As political generalization his remarks are beneath serious consideration, but they do reveal a profound – and significant – contempt for women's contribution to life. What function did women have in Treitschke's view of politics? Implicitly, women existed in order to bring forth and rear those 'men of action who alone make history'. Explicitly, Treitschke insisted on the necessity for women to fulfil a still humbler function: 'The masses must for ever remain the masses. There would be no culture without kitchen-maids.' Moreover, according to Treitschke, women are also the *intellectual* handmaids of men: 'It may be said roughly that the normal woman obtains an insight into justice and government through men's eyes, just as the normal man has no natural aptitude for petty household management.'[18] Thus, from Treitschke's own perspective, if 'justice' and 'government' are *not* to go on subserving war, as he confidently predicted, 'until the end of history' – then 'justice' and 'government' will need to be redefined. And they will need to be redefined not by 'the normal man' but by abnormal men and women who do not obtain all their insights into politics through the eyes of conventional-minded Treitschkean men. For without intellectual kitchen-maids, as Virginia Woolf was later to point out, there can indeed be no Treitschkean culture of rival patriotic patriarchies: 'If we could free ourselves from slavery we should free men from tyranny' ('Thoughts on peace in an air-raid').

This Bismarck-Treitschkean tradition of the exaltation of war as a natural part of the divine scheme, morally right and 'essentially virile', did indeed become part of 'normal' male thinking, backed up by 'normal' women, in much of Europe between 1890 and 1914, with tragic consequences that are not over yet. Germany's naval warlord, for example, Admiral von Tirpitz, the builder of the

[17] Röhl, *Bismarck to Hitler*.
[18] Treitschke, *Politics*.

'Ironclads' and the initiator of U-boat warfare, was a devoted ex-student of Treitschke, whom he called 'that splendid man' and who, he said, had 'given me private advice'. In France, even the once-radical humanitarian Emile Zola agreed with Treitschke, writing in *Le Figaro* in 1891: 'War is life itself. Nothing exists in nature, is born, grows or multiplies except by combat. We must eat and be eaten so that the world may live. It is only warlike nations which have prospered: a nation dies as soon as it disarms. War is the school of discipline and courage.'[19]

One wonders what the function of sexual intercourse, pregnancy, parturition and the rearing of the young can possibly be if indeed 'nothing exists in nature, is born, grows or multiplies except by combat'. And General Count von Moltke, yet another enthusiastic former student of Professor Treitschke, went even beyond Zola in his praise of war: 'Perpetual peace is a dream, and not even a beautiful dream. War is an element of the divine order of the world. In it are developed the noblest virtues of man – courage and self-denial, fidelity to duty and the spirit of sacrifice. Without war the world would stagnate and lose itself in materialism.'[20] Thus war is not just good, it is the source of all good – all idealism. Logically, one might suppose, humans should never stop killing one another lest they lose their 'noblest virtues'. Indeed, to the German patriot Bernhardi in 1912, peace appeared 'almost a state of depravity'. Nietzsche, in his less sane moments, agreed: 'I advise you that not work but war, war and bravery, have done more glorious deeds than love for one's kin . . . A good war justifies any cause . . . Men should be trained for war and women for the recreation of the warrior: all else is folly.'[21] Klaus Wagner's *Krieg* (*War*; 1906) echoed Nietzsche:

> War is the natural sifting! War is the law of nature. War is the bottom basis of rightful realisation in the future. War is the creative principle of the world. With this we reach the cardinal point of our thought. Society is driven to war by want of nourishment and by hunger for labour-to-war, for the protection

[19] James Joll, 'The mood of 1914', in *Origins of the First World War*, Longman, 1984.
[20] Brian Bond, *War and Society in Europe, 1870–1970*, Fontana, 1984, ch. 1.
[21] Friedrich Nietzsche, *Thus Spake Zarathustra*, Dent, 1933.

> of race and culture and to get steeled now and in future to war, in order to live and to grow. Such is the purpose of war for which we labour. Men work with aim and object. War promotes the right vigour of life at the expense of bad aimlessness concerning the future; war makes life. Such is the salvation of war.[22]

In other words, humans must wage war in order to wage war – war for war's sake. Kaiser Wilhelm II was sufficiently carried away to tell his young naval recruits: 'If your Emperor orders it, you must open fire on your own father and mother.' And in 1910 he ordered the formation of a kind of German boys' army, resulting in the Jungdeutschlandbund of 1911, which declared: 'War is beautiful . . . We must wait for it with the manly knowledge that when it strikes, it will be more beautiful and more wonderful to live for ever among the heroes on a war memorial in a church than to die an empty death in bed, nameless.'[23] Just before August 1914, the *Jungdeutschland Buch* for German boys, by Scherl, declared in its chapter on war: 'We, at [the Kaiser's] call, may take up our arms with light and happy hearts and rejoice in war. Let us, therefore, laugh heartily at the old women in trousers who are afraid of war and death, and so murmur that it is cruel and ugly. No, war is beautiful. Its majestic magnitude lifts the heart of man above that which is earthly, out of the everyday.'[24]

The period before 1914 witnessed an ever-escalating male militarism not only in Germany but throughout Europe as boys joined para-military youth groups, older civilians paraded in their Reserve Officers' uniforms and the length of conscription was extended. '[A] spell with the colours became the introduction to manhood.'[25] But just playing at war by preparing for it, (and vice versa), were not enough – as General Ludendorff was ominously to indicate in July 1914: 'I am thirsty for a man's work to accomplish and it will in full measure be awarded me.'[26] (Ludendorff was to become the *de*

[22] Caroline Playne, *The Neuroses of Nations*, Allen & Unwin, 1925, Part I, ch. 4.
[23] Bond, *War and Society*.
[24] Playne, *Neuroses of Nations*, Part I, ch. 4.
[25] Victor Kiernan 'Conscription and society in Europe before the war of 1914–1918', in M. R. D. Foot (ed.), *War and Society*, Elek, 1973.
[26] Peter Vansittart, *Voices from the Great War*, Cape, 1981.

facto military dictator of Germany in 1917 and was later to be of immense if not indeed of essential assistance to the rise of the Nazi Party.) In France, children were constantly taught the superiority of the French to the Germans and schoolboys actually petitioned the President in favour of an extension of compulsory military service from two to three years. In 1912 Abel Bonnard wrote: 'We must embrace [war] in all its wild poetry. When a man throws himself into it, it is not just his own instincts that he is rediscovering, but virtues which he is recovering . . . It is in war that all is made new.'[27] Meanwhile, the all-too aptly named Futuristic Manifesto drafted by Marinetti in Italy in 1909 proclaimed: 'We want to glorify war – the world's only hygiene – militarism, deed, destructor of anarchisms, the beautiful ideas that are death-bringing, and the contempt of woman.' That Manifesto reads like an extraordinary premonition of the woman-despising necrophilia of fascism. 'Viva la muerte,' said Franco's generals in Spain, while Hitler's special SS elite in occupied Europe were to wear the death's head for their emblem as they machine-gunned hundreds and thousands of women and children into open graves.[28]

Neither were the British immune – it was, after all, their Empire's great hour. Lord Roberts, the Commander-in-Chief of the British Army, was another of those who thought of war as a 'tonic'. Between 1899 and 1902 the Boer War was to rouse frenzies of popular Imperial xenophobia and war-lust in Britain, and in 1907, Kipling, the poet of the British Empire, fantasized about a society which would start to drill its boys for the army from the age of six until at last they were 'magnificent men marching in sunlight'.[29] In 1905, General Baden-Powell urged British boys, then reared on a diet of Henty and Rider Haggard, to emulate the bushido of Japanese soldiers in their willingness to die for their Emperor: 'Be prepared', the motto of the 'real true Scout' meant 'Be prepared to die for your country.'[30]

[27] James Joll, *Origins*. See also Playne, *Neuroses of Nations*, Part II for a summary of French chauvinist militarism in E. Psichari's *L'Appel des armes* and M. Lavader's *Servir* (1913).
[28] For the evidence during the Eichmann trial, see Vera Laska, *Women in the Resistance and in the Holocaust*, Greenwood, 1983.
[29] Alfred Vagts, *A History of Militarism*, Meridian/Hollis & Carter, 1959, ch. 13, 'The militarism of the civilians'.
[30] Bond, *War and Society*, ch. 3.

And the writer H. H. Munro, alias Saki, summed up the essential *boyishness* of war thus: 'Nearly every red-blooded human boy has had war, in some shape or form, for his first love; if his blood has remained red and he has kept some of his boyishness in after life, that first love will never have been forgotten.'[31]

As we all know, in August 1914 almost 'every red-blooded boy' in Germany, France, Austria, Russia and Britain was indeed only too well psychologically prepared to die for his country. Unsuspectingly he bartered his new conviction of patriotic purpose and male comradeship in exchange for the risk of being dismembered, disembowelled, blinded, burned or blown up – and for the obligation of doing the same to others. This inversion of values had reached such a pitch by 1914 that peace could now seem not the basis for all life but rather death-in-life, while it was war that promised 'real living'. 'War seemed to offer the antithesis of materialism and mechanisation . . . complete liberation from the constricting bourgeois world . . . [and] a return to a healthy open-air life.'[32] The illusion would have been ludicrous had it not also been so ghastly. The poet Julian Grenfell, in his verses 'Into Battle', took Zola's assertion that 'War is Life' to its logical conclusion: 'he is dead who will not fight.' He himself, like so many of his contemporaries on both sides of the conflict, volunteered for the war as if it were in fact just an exhilarating boyish escapade: 'I *adore* war. It's like a big picnic without the objectlessness of a picnic.'[33] And L. T. Hobhouse wrote home: 'Preparing to fight in time of war is the greatest game and the finest work in the world.'[34] No wonder the leading British suffragist Helena Swanwick should have felt in 1914 that 'men had dropped their end of the burden of living. Many of the best men in every country [foreswore] their culture, their humanity, their intellectual efforts . . . to wallow in the delights of regimentation, brainlessness, [and] the primitive delights of destruction!'[35]

But in the final analysis it was not men who had betrayed *humanitas* in 1914; they themselves had been betrayed by the brutalizing ethos of militaristic masculinism and by the crude social

[31] Vansittart, *Voices from the Great War*.
[32] Bond, *War and Society*, ch. 3.
[33] Nicholas Mosley, *Julian Grenfell*, Weidenfeld & Nicolson, 1976, p. 239.
[34] Joll, *Origins*.
[35] Helena Swanwick, *I Have Been Young*, Gollancz, 1935.

Some of the 900,000 German women involved in making shells, 1918.

Darwinism to which both men and women had for so long been exposed. As Helena Swanwick herself admitted: 'In one sense, men had made the war. But they couldn't have made it if the mass of women had not been admiringly, even adoringly with them.'[36] Caroline Playne went even further:

> The souls of women were as much possessed by passion as the souls of men. It often appeared as though their case were worse; that the minds of women were more fixed in the strange belief that the infinite calamity of war 'had to be'. Their version of the patriotic creed demanded the destruction of the enemy and his belongings, even at the cost of the destruction of their own life and belongings. With humanity blotted out by the dense

[36] ibid.

Nearly a million British women were involved in munitions manufacture between 1916 and 1918.

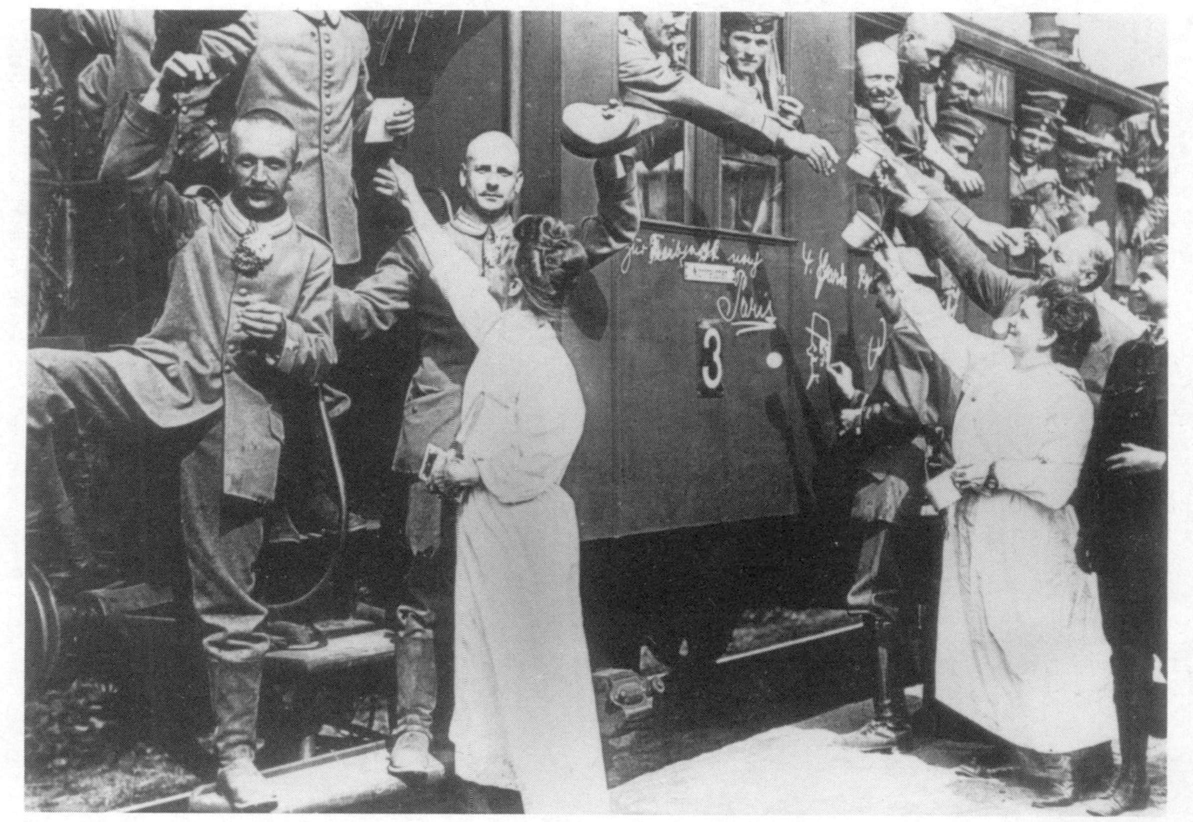

'Young people – but old as well – were reporting themselves as volunteers, soldiers were going off with songs and jokes, wives and girls were . . . throwing flowers over them' von Gerlach, 1 August 1914 (Playne, 1925). Or, as Saki's sister, Ethel Monro, wrote to him in 1916, 'Kill a good few for me.'

> fumes of nationalist fervour, women in their distraction offered themselves up on the funeral pyres of all they normally held most dear, whilst the frenzied world applauded, praising their courage and endurance.[37]

Thus German women were photographed in 1914 sending off the men on their 'free trip to Paris' and millions of women on all sides of the war made the shells that killed the men.

It is now time to attend to some of the few women who did not agree with the mass.

[37] Caroline Playne, *Society at War 1914–16*, Allen & Unwin, London, 1931, ch. 4.

Part II

Alternative Models

2

The Enemy's Friend: Kate Courtney (1847–1929)

> Is there no voice of insight and goodness strong enough to save the world?
>
> Kate Courtney, *War Diary*, 11 March 1918

A high proportion of Europe's women suffragists and radicals were anti-militarists who opposed World War I. Many of these women later published their own accounts of their anti-war struggle – for instance Lida Gustava Heymann in *Erlebtes, erschautes* (*Things lived through and seen*), Sylvia Pankhurst in *The Home Front* and Helena Swanwick in *I Have Been Young*. And recent studies have come out on their great precursor, Bertha von Suttner, on Rosa Luxemburg, on Mrs Despard, Selina Cooper, Catherine Marshall, Rozika Schwimmer and Mary Sheepshanks, as well as on their American counterparts, Jane Addams, Emily Greene Balch, Crystal Eastman and Helen Keller.[1] But Kate, Lady Courtney of Penwith, is still almost unknown today.

[1] See, for example, Gisela Brinker-Gabler, *Kämpferin für den Frieden: Bertha von Suttner*, Fischer, 1982; Frederik Hetmann, *Rosa L*, Fischer, 1979; Andros Linklater, *Charlotte Despard: An Unhusbanded Life*, Hutchinson, 1980; Jill Liddington, *Selina Cooper: The Life of a Respectable Rebel*, Virago, 1984; Jo Vellacott, *Bertrand Russell and the No Conscription Fellowship* (for Catherine Marshall); Anne Wiltsher, *Most Dangerous Women*, Pandora, 1987 (for Rozika Schwimmer); Sybil Oldfield, *Spinsters of this Parish*, Virago, 1984 (for Mary Sheepshanks); Allen Davis, *American Heroine: The Life and Legend of Jane Addams*, OUP, 1973; Mercedes Randall, *Improper Bostonian* (for Emily Greene Balch), Irvington, 1964; Blanche

Kate Courtney was born Kate Potter, one of the many older sisters of the famous Fabian Socialist Beatrice Webb. Not beautiful and not obviously clever, Kate Potter was never in any danger of 'thinking a little too well of herself'. For a long time she was very unhappy at home, both as a girl and as a young woman, because she wanted to do something practical about other people's misery, but her class dictated that she merely practise 'self-improvement' and wait for a suitable marriage proposal. At last, when she was 28, she was permitted to leave her wealthy family and begin social work in Whitechapel – one of the poorest parts of London. She worked first under the supervision of the housing reformer Octavia Hill, and then with Samuel and Henrietta Barnett, founders of Toynbee Hall and pioneers of city 'Settlement' work. Kate Potter had such an endearing warmth about her, such real respect for other people and such a palpable anxiety not to hurt, that she managed to humanize even her unlovable role of rent-collector there. In 1880, when she was 33, she was introduced to the Liberal cabinet minister Leonard Courtney, who was first attracted to her, as he later confessed, by her hearty laugh. Kate Potter soon came to love him, but doubted for a long time whether 'her great friend', as she thought of him, cared equally for her. Three years later, however, his middle-aged caution was overcome and they were married – cheered on by her scores of well-wishers from Whitechapel. The Courtneys' marriage, although childless, turned out to be a great success – 'Kate is wonderfully happy, always in the highest spirits, strong in his strength and basking in his warm affection.'[2]

Both the Courtneys were staunch Liberals and deeply committed to the achievement of international peace. Their first real testing-time on the peace-or-war issue came with the outbreak of the Boer War in October 1899, a war that was provoked by the British in order to establish, in the words of the Prime Minister Lord Salisbury, 'that we not the Dutch are Boss'.[3] Every war brings the next war a little nearer. The Boer War contributed its part to World War I and even to World War II, by setting aside the growing international

Wiesen Cook (ed.), *Crystal Eastman on Women and Revolution*, OUP, 1978; and Joseph P. Lash, *Helen and Teacher*, Penguin, 1980 (for Helen Keller).

[2] Beatrice Webb, *Diary, 1882*, Vol. I, 1873–1892, Virago, 1982.

[3] Quoted by Andrew Porter, 'British imperial policy and South Africa (1895–9)', in Peter Warwick (ed.), *The South African War*, Longman, 1980.

Kate Courtney

inhibition against going to war as a mode of settling disputes; the Boer War constituted a devastating reverse to the international peace movement, erupting as it did only a few months after the first Hague Peace Conference of 1899.[4] Secondly, the Boer War, like every other war, institutionalized and reinforced the 'positive' value of masculinist militarism:

> When the Tommy joins the 'unt
> With the stabbin' of the baynit,
> The Baynit, the bloody baynit,
> Gawd 'elp the man in front![5]

Thirdly the war stimulated widespread (and lasting) righteous hatred of Britain as an imperialist bully – especially in Germany, where 'English people were spat upon in the streets.'[6] Finally, British policy in the Boer War established what was generally considered to be a horrific precedent for the treatment of enemy non-combatants.[7]

The Boer War was at first an intensely popular war in Britain. 'Large cheering crowds lined the streets as soldiers marched from barracks to embark for South Africa, and when on 22 October the Guards set out for war there was a crowd assembled of such proportions they could scarcely make their way through it.[8] Kitchener's mode of conducting the war, however, including his 'scorched earth' policy, the internment of civilians in military camps and the imposition of martial law in annexed areas ('methods of barbarism', in the phrase of the Liberal opposition leader, Campbell-Bannerman) all stimulated a growing protest movement within Britain against the war. This movement was labelled, inaccurately but all the more damagingly, 'pro-Boer' and it was treated with a passionate hostility that often culminated in violence: 'Outspoken critics of the war had windows and property smashed, noses bloodied, and meetings broken up by drunken mobs, while the police merely

[4] The Hague Conference on Peace and Disarmament was summoned by Tsar Nicholas II of Russia in May 1899.

[5] Quoted by Malvern van Wyk Smith, 'The poetry of the War', in Warwick, *South African War*.

[6] Ethel Smyth (in Berlin during the Boer War), *Female Pipings in Eden*, Peter Davies, 1933, p. 39.

[7] See S. B. Spies, *Methods of Barbarism?*, Human & Rousseau, Cape Town, 1977, esp. p. 148 and pp. 296–7.

[8] Peter Warwick, *South African War*, p. 58.

looked on, and the government . . . hinted that really the critics had only themselves to blame."[9] Kate Courtney and her husband were notorious 'pro-Boers'. The year 1900 brought them scores of anonymous threatening letters, addressed to Leonard, then aged nearly 70:

> What a pity a soft-nosed bullet cannot be lodged in the place where your brains are supposed to be.
>
> To the Little Englander Mr Leonard Courtney, Knight of the White Feather, House of Commons.
>
> The Constable of the Tower will make room for you. A rope and short shrift for traitors.[10]

Kate Courtney confessed: 'I really feared he might be assaulted some day in the street' (Diary, April 1900).[11] Both the Courtneys had to learn very quickly that their immovable anti-war stance would isolate them from friends, relatives and former political supporters. 'Not a single invitation except family' (Diary, August 1900). The political rejection had been expressed most forcibly in Leonard Courtney's own long-held constituency in Cornwall. One meeting called to support him at Liskeard in July 1900 was broken up in disorder and one of the speakers who was hissed and shouted down for trying to explain and support the Courtneys' anti-war views was their friend Emily Hobhouse, of whom much more was soon going to be heard world-wide in relation to the war. Leonard Courtney was dropped as Liberal candidate for Penwith and Kate Courtney's first reaction was to escape thankfully into the private 'life of natural happiness':

> I have spent a peaceful hour or so sweeping up the leaves in my back garden and rolling the grass. For you see, my dear [Diary], we are out of it – I can enjoy the brilliant colours of our Virginia creeper with a clump of sunflowers standing against it and our white Japanese anemones opposite. Yes, we are completely and entirely out of it – my great man is in splendid isolation. (Diary, Sept. 1900)

However, Kate Courtney did not, in the event, choose to escape

[9] Bernard Porter, 'The pro-Boers in Britain', in Warwick, *South African War*, p. 239.

[10] John Fisher, *That Miss Hobhouse*, Secker & Warburg, 1971, ch. 4.

[11] Kate Courtney, Diary. Unpublished MSS, London School of Economics Library.

from bitter anti-war politics into her garden. In April 1900 she and Emily Hobhouse had already founded a Women's Committee of the South Africa Conciliation movement that was urging a negotiated settlement of the war. In June they had organized a large women's protest meeting in the Queen's Hall, London, which Kate Courtney, with much trepidation, had chaired. The *Westminster Gazette* called it one of the most remarkable women's meetings held in London for a very long time and praised the excellence and brevity of the speeches.[12] Day and night, far from being 'out of it', Kate Courtney continued to be haunted by the distant atrocities:

> But behind everything is that cruel work going on in the two Republics – burning farms – the combatants treated as rebels and marauders, non-combatants paying in person and goods for resistance to our soldiers. I fear a terrible story is being enacted, and a worse one told abroad till some people will loathe the name of England. (Diary, 15 Sept. 1900)

> That cursed war . . . in spite of continual defeats and deporting men, women and children, the Boer commandoes go on fighting – the British soldiers write home longing to get back and hating the kind of work – the only wholesome sign for some time. Still, it is 'submit or be exterminated'. (Diary, 20 Sept. 1900)

In November 1900: 'I got up in the middle of one night . . . I could not sleep without some outlet . . . and wrote [to the *Westminster Review*]:

> I suppose we are all grieving at the way in which the war in South Africa is dragging on and the conditions under which and methods by which it is being fought . . . Why, why, does it go on? . . .
>
> We have substituted uncivilised for civilised methods of warfare . . . [and] if we refuse all concessions, if the hideous work goes on of telling off our soldiers to confiscate, burn and kill only ruined homes and starving women and children and a few thousand prisoners . . . are left – then indeed a time will

[12] Fisher, *That Miss Hobhouse*, ch. 6.

> come when we may *proclaim* peace, but it will be the peace of death.

'We have substituted uncivilised for civilised methods of warfare' – how ominously and pitifully prophetic that cry of a general confession sounds in our ears now.

Meanwhile Emily Hobhouse had founded the South African Women and Children's Distress Fund to help women and children who were homeless as a result of Britain's policy of farm-burning, and in December 1900 Kate Courtney supported her friend in her mission to go to South Africa in order to investigate the condition of women and children there. A month later Emily Hobhouse uncovered the first mass atrocity of the twentieth century – the British use of 'concentration camps'.

> Two miles outside Bloemfontein Emily Hobhouse had found a village of two thousand people – nine hundred of them children and the rest mainly women with a few surrendered Boers. They were living six or more to a tent . . . The atmosphere, even with the tent flaps open, was indescribable. The refugees seemed to have become anonymous, for the camp had no streets nor the tents names or numbers. Even the expectant mothers had to sleep on the bare ground. The flies swarmed everywhere.[13]

As Emily Hobhouse commented prophetically:

> I call this camp system wholesale cruelty. It can never be wiped out from the memories of the people. It presses hardest on the children. They drop in the terrible heat. Will you try somehow to make the British public understand the position and force it to ask itself what is going to be done with these people? . . . There must be a full 50,000 of them . . . Entire villages and districts rooted up and dumped in a strange bare place. To keep these camps going is murder for the children. (26 Jan. 1901)[14]

Once Emily Hobhouse returned to England, Kate Courtney was instrumental in procuring her the political publicity that was now essential.

[13] ibid., ch. 7.
[14] ibid.

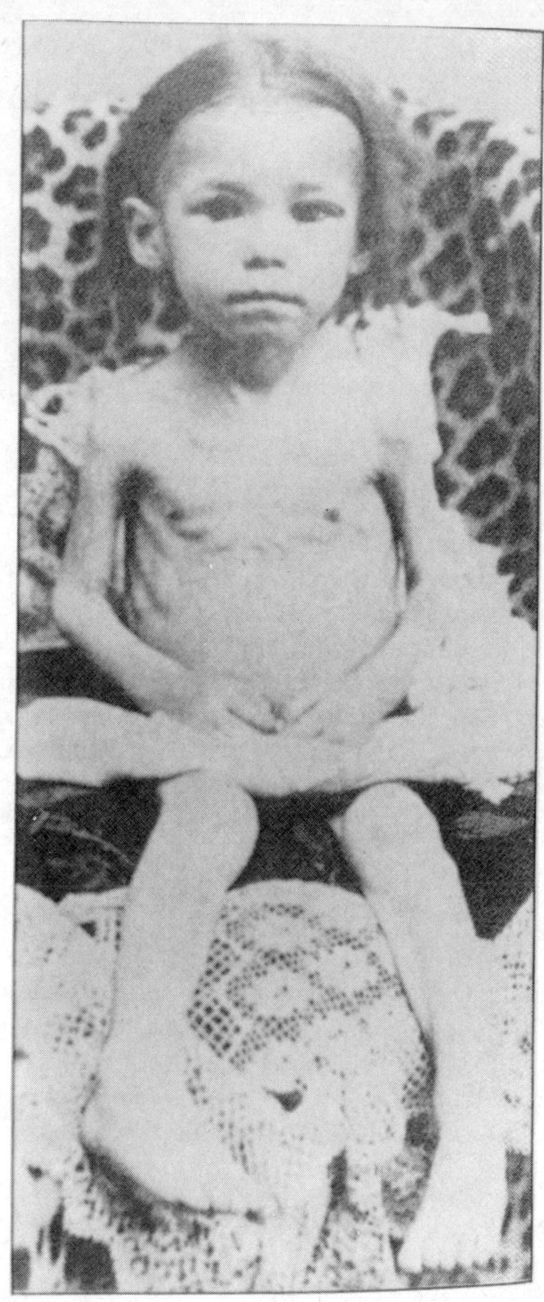

Child victim of the Bloemfontein concentration camp.

> Emily Hobhouse is now speaking about the concentration camps (the name which has finally settled on to them) whenever halls and chapels can be got. The Westminster Chapel was offered by the Minister but the police stopped it. (Diary, July 1901)

> *The Times* attacked Emily Hobhouse with really farcical statements of ordinary Boer mortality . . . This attitude towards the mortality in the concentration camps (now 50% for children in the Transvaal) is odious and contemptible. (Diary, Oct. 1901)

> Another Blue Book out about camps showing increased and truly terrible mortality for October and only a little bit less for November. Milner still bent on penalising wives of . . . burghers – and penalising has meant death to the little ones. Heartless, ungenerous – mean to an incredible degree. (Diary, 13 Dec. 1901)

Kate Courtney's values are here made clear. Against the professional militarists' 'methods of barbarism' she upholds an absolute right to life for 'the little ones'. A total of 27,927 Boers died in the British concentration camps – more than 22,000 of them children under the age of 16 – and more than 4,000 women: at least 14,000 African children also died in the black concentration camps set up by the British.[15] The repercussions within Afrikanerdom and therefore within South Africa have not been fully worked out yet.

Although she could not know it, Kate Courtney's efforts in favour of conciliation and negotiation, her relief work for enemy refugees and her steadfast refusal to participate in the patriotic war-psychosis of the Boer War were all to be a rehearsal for her spiritual resistance to World War I.

In 1911, eight years after the Boer War was over, Kate Courtney wrote in her unpublished diary about the Agadir Crisis, when Germany and France almost went to war over Morocco. These entries show her to have been England's first Cassandra this century. She immediately recognized that Italy's seizure of Tripoli from the Turks would 'put back the Peace and Arbitration movement terribly and set a precedent which will greatly strengthen mutual suspicion

[15] See S. B. Spies, 'Women and the War', in Warwick, *South African War*, pp. 100, 173.

and add to armaments' (Diary, 1911). Bertha von Suttner, the peace activist, was making exactly the same judgement in her speeches in Bucharest and Budapest in November 1911:

> What an example to set: What a precedent, opening the way for the exercise of force in the future! All the statutes, treaties, obligations, all the basic principles laid down at The Hague [the Second Peace Conference there, in 1909] have been denied as if they had never existed . . . The action at Tripoli was more than aggression against Turkey, it was an assault on The Hague.[16]

Kate Courtney recognized the guilt of all the competing imperialisms – 'France in Morocco, Austria in Herzegovina and Bosnia, Russia in Persia. We in South Africa and Egypt.' Only Germany as yet is 'still a poor lion without a Christian'.

By October 1911 it had come out that the British fleet had very nearly been mobilized:

> We have been at the point of war unbeknown to the country – German bitterness is extreme and to a great extent justified for we have supported France right or wrong and threatened Germany. It is a question if we have not bound ourselves secretly to give not only diplomatic but military assistance so that the Entente is an alliance. There has been planning between the two Armies and Navies as if we were allies for war: and all for what? To give France what is doubtfully moral [Morocco] and to stop off Germany everywhere . . . What is the good of talking friendship if the diplomatic section of the country is based on . . . fears and animosities? (Diary)

More ominous still was the view of Lord Morley that 'Churchill is so full of his special office [as Naval Secretary] that he is impatiently saying "We are ready for war, better now than later", a fatal step towards the abyss. It looks pretty bad' (Diary, 2 Jan. 1912). By July 1912 Kate Courtney could see that 'both sets of imperialists [the British and the German] have played into each other's hands.' In this, the Agadir section of her Diary, Kate Courtney pinpointed all

[16] Quoted by Beatrix Kempf, *Suffragette for Peace: The Life of Bertha von Suttner*, Oswald Wolff, 1972, p. 103.

three factors that were so soon to combine and bring about catastrophe – the secret machine of Cabinet government which could mobilize the country without warning or consultation; the secret international diplomacy rooted in an enemy psychosis; and the uncontrolled, unstable armaments race between two rival imperialisms. The analogies with the late twentieth century need not be laboured. International affairs continued to go from bad to worse in 1912:

> One or two bad debates on Navy. It is almost enough to make one despair – the Government's poverty of resource or effort towards a real understanding with Germany. It seems as if we were assisting at a Greek tragedy and some terrible catastrophe was nearing us every day – and for no reason – just blind fate – insanity. (Diary, 1 Aug. 1912)

On the Continent at precisely the same moment, the summer of 1912, Bertha von Suttner was Europe's Cassandra. Normally soft-spoken and gentle in manner, for once she accosted young Stefan Zweig quite loudly in a Vienna street:

> 'People don't realize what's going on! That was war and they have once again hidden everything from us and kept it dark. Why don't you do something, you young people? It concerns you above all! Defend yourselves, pull yourselves together! Don't always leave everything to a few of us old women to whom no one pays any attention. Things are looking worse than ever now. The war-engine is revving up already.'[17]

Kate and Leonard Courtney had tried to advocate a radically different basis for foreign policy that is still pertinent: 'Leonard laid down the great principle of friendship with all – no entangling alliances dividing Europe into two armed camps – rather the concert of Europe' (Diary, Nov. 1911). But they and all the other anti-militarists were not, of course, heeded and August 1914 came inexorably nearer. When World War I was finally declared Kate Courtney was 67 and her husband, now Lord Courtney, was 82 and nearly blind. Once again her diary records the very pulse of those

[17] Stefan Zweig, *Erinnerungen eines Europäers*, quoted by Gisela Brinker-Gabler, *Kämpferin*, p. 11.

days,[18] not merely what was happening but what had to be endured emotionally in response to what was happening:

> August 1st. On the brink . . . Bank Rate up to 8%, which Leonard could hardly believe . . . Stock Exchange . . . closed, and all business suspended.
>
> (Later) *The Observer* has come, and Reuters says Germany has declared war on Russia, and it looks as if France must be involved.
>
> August 3rd. A special *Sunday Times* was brought up . . . last night as I was getting into bed, with the remark 'no news'. But there was some, and very bad, only it may be false.
>
> Reuter says Germany has invaded Luxembourg. Fatal, or nearly so, to our neutrality, if true, when it is hanging in the balance. Couldn't sleep for thinking of it.
>
> August 9th. A terrible week – and it has come . . . Lord Crewe declined to make any statement in Lords, simply referring to Grey. L. raised a voice against being committed to a policy without having a statement of it and of the reasons. There was a hubbub at first and L. stood facing a hostile house . . . L. persisted, and finally got his one sentence out. It was an ordeal, and made me anxious. Came away very sad.

What Kate Courtney did for the whole duration of World War I was refuse to wage it. She publicly resisted the war-spirit despite her own personal anguish over relatives at risk and in the face of almost universal anti-German hysteria within the country at large. As one of her friends commented in retrospect, Kate Courtney took her 'stand against fearful odds and risks – the only risk that matters at all, the one big risk – loss of friends'.[19] Her *War Diary* is a most moving and revealing document which deserves to be much more widely known. She emerges as one of those rare people in Keats's words to whom 'the miseries of the world are misery, and will not let them rest'. Kate Courtney's untiring efforts to wage peace can

[18] See Kate Courtney, *War Diary*, privately published, 1927. Held in Fawcett Archive.
[19] Letter to Kate Courtney from Ursula Grant Duff, 1928, held in the Courtney archive at the London School of Economics Library.

be considered under three main headings: her work for the Emergency Committee for 'enemy aliens', her membership of the Union for the Democratic Control of Foreign Policy, and her vital contribution to the formation of an International Women's Peace Movement.

No war is possible without dehumanization of 'the enemy'. What Kate Courtney refused to do was ever to dehumanize the Germans. Instead, she immediately interceded on behalf of those now officially stigmatized. Barely a week after World War I broke out she was already helping her Quaker nephew Stephen Hobhouse 'to start an (Emergency) Committee for relieving destitute and helpless Germans stranded here. Two meetings at Friends' Meeting House – last very grievous with jeering words from Sir F. Robertson, Director of Foreigners in Distress, and from Miss Garland, who suggested, quite gratuitously, it would be illegal. Gave us much trouble . . . many difficulties' (*War Diary*).

Her concern soon extended to the first German prisoners to be held in Britain and on 2 February 1915 she had 'a long day going to Southend to the prison ships'. Her work for the Emergency Committee Relief intensified in May and June 1915, when, in the aftermath of the sinking of the *Lusitania*, there were 'horrible anti-German riots in London . . . violence meets violence' (*War Diary*), and the new government policy was deportation and internment. Kate Courtney's special role within the Emergency Committee was clearly to be their 'front person' intervening with men in power; for example, 'June 20th, 1915 . . . I interviewed Sir J[ohn] Simon, the new Home Sec.'

Earlier that year Kate Courtney had made a point of writing to *The Times* in order to publicize the work of her counterparts in Berlin, who were overseeing the welfare of *British* POWs and civilians then stranded in Germany. Under the heading, taken from Romain Rolland, 'Notre prochain. L'ennemi – our neighbour the enemy', Kate Courtney translated the Berlin Committee's compassionate appeal to and for a common humanity: 'Our thirst to help others and to alleviate suffering recognizes no frontiers . . . That which unites people has deeper roots than that which separates them.' To Kate Courtney, 'the enemy' were in reality nothing more than 'the most unfortunate, because most hated people' (her letter to *The Times*, 26 March 1915). Kate Courtney's first anti-war work therefore had to be the attempted diminution of that hatred. Her attempts to be reasonable and humane, however, were often quite roughly rejected – it was no easier to be thought 'pro-German' in 1914–18 than it had been to be thought 'pro-Boer' in 1900:

> Outdoor meeting at Lady Maud Parry's. Miss Maude Royden and Mr Ponsonby speakers. A Mrs Dash quite astonishingly violent and insolent. I did not mean to speak, but her attack on the speakers brought me up, and Vernon Lee and others expressed great satisfaction at the way I ignored the virago, who really made as if she was going to hit me at one time. War may make some noble, but it makes others very silly. (*War Diary*, 25 July 1915)

In April 1916 Kate Courtney tried to persuade her nephew Stephen Hobhouse not to give up his work as Chairman of the British Emergency Committee; she suggested that 'perhaps the best peace work now is this relief of enemy aliens, and his correspondence with Germany . . . We are almost the only link between the countries now allowed by our authorities' (*War Diary*). And a year later her good offices were again required to try to intercede for 13 German women and nine children from East Africa 'claimed by the Belgians as their prisoners to go to France . . . They had to go' (*War Diary*, 19 May 1917). In November and December 1918, her work with the Emergency Committee had to focus on the urgent necessity of feeding starving defeated Germans within Germany itself. 'We have been trying and feeling for some way to get permission for a few of the Quakers of the Emergency Committee and War victims to go over there to investigate and help in relief . . . I have made several attempts but so far no way has opened' (*War Diary*, 4 Dec. 1918).

Kate Courtney (now aged 71 and widowed) spent the Christmas of 1918 working to build up the necessary relief organization; the first meeting of the Fight the Famine Committee was held at her house in Cheyne Walk in January 1919 and out of that Committee came the new German verb – '*quakern* = to feed' – and the Save the Children Fund.[20] Her insistence on treating Germans as fellow humans in 1918–19 finally caused her to be pilloried in the popular press:

[20] See Oldfield, *Spinsters*, ch. 11; Picton and Fuller, *The White Flame: The History of the Save the Children Fund*, Longman, 1931; and Francesca Wilson, *Eglantyne Jebb*, Allen & Unwin, 1967.

HUN 'DELEGATES' DINNER PARTY.

CROWD WAITS IN VAIN TO GIVE THEM A WELCOME.

LADY COURTNEY'S GUESTS.

GERMAN AND AUSTRIAN DELEGATES ATTENDING THE FIGHT THE FAMINE CONFERENCE IN LONDON WERE GUESTS AT A DINNER PARTY GIVEN BY LADY COURTNEY IN CHEYNE WALK, CHELSEA LAST NIGHT. A BEREAVED FATHER AND DEMOBILISED SOLDIERS PREPARED 'SOME' WELCOME. (*DAILY SKETCH*, JULY 1919)

Kate Courtney quietly replied:

> Is it reasonable to desire to insult just those Germans who have been consistent opponents of the militarists in their own country; and this for years before 1914; and who at much cost of reputation and comfort have differed from their own people in a time of passionate emotions? Do they [the angry British at her gate] understand what this means? I do, and my heart goes out to those in Germany and in all countries who are my spiritual comrades and will remain so.

The *Daily Sketch* headed that letter with a sneer: 'Our German guests. Lady Courtney of Penwith and her Spiritual Comrades'.

Anti-militarism, however, requires not only practical acts of humane intercession for the so-called 'enemy' but also an alternative mode of political thinking. Kate Courtney found her congenial group of radical political thinkers in the newly formed Union for the Democratic Control of Foreign Policy, chaired by E. D. Morel.[21] The UDC was a group of left-wing pacifist intellectuals who wanted the nations to learn from their past blunders of secret diplomacy and heavily armed rival bloc-thinking and to negotiate a just peace which would prevent global war in future. As early as 14 November 1914, Kate Courtney voted at a crowded peace meeting in her own home to join the UDC. The UDC was treated with great hostility and suspicion by 'the Establishment' for being unpatriotic and even pro-German and its public meetings were often attacked. On 4 December 1915, for example, Kate Courtney reported: 'UDC meeting broken up in London, or rather hall captured before it met by soldiers and

[21] See Helena Swanwick, *Builders of Peace: The Union for the Democratic Control of Foreign Policy*, Swarthmore Press, London, 1924.

others with forged tickets – I was outside for half an hour in a crowd unable to get in.' In September 1917, E. D. Morel was arrested under the Defence of the Realm Act for the technical offence of sending two of his pamphlets to Romain Rolland in neutral Switzerland. He was sentenced to six months' imprisonment.[22] The Courtneys were outraged and Kate Courtney interceded with her brother-in-law, Lord Parmoor, on Morel's behalf.

One plank of the UDC platform was the necessity for a new international order which would be empowered to invoke the compulsory arbitration and negotiation of international disputes. Kate Courtney yearned for such a 'new order of the world . . . the one thing that matters now' (*War Diary*, 15 Oct. 1918), but she also recognized with ominous prescience that Germany might be excluded from such a new League of Nations at the outset. And the eventual terms of the Armistice – so totally opposite to those long proposed by the UDC – she saw as cruel, humiliating and stupid: 'The great desire seems to be . . . to force a (new) fierce war of self-defence on Germany' (*War Diary*, 29 Oct. 1918).

Kate Courtney's third sphere of anti-war work in wartime consisted of her efforts to help leading women internationalists from America and Europe to use whatever influence they could muster in order to bring World War I to a speedy, negotiated and just end. The story of these 'most dangerous women' who assembled at The Hague in 1915 and then sent Jane Addams, Dr Aletta Jacobs, Chrystal Macmillan, Emily Greene Balch and Rozika Schwimmer to interview the foreign ministries of all the belligerent powers about the possibility of mediation by neutrals, has been recounted by Anne Wiltsher.[23]

[22] 'Doubtless he broke the law, but it was a law for which we can have no respect and in its application in his case, is contemptible . . . The sentence of the Police Magistrate was so out of relation to the offence that it may well be called outrageous. Magistrates, paid and unpaid, and indeed the very highest judges, live in an atmosphere of war, from which scarce one emerges.' Leonard Courtney to Lord Morley, quoted in G. P. Gooch, *Life of Leonard Courtney*, Allen & Unwin, 1922, ch. 24.

[23] Anne Wiltsher, *Most Dangerous Women*, Pandora, 1985. Jane Addams was an outstanding social reformer, suffragist and anti-militarist, who was eventually awarded the Nobel Peace Prize in 1931; Dr Aletta Jacobs was a pioneer woman doctor and President of the Dutch Women's Suffrage Association; Chrystal Macmillan was a Scottish barrister, suffragist and pacifist; Emily Greene Balch was Professor of Economics and Sociology at Wellesley in the United States; and Rozika Schwimmer was the intrepid Hungarian feminist and pacifist who initiated the

Kate Courtney played an essential part in this, the first-ever collective peace initiative organized by women internationally. Between March 28 and April 18 1915 she was continually involved in the planning necessary to enable the British deputation of 180 women to attend the Hague Congress. As soon as she was told that the government had cancelled all travel permits for the women, Kate Courtney went to interview the Home Secretary, Mr McKenna. She succeeded in persuading him to be 'a bit relaxed' and to allow a few British women to go. The following day she went on her own to Lord Haldane to enlist his good offices with McKenna. 'Finally Mr McKenna agreed to 25 going.' But then Winston Churchill, at the Admiralty, tried to torpedo the whole venture, the women believed, by closing the North Sea to all shipping. A handful of leading British women had managed to reach The Hague already, however, and a very remarkable Congress did take place that April. Between May and June 1915, Kate Courtney was busy publicizing its resolutions – many of which were later to be incorporated by Woodrow Wilson into his Fourteen Points. She also personally arranged for Jane Addams, the United States envoy and famous social reformer, to be seen by Lord Robert Cecil at the Foreign Office, by Lloyd George at the War Office and by the Archbishop of Canterbury at Lambeth Palace. From October 1915, when she was elected on to the National Executive of the British section of the Women's International League, until the end of the war, Kate Courtney put a great deal of effort into this women's initiative to educate public opinion, both men and women, about the internationalist alternative to endless militarism and war. The effort often exhausted her but still she persisted:

> April 19, 1916. Nearly a week of Women's International meetings. Too many for us.
>
> July 4, 1917. I have not been altogether idle, but tired and not up to my duties . . . The day before yesterday we had a crowded [WIL] meeting here – right up the staircase . . . It was a greater success than I could have hoped, and encourages one to go forward – but it is tiring.
>
> Dec. 1, 1916. Last Saturday a crowded [WIL] meeting here

women's attempt to secure an end to the First World War via the mediation of neutral powers and who became, in 1919, the first woman ambassador in history.

> . . . two thirds were not members, and quite a third were opponents of Peace by Negotiation which was the subject . . . Of course, they were mostly our friends, and only those came who felt they could stand our views. I was a little anxious about disturbance as some of the Pankhurst ladies tried every device to get invitations, but all went quietly, crammed as it was. (*War Diary*)

Finally, on 9 February 1918, she reports that she held:

> A crowded meeting . . . of WIL on the International Outlook and Peace [via] the League of Nations. Of course they were not all WIL as I always ask a good many outsiders and boldly asked more than usual, and they came, and I thought showed a more coming on spirit than ever before . . . Up got a young officer in Khaki and instead of denouncing us pacifists, denounced the Govt. for not negotiating . . . he also pitched into the Labour Party for not backing their manifesto by deeds and calling a strike.

A year later Kate Courtney wrote to the *Westminster Gazette* supporting a Serbian proposal that the new League of Nations should be a league not just of governments but of peoples – teachers, doctors, writers, artists. Kate Courtney enlarged on that suggestion by looking hopefully to the humane internationalism of the next Women's International League Congress then about to take place in Zurich – the first International Women's Peace Congress since The Hague in 1915. Once again, as during the Boer War, saving the lives of the children was an essential aspect of Kate Courtney's anti-militarism and a platform on which she believed that the women of the world could and would eventually unite.[24] 'Perhaps women may succeed, where statesmen have failed, in bringing an atmosphere of peace and mutual help instead of suspicion and conflict into this distracted world. At any rate we shall have one great and passionate desire in common and that is to save the lives of the children of Europe.'

But for all Kate Courtney's unceasing efforts to wage peace even during wartime, she did not insulate herself in a sealed-off world of

[24] cf. the efforts of leading women internationalists like Inga Thorsson today to connect the issues of disarmament and development (see below ch. 9).

high-minded idealism which the war was never allowed to penetrate. Personal anxieties and personal grief came home at least as much to her as they did to those who could believe in the meaningfulness of the young men's self-immolation. Nephew after nephew – Paul Hobhouse, Basil Williams, Noel Williams, Leonard Cripps, Fred Cripps, Harry Cripps, Phil Holt, and Bill Playne – enlisted for the war only to be wounded time and again: her best loved nephews of all, Paul Hobhouse and Noel Williams, were killed in the very last months of the war. Another nephew who caused Kate Courtney intense concern was Stephen Hobhouse, the Quaker conscientious objector, whose health was damaged for life by the treatment he received in prison.

> I went yesterday with Rosa Hobhouse to see Stephen in prison at Wormwood Scrubs. I was nervous and indeed did not do very well for the dear noble fellow in my short ten minutes. We went into a pen like a horse-box . . . There are a number of men like him – now treated like felons and no Liberals protested except a few pacifists . . . Stephen has suddenly, without reason given, been returned to his Unit – we suppose he will be again court-martialled and sentenced. It makes me hot to think of it . . . The event of the week for me has been the news of the second sentence on Stephen Hobhouse – two years hard labour for obeying Christ rather than the War God. (*War Diary*, March–April 1917)

In August 1917 she and Leonard travelled to Exeter Prison to visit Stephen:

> It was very touching and in a way comforting . . . We went into a long bare room with a table on one side of which we sat, while Stephen came and sat on the other, and a good-natured warder sat a little way off . . . We came away glad to have this fruitful and not unhappy ¾ hour talk and I don't know if I broke prison rules, but I kissed him heartily coming and going. Rosa had warned me not to do so, as she had asked the warder if she might kiss her husband . . . Ask a warder if I might kiss my own nephew, certainly not! So I just put my arms around his neck and gave him a good hug, and the warder, like a true gentleman, looked out of the window!

In addition to her acute personal anxiety over all the individuals whom she knew to be at risk, Kate Courtney was also unspeakably depressed by the general human tragedy. Submarine warfare, mines, food blockades, poisonous gas, the sinking of the *Lusitania*, Zeppelin raids, the execution of Edith Cavell, the first aeroplane bombing of central London and the British reprisal bombing of Mainz; finally the 'competition in starving babies' – all these horrors caused her to cry out in her Journal: 'Has the Spirit of Goodness wholly deserted this world?' (26 Oct. 1915). Essentially life-loving though she was, Kate Courtney was actually driven to write: 'I felt last night some understanding of people taking their own lives in despair' (Jan. 1916). And on 11 March 1918:

> I have felt very low and hopeless lately – both about the realisation of any of one's visions of a better feeling here and in Germany, and in the fate of our poor old country. Is there no voice of insight and goodness strong enough to save the world? If only I had faith, not now and then in moments of exaltation, but always within me. But I have done nothing to deserve such a blessing with my love of an easy comfortable life for myself and all around me. (*War Diary*)

Nevertheless, despite her near despair, Kate Courtney's marvellous capacity for enjoying life did keep breaking through – and it also came to the aid of her anti-war struggle. For if she had not in her heart of hearts really wanted to go on living herself, then it would have been impossible for her to have done convincing, heartfelt work for the life of the world. What kept Kate Courtney wanting to live even in the darkest days was, first and foremost, her marriage with Leonard, now in his eighties. Already during the Boer War, in the midst of all the reported horrors in the Transvaal, she had written: 'L's birthday. We have each other wholly and entirely. I should be an idiot not to be happy now whatever the unknown future . . . We must catch the present – people don't live half enough in the present' (Diary, July 1901). And now, during World War I, she recorded:

> for me there is much happiness as long as I have Leonard . . .
>
> Still alone here together and happy to be so . . .
>
> I thought as I walked in my little back garden we might still have a few happy years in our dear Chelsea home if only this war could end. (*War Diary*, Jan. 1916–March 1918)

Kate Courtney's greatest gift, according to her nephew, Stephen

Hobhouse, 'was an extraordinarily unselfish heart overflowing with imaginative sympathy with the lives of others – relations and strangers, neighbours rich and poor, allies and opponents, servants and children and animals'.[25] But her other great source of life-spirit, in addition to her gift for love, was her unfailing joy in the beauty of the world. At times her Diary reads like the journal of a twentieth-century Dorothy Wordsworth:

> Olney, Bull Hotel. Here one has got into a new world to us, and thoughts of the gentle Cowper, and the wholly new kind of landscape, have pushed out the war now and then . . . Most of all I like to dwell on the fine church with spire rising above the town, and on the bank of the Ouse, where the mill dam is, and with old mill and big browny pink poplars to set it off. (31 May 1915)
>
> Bude. We have got to love the place . . . Wild flowers in the back country, honeysuckle and all sorts of marsh flowers, including a sort of sunflower, I think like the one with big leaves and small flowers in my garden. (Sept. 1916)
>
> Penzance. I have watched every morning for the sunrise over the sea, and had some great ones – a glorious one today. (New Year, 1917)
>
> Ivinghoe. Hoar frost on the grass, ice on the roadpuddles, keen cold wind, but brilliant sun. We have just had a glorious walk along the top of the downs – blue sky, white clouds and great wide views on two sides. (Easter 1917)
>
> Chelsea. Yesterday such a tender evening sky and lovely moon and greenery and daffodils all coming out . . . The tender radiance of the sky is more and more extraordinary – a sort of sunny mist like looking at objects through a mist or in a dream. (March 1918)

After Leonard's death, in May 1918, Kate Courtney found that she could go on living if she continued to wage what had been for

[25] Stephen Hobhouse, *Margaret Hobhouse* (Stanhope Press, 1934), ch. 12. Stephen Hobhouse also gives Sir John Fisher Williams's testimony: 'In the quarter of a century almost in which I knew her intimately I never heard her impute an unworthy motive to an opponent; the worst fault which she ever credited to those who disagreed with her was a lack of imagination or, possibly, of understanding.'

so long their joint struggle against righteous killing. The eventual terms of the Treaty of Versailles were as abhorrent to her as they would, she knew, have been to Leonard, both on account of their hardness of heart and because of the nemesis such an indulgence in revenge would surely entail. Now 72 years old, Kate Courtney poured out her horror and fears for the world in three powerful letters to the press. She, who in 1911/12 had foretold World War I, now foretold that the Bismarckism of Clemenceau and of the other victors would once again bring disaster upon Europe. Against the Allies' iron-fisted approach to defeated Germany, Kate Courtney desperately pleaded for conciliation, comradeship and the renunciation by Britain of her demand for German war reparations. What she was ultimately up against, as she knew, was the Gospel of Force:

> To those (and they must be many) who expected that the collapse of German militarism and the signing of the Armistice would bring a better spirit over the Nations, and that President Wilson's wise and powerful personality would materialise that spirit into action, these last weeks must have brought, as they have to me, bitter disappointment. Wherever we turn our eyes, belief in force is still the gospel. Bolsheviks, just escaped from exile, prison and gibbet of the Tsarist regime, enforce their crude social theories by similar means, while the allies seek to destroy those theories by armed intervention. Liberated Poland would rejoice us whole-heartedly if the Poles were not celebrating their recovered nationality by murdering fellow citizens who happen to be Jews. Spartacists try by violence to convert the majority in Germany to their idealistic views – a bomb first, and then Utopia!
>
> And is it better in France, or – why should I hesitate – in England?
>
> M. Pichon in the French Chamber asks: 'Have the victors no rights over the vanquished?' So said Bismarck in 1871. Result: Alsace-Lorraine. 'Destroy Germany's economic position so that for two generations she cannot recover!' 'Bleed France white,' said Bismarck. Or another version, as given by our own Prime Minister: 'An indemnity to cover the total cost of the war.' Everywhere, all over the world, is the same temper . . . Cannot we yet recognise the new spirit in Germany? . . . We

demanded the defeat of militarism: it is gone. We insisted on a popular and democratic government; they have got one more democratic than our own . . .

If for the last half century they have followed false gods in their international relations, they have now dethroned them. Have we had no false gods over here? [Does] conciliation and comradeship, even with our late enemies, sound sentimental and vague? The 'Spirit that moved on the face of the waters' was vague, but it preceded the Light. (19 Feb. 1919, Letter to the *Westminster Gazette*)

The cruel and unwise conditions of the Peace Treaty insisted on by France will have results [which] will be suicidal to France . . . and disastrous to all Europe . . . M. Clemenceau is a great Frenchman, as Bismarck was a great German. Both in their hour of victory have done an evil thing for their respective countries and for the world. (9 Jan. 1920, Letter to the *Daily Mirror*)

The international situation seems worsening every day and fills many with alarm for the future. The crushing victory which has destroyed the economic life of Germany and Austria and brought disease and famine to all Central Europe is recoiling on the victors, not only economically and financially but morally . . . There is one thing which might change the atmosphere, and that is some act of real renunciation on the part of one of the great nations; and we are the nation who could do it. Let us renounce our share in the indemnity [reparations payments] in favour of those of our allies who have suffered invasion and in return get them to exact no more than Germany can pay without further ruin to her economic life so essential to the restoration of trade all over Europe. I would go further, and return to her some of the merchant shipping which is sorely needed for that restoration. And – if we really believe in the League of Nations, why not take the profoundly wise step of declaring that as soon as it was complete by the inclusion of our late enemies and if possible, Russia, and in working order, we should submit all colonial mandates to it for confirmation?

Somebody must begin to be good if the better world we were promised is ever to come. Why should not we make the

> adventure? The spirit of Sacrifice is as infectious as the spirit of Greed. (1920, Letter to the *Daily News*)

'Somebody must begin to be good if the better world we were promised is ever to come' – Kate Courtney herself was a shining example of somebody 'beginning to be good'. She was condescended to all her life by her brilliant and much more famous younger sister Beatrice Webb:

> Dear Kate is an incurable sentimentalist, (Beatrice Webb's *Diary*, 19 July 1900)

> [Kate] is a dear kind honest soul, but her sentimentality on all issues is a veritable vice. Her servants cheat and oppress her, and if she governed a state she would be defied by her subjects and cheated and oppressed by all other states. (Beatrice Webb's *Diary*, Sept. 1917)

> there is no point of contact between our intellects, and . . . in no single instance have we both been keen on the same public ends. (Beatrice Webb's *Diary*, May 1922)

Nevertheless, it may be Kate Courtney, rather than Beatrice Webb, whose life and thought the world might do well to ponder at the end of this century. The charge of 'sentimentalism' brought by Beatrice Webb against her sister would seem to mean that Kate Courtney thought better of others than they ever deserved and that she indulged in quite impossible hopes of world fellowship. In other words, she shied self-protectively away from the realities of human conflict, cruelty and greed. But it should now be clear, both from Kate Courtney's own Diary and from her letters to the press, that she did not in fact shy away from the evidence of evil in the world. She perceived all too clearly the cycle of oppression, suffering and retribution and then more oppression, suffering and retribution which is always being acted out within or between one group of humans and another. But what Kate Courtney did in response to that perception was to practise in her own life an alternative reality – real human solidarity with all who needed her help and particularly with those labelled 'the enemy' by her society – whether such people were Boers dying in Bloemfontein concentration camps or 'Huns' on British prison ships or the starving children of a defeated Germany. By what right do we, or Beatrice Webb, regard sympathy, when lived out like this, as being less 'real' than antipathy?

When Kate Courtney died, in February 1929, Beatrice Webb was finally moved to write an elegy for her that was all the sadder because she had learned to see the miracle of her sister's nature too late:

> Kate was the most beneficent of my sisters and was the most beloved by nephews, nieces and friends. She was in a sense faultless – she had no malice, no envy, little egotism . . . she was always . . . arranging to do kind acts to all sorts of persons . . . I sorrow because her beneficent presence meant so little in my life. (Beatrice Webb's *Diary*, 6 March 1929)

But Kate Courtney's beneficent presence does not have to mean 'so little' in our lives if only we see in time what it is that she offers us – a model of war-resistance that could be quite crucially relevant to the late twentieth century. Kate Courtney's rejection of the very concept of an 'enemy' even in the midst of a mass-murdering war, as well as during the crucial years when enmity, unscrutinized, built up to that war, holds a vital lesson against acquiescence in our own Cold War. To impute collective guilt by association to the populations of those countries whose governments arouse our – or our government's – detestation is not rational and will end, sooner or later, in detestable acts towards those populations. Kate Courtney knew perfectly well that there were many Germans in power who were as brutal as they were stupid, but instead of joining in the chorus of righteous hatred of 'Prussianism' between 1910 and 1918, she was a fearless witness to and intercessor for the countless non-brutal Germans who were not in power. No one has practised more convincingly her faith in the equal humanity of all ordinary, powerless people. How she would have echoed Einstein's and Bertrand Russell's last joint plea to the world: 'Remember your humanity, and forget the rest.'[26]

One central factor in Kate Courtney's motivation was her impulse to 'save the children' and it was her belief that an international women's network for peace and justice for all children could contribute much 'if that better world we were promised is ever to come'. She did not rely on better feeling alone – she knew perfectly

[26] Published 9 July 1955; see Nathan and Norden, *Einstein on Peace*, Avenel, N.Y. 1981, pp. 631–2.

well that new institutions also were now called for and that the nations must evolve a new system of supranational international law, of controlled gradual disarmament and the machinery of conciliation and arbitration. A federal, decentralized world-economic and legal community may in fact turn out to be the only realistic alternative to world anarchy and destruction in the twenty-first century.

Finally, Kate Courtney's extraordinary life-spirit, her humour, her delight in the beauty of the world and her eagerness that others should also have a chance to enjoy life never deserted her. She had a little fountain in her front garden that exercised a great fascination for the local street boys. A policeman knocked on her door one day to report: 'See here, lady, I've caught the worst boy in Chelsea in your front garden.' Kate Courtney refused to be appalled. 'Well,' she replied, 'he could not be in a safer place; he won't do any harm *here*. You had better leave him to me, Constable.' She had another, larger garden at the back of her house and there she would encourage shabbily dressed tired little girls to come with their heavy younger sisters and brothers and prams, to rest among the flowers out of danger from passing traffic.[27]

Always 'spare and energetic', 60-year-old, 70-year-old, 80-year-old Kate Courtney spurs us all on to revitalized efforts in our turn to transmit the earth and life itself to generations of children yet unborn.

[27] Elizabeth Fox Howard, 'My Lady of Chelsea'. Obituary note on Kate Courtney in the *Friends' Quarterly Examiner*, 1929.

3

The Political Preacher: Maude Royden (1876–1956)

It is not possible to argue that women cannot prophesy, for they have prophesied.

Maude Royden, *Equality in the Spiritual World*.

One of the last entries in Kate Courtney's *War Diary*, dated January 1919, went: 'Maude Royden too was splendid.' Born the youngest child of Sir Thomas Royden, the Cunard shipping magnate and Conservative MP, Maude Royden might seem to have been destined for a life of decently obscure high privilege.[1] Instead, she was to become notorious as a speaker for the unenfranchised and the forlorn cause. In her own time she was most famous – or notorious – for her unsuccessful struggle to be ordained as a woman priest in the Church of England. She was that very rare creature, a great woman orator; if some protest meeting were held in the Albert Hall she would be on the platform and was always billed as the last to speak so that no one would think of leaving before the end. She was the Church of England's great opportunity, as Archbishop William Temple knew, but the Synod failed to grasp it.

Although no saint, Maude Royden was blessed with an exceptionally alive, laughing personality, and this, combined with an outstanding

[1] The first full-length biography of Maude Royden written by Sheila Fletcher, will be published by Basil Blackwell in 1989.

gift for reaching out in sympathy to those in trouble, made her a wonderfully attractive human being to many people. She could be funny, self-critical and tender by turns. If she were in the room all eyes were drawn to her and the fact that she was lame and walked with a noticeable limp only made others feel all the more protective of her. Unlike those sad souls who leave a message at the end: 'No flowers please, by request', Maude Royden said she wanted 'lots of flowers' – and she got them. 'People are not followed and loved as Maude Royden was followed and loved,' said her lifelong friend Dame Kathleen Courtney, at the memorial service, 'because of what they have done, but because of what they are.'[2] And Dame Sybil Thorndike said: 'What a speaker – what a preacher.'

After reading modern history at Oxford (1896–9), Maude Royden became a social worker in one of the poorest districts of Liverpool and 'nearly killed herself with overwork and worry'.[3] After a serious breakdown in her health in 1901 she moved to a tiny country parish in Rutland, where she became the unofficial curate of its vicar, her friend and teacher Hudson Shaw, whom she 'found a magnetic and powerful personality'.[4] They were to love each other all their lives but could neither become lovers nor marry because Shaw was already married when they first met. In 1903 the Oxford University Delegacy made the successful experiment of appointing Maude Royden as their first woman University Extension lecturer in literature. And five years later, in 1908, Maude Royden directed her quite exceptional gifts as a speaker to the campaign for Votes for Women.

> To work for the enfranchisement of women was a tremendous experience, a tremendous education . . . I was often attracted and almost seduced by the dramatic and heroic methods of my militant sisters and, if I was never actually won by them, it was because I neither expected nor wished to bully or to frighten men into giving us the vote, but always hoped to convince them of the justice of doing so. The struggle both absorbed and

[2] The Guildhouse Fellowship, Sept. 1956, *In Memoriam Maude Royden. CH, DD, LL D.* Dame Kathleen Courtney, veteran suffragist and internationalist is not to be confused with Kate, Lady Courtney, in ch. 2 above. They were not related.
[3] Kathleen Courtney, Broadcast talk on Dr Maude Royden for BBC Home Service, 2 Oct. 1956.
[4] Maude Royden, *A Threefold Cord*, Gollancz, 1947.

Maude Royden

> widened my life. It gave me a sympathy – and I believe an understanding – which linked me to all disfranchised persons and nations.[5]

Maude Royden was soon asked to speak every day, and sometimes twice a day, up and down the country travelling incessantly in third-class carriages. She also made great efforts to train her fellow women campaigners as public speakers and she quickly became one of the best-loved leaders of the British women's movement on the suffragist side. She served on the National Council of the National Union of Women's Suffrage Societies, she wrote pamphlets, she electioneered for pro-suffrage parliamentary candidates, she lobbied at the House of Commons and finally, from 1912 to 1914, she became the very lively and humane editor of the suffragists' weekly paper, *The Common Cause*. Then came the outbreak of World War I. Maude Royden did not declare herself a pacifist, even to herself, at once: 'Till [1914] I had never believed there would be a great European or world war and had not taken the trouble to think out my position if there were. I should have done so long ago when the Boer war broke out but I am a slow grower and though certainly old enough to know better "My country right or wrong" was still my simple creed.'[6]

Between the Boer War and August 1914, however, had come Maude Royden's anti-militarist education through her commitment to women's suffrage. The world-wide women's movement was, as she herself had recently reported from the Budapest Conference of the International Women's Suffrage Alliance in 1913, positively international:

> Internationalism should emphasise the solidarity of human interests as a fact more fundamental than the bitterest national or racial dissensions . . . It is clear that all of us have been working along the same lines, and inspired by the same motives

[5] From an essay by Maude Royden in *Myself When Young*, ed. Margot Asquith, Muller, 1938.

[6] From 'International peace', in Maude Royden's unpublished, unfinished typescript autobiographical work, 'Bid Me Discourse', now in the Fawcett Archive (at present in the City of London Polytechnic), ch. 8.

. . . For peace, and against prostitution, alcoholism and the neglect of children.[7]

The declaration of war came as an immense shock to her. She was appalled; she could not endorse the rightness of the war and yet she longed to be convinced that she was wrong and that the war *was* just:

I could not want to cut myself off from the great torrent of my country's suffering and aspiration. I had not a relative in the world who did not share that aspiration. I had not one who did not regard Pacifists [and even Hudson Shaw was no pacifist] with horror . . . I wrote to a little religious paper of courageous and liberal views [*The Challenge*] and asked to be convinced that war was right. The correspondence raged for weeks. No one convinced me, eager as I was to be convinced. I became a Pacifist.[8]

The first people to become alarmed by Maude Royden's anti-war position were some of her closest colleagues in the women's suffrage movement in Britain. In November 1914, Helena Auerbach, the National Treasurer, wrote a confidential warning letter to the President:

Dearest Mrs Fawcett,

It looks to me as if some of the dearest people in our Union – such as Miss Courtney,[9] Miss Royden, Miss Marshall,[10] and Miss Ashton,[11] are bent upon a campaign of political education with regard to the attitude of the NU towards the war. They appear moreover to have strong leanings towards what the 'Union of Democratic Control' calls its 'policy'.

This kind of propaganda – whether wise or not – is certain to have a most exasperating effect on a good many persons and it would be nothing short of disastrous to the NU if it becomes

[7] *Ius Suffragii*, 1 Sept. 1913.
[8] Royden, 'Bid Me Discourse', ch. 8.
[9] Kathleen Courtney was the full-time Hon. Sec. of the NUWSS in Britain.
[10] Catherine Marshall was the Hon. Parliamentary Sec. of the NUWSS.
[11] Margaret Ashton of Manchester was on the National Executive of the NUWSS.

a centre or a medium of propaganda for any policy of any kind in connection with the war.[12]

The argument over which stand to take over World War I was in fact to split the leadership of the British women's movement,[13] and Maude Royden was to be one of those who aligned themselves with the 'pacifists' against the 'patriots'.

Already in December 1914 Maude Royden joined Dr W. E. Orchard and one or two other church people in a spiritual retreat to ponder their response as Christians to the war. Out of this meeting came the Christian pacifist organization, the Fellowship of Reconciliation, which asserted as its basic principle: 'Love is the only power by which evil can be overcome.' Most members of the FOR, according to Martin Ceadel, were quietists;[14] their pacifism was a matter for the individual conscience and not a subject for political evangelism. Maude Royden, however, belonged to the Fellowship's activist minority and in January 1915 she published her first pacifist pamphlet, *The Great Adventure*. In this she advocated non-violent, direct action (NVDA) and so became the first British anti-militarist thinker ever to call for NVDA against the war-machine. To Maude Royden, Christ was not neutral about evil or injustice ('was Christ "neutral" on the Cross?'), but offered humanity an alternative method of resistance to evil and injustice other than that of waging war. It was He, in the Sermon on the Mount, and its aftermath, who both preached and practised the 'great adventure' of disarming oneself and making peace with 'the enemy'.

> If we had disarmed in the first week of last August – not by an arbitrary decision of the Foreign Office, but on a demand from the people – there would have been no war. So great a moral miracle would have had its effect. The world would have been changed. No nation would have rushed into war 'in self-defence' . . . Had we – not by words that would have been disbelieved, or protests on which our own record cast a doubt,

[12] For the rest of this letter see Sybil Oldfield, *Spinsters of this Parish*, Virago, 1984, p. 309.
[13] ibid., ch. 9.
[14] Martin Ceadel, *Pacifism in Britain, 1914–1945*, OUP, 1980, ch. 4; and see Vera Brittain, *The Rebel Passion*, Allen & Unwin, 1964, on the history of the Fellowship of Reconciliation.

> but by *acts* – proved that we, at least, intended no attack. I do not believe the German Foreign Office could have refused to confer with us. I do not believe that the Socialists would have supported the war votes in the Reichstag, or that the Socialist soldiers (estimated to be two-fifths of the German army) would have marched. Had they done so, we could have called, not on our allies only, but on the world to support us in our demand for peace. We could have called on every neutral nation to refuse aid of any kind to the warmaker, and on our allies to make no preparation for war, leaving to the first aggressor the appalling responsibility of marching against an absolutely non-resistant people. *We could have called for the peace-lovers in the world to fling themselves – if need be – in front of the troop trains. If millions of men will go out to offer their lives up in war, surely there are those who would die for peace! and if not men, we could have called out women! . . . had they been organised and ready, there would have been no war.*[15]

But, as Maude Royden confessed above, she herself had been totally *un*organized and *un*ready to rally national self-disarmament in August 1914 – and that failure holds a serious lesson for nuclear pacifists also at the end of the twentieth century.

Maude Royden refused to accept the ideological defence of World War I that it was a crusade against the false ideal of Prussian militarism. She herself wanted to combat that false ideal – of course – but she refused to 'put a nation to the torture in order to do so'.[16] If the Germans were successfully crushed by the Allies, they would not be persuaded that militarism was wrong, only that they needed a still mightier army. Meanwhile the heresy of militarism was growing ever stronger within Britain too – 'We seek to convert the Prussian from his heresy, but we ourselves know not what spirit we are of.'[17] How then *can* a false ideology be fought? 'There is only one way to kill a wrong idea. It is to set forth a right idea. You cannot kill

[15] Maude Royden, *The Great Adventure: The Way to Peace*, pamphlet, 1915 (now located in Fawcett Archive); my emphasis.
[16] ibid.
[17] ibid. (and cf. Christa Wolf in *Cassandra*, ch. 7 below).

hatred and violence by violence and hatred . . . Satan will not cast out Satan.'[18] Warfare, however, Maude Royden acknowledged, is not simply 'satanic' – it too is a 'great adventure', a heroic risking of self for others, and it is this very 'heroism of war, not its cruelty, that leads all the world after it'.[19] Like Bertha von Suttner before her, and Virginia Woolf after her, Maude Royden identified the masculine heroism of war, the soldier's identification of his manhood with his readiness to risk death in battle in order to defend the defenceless homeland, as the root cause of humanity's age-long acceptance and even affirmation of warfare. Against that false heroic ideology – false because the willingness to sacrifice oneself conceals and even entails a willingness to destroy countless others, including many defenceless in their homelands – Maude Royden invoked her alternative:

> I tell you that there is a mightier heroism still – the heroism not of the sword, but the cross . . . Who is the great adventurer – he who goes against the enemy with swords and guns, or he who goes with naked hands? . . . Peace is the great adventure . . . And only when the world conceives it so, will the world be drawn after it again.[20]

But Britain was already at war; it was too late to advocate unilateral disarmament. Instead, all that Maude Royden could do was to carry on preaching that waging war was wrong, however much she longed to be one with her country in its suffering, and even though she was warned that the world was 'not ready yet for such teaching'.

> I can not so separate myself from the world, and to me the separation involved in preaching that *here* and *now* war is wrong, when so many think it right, is less real than the separation implied in the belief that I can see a vision others cannot. I am convinced that what I can see others can see, and nothing will persuade me that the world is not 'ready' for an ideal for which I am ready . . .
>
> For the truth, as they see it, men are laying down their lives to-day in Belgium and in France. And we who see another

[18] ibid.
[19] ibid.
[20] ibid.

> truth – shall we be less true to it than they? We cannot sacrifice the Christian ideal even to a national necessity. Truth is more than victory.[21]

It was this truth, that one must neither return evil for evil, nor submit to evil, but rather 'overcome evil with good' that Maude Royden consistently preached to ever more hostile gatherings in 1915. Occasionally, as in Birmingham Town Hall, she could speak without interruption and walk out afterwards, limping, past a waiting angry crowd without being set upon. At other times in 1915 she had to run the gauntlet of almost murderous violence:

> The Fellowship of Reconciliation organised a caravan tour through the country for some of us and we had increasingly rowdy meetings. Two newspapers – one daily and one weekly – carefully informed the public of our route and plans. They said it would be deplorable if we should meet with violent handling but that no one could be blamed if we did and we could be found at such and such a place on such and such a date . . . We were mobbed in a little Midland town, our caravan burnt and ourselves threatened with death.
>
> It was a horrible experience . . . There is something indescribably bestial in the hatred of human beings close to one and with the lust to hurt and destroy. There were (the police afterwards told us) between two and three thousand there, and about fifteen of us. The people were those whose husbands, fathers, sweethearts and sons had been mown down in Sulva Bay. They could not hear or see us without hatred, convinced we were betraying the cause sealed with that blood.
>
> I can never account for our escape. I know we remained completely passive until a man came and suggested that we should be taken to the police . . . As we approached [the police station] the crowd realised that we were being rescued and suddenly made a rush at us but it was too late. Missiles were thrown and I got a crack on the head. The next moment the door opened and we went in. The mob waited for hours but nothing happened and at last they went away. The police

[21] ibid.

> stopped an express train in the small hours of the morning, put us aboard and washed their hands of us.[22]

That episode ended the efforts of the Peace Caravan. Maude Royden felt it was unbearable as well as counter-productive to trigger so much hatred all in the cause of peace:

> It is always difficult to know whether one is influenced by wisdom or by cowardice in keeping silent at any particular moment. I cannot judge for myself. I only know that to go on preaching peace to people in such straits as my countrymen were by this time seemed intolerable . . . The young . . . died in squalor and in filth that the most realistic war books cannot make us see as they saw it . . . I ceased to protest. Only when conscientious objectors were being treated with a brutality that decent men and women blush to remember now, and again when an appeal for negotiated peace 'before it was too late' was issued by Lord Lansdowne in the Daily Telegraph did I feel moved to words. When at the City Temple [after 1917] no one was left in any doubt that I was a Pacifist but I did not try to convert those whose suffering was almost beyond endurance.[23]

It was characteristic of her, both then and later, that when circumstances – or her own views – changed, she would force herself to acknowledge the fact and change her behaviour in response to them.

Maude Royden could no longer believe, as she had believed before 1914, 'that women were innately more pacific than men'.[24] She had been forced to acknowledge that women '*can* be as virulently militarist, as blindly partisan . . . as the male non-combatant. There appears to be no cleavage of opinion along sex lines.'[25] But though women could not be looked to as a natural force in the world for peace, the women's *movement*, said Maude Royden, still could. Its influence would be more indirect than had at first been supposed but it would still work against militarism because its basic principle

[22] Royden, 'Bid Me Discourse', ch. 8.
[23] ibid.
[24] 'War and the women's movement', in C. Buxton, G. L. Dickinson et al. (eds), *Towards a Lasting Settlement*, for the Union for the Democratic Control of Foreign Policy, 1915.
[25] ibid.

was the assertion that moral force, not physical, must be the foundation stone of political power. The consent of the governed is essential to the legitimacy of the government. No member of the physically weaker sex could ever accept that 'Might is right'.

> Militarism and the Women's Movement cannot exist together. Take a militarist religion like that of Islam, and you see women reduced to the lowest level of degradation; a militarist legal code like the Code Napoléon, and you have women without human rights and only sex functions – breeders of potential soldiers merely; a militarist civilisation like that of Prussia, and again women without rights, almost without privileges . . . 'You do not know what it is like to be a woman,' said a prominent German Suffragist, 'in a country which has built its whole existence on a successful war.'[26]

Women are not essentially anti-militarist, but militarism is essentially anti-feminist. Therefore feminism as an ideology must always take issue with Bismarckian *Machtpolitik*. Inasmuch as women are not equal to men in their capacity to use force, they are less willing to believe in the valid arbitration of force. And therefore, according to Maude Royden, 'Women can do no greater service to the world than to increase healthy scepticism of violence as a method of imposing ideals.'[27] The validation of violence has to be called in question by the physically weaker sex.

Once World War I was over and the doomed 'Peace Settlement' made, Maude Royden's hope for a better world began to focus on the contribution that thinking women might now be allowed to make towards a real 'League of Nations'. She held to this hope not because she believed that women were better or wiser or stronger than men, but simply because they, hitherto totally excluded from international decision-making, could not help but bring fresh eyes to the public world.

> There is just one thing to be said for women in this matter, and that is that they have none of the traditions which make it difficult for men to see sense . . . The statesmen of Europe are apparently incapable of working any machinery except on the

[26] ibid.
[27] ibid.

old lines . . . . We – the people in the street – imagined that the brotherhood of nations would be realised after the war. Our governors, on the contrary, see all Europe split up into little armed camps – hating each other, fearing each other, preparing to fight each other, spending their last farthing on arms and explosives, while their children die of starvation and philanthropists strive to prolong their feeble existence by huge (but still inadequate) doles of food and money . . . [And our governors] make no excuses, they are not ashamed, they are not surprised. I am persuaded that someone has got to get into this thing – this shadow that we call 'The League of Nations' – who has not been trained in the old ways. Women in short.[28]

But thoughtful women could bring to world politics not only the clarity of a vision unclouded by centuries of the practice of *Realpolitik*; they could also bring, Maude Royden believed, some elementary but vital psychological insight gained through their long experience of the private world of family life:

[Statesmen] begin at the wrong end, and draw new frontiers for military purposes, regretting that alas! the integrity of nations and the principle of self-determination must be violated to do so. Women, accustomed to deal with children both good and bad, would not, I think, have thought of a plan so ingenious as to give one child what belonged to another, and then provide them with weapons because justice demanded that they should be allowed to defend themselves from the rage and the fear they would certainly feel.[29]

Maude Royden's hope that it might be granted to women to 'mother' the twentieth-century world was developed in her remarkable sermon to women delegates attending the conference of the International Alliance for Women's Suffrage in Geneva in June, 1920. Once again the world's feminists renewed their commitment to internationalism. Maude Royden was given permission to preach in Calvin's pulpit, where no woman had ever spoken before, in that same Geneva where John Knox's diatribe against the Monstrous Regiment had declared: 'that a woman promoted to sit in the seat

[28] *London Mail*, 22 Apr. 1920.
[29] ibid.

of God, that is to teach, to judge, or to reign above man, is a monster in nature, contumely to God, and thing most repugnant to His will and ordinance.'[30] Maude Royden took as her text: 'Except the Lord build the house their labour is but lost that build it; except the Lord keep the city the watchman waketh but in vain.' Her definition of 'the Lord', however, was not the supreme Legislator and Judge of mankind, but rather human love, human forgiveness. She had the audacity to preach love to the survivors of the 'Great War' of righteous hatreds. It was women, as she reminded her hearers, not men, who were now thought by scholars to have mediated to St Luke that supreme Christian parable of the Prodigal Son.

> Love alone can build. Love alone creates. There is no power to create but love. We know this, we women [because] we are old in the work of making homes . . . For lack of this conception, the world perishes. Again and again men have built up their magnificent civilisations and again it has crashed to earth in ruins . . . Already the League of Nations threatens to crumble; already men cry, with glee, or with despair: 'The League is dead'; it was still-born.[31]

In her peroration, Maude Royden directly confronted her hearers – the women of post-1918 – with their own lost hopes of motherhood and tried to give them an alternative meaning in life:

> Women whose husbands or lovers the war has slain, mothers now childless, women who have not borne and now may never bear a child, to you above all belongs the service of the world. In none of you must the divine spirit of motherhood perish unused . . . the world needs it more than you dream . . . [Bring] to birth a new world . . . make the nations a family – and of the world a home.[32]

Years later, when writing 'Bid Me Discourse', Maude Royden

[30] John Knox, *The First Blast of the Trumpet against the Monstrous Regiment of Women*, Geneva, 1558, quoted in O'Faolain and Martines (eds), *Not in God's Image*, Fontana/Collins, 1973, ch. 10, p. 275.
[31] 'Women, the world and the home', Maude Royden's sermon preached in Geneva, June 1920, published by the League of the Church Militant, 1920.
[32] ibid.

recorded: 'What I was thinking every woman there was thinking, what I was saying was in all their hearts. Alas, what came of it at last?'

From 1920 to 1925 Maude Royden consecrated herself, and urged both men and women to consecrate themselves, to try to make a world in which everyone could be happy. She realized that this vision contradicted the 'scientific' view of the social Darwinians that 'suffering and exploitation are the law of life as reflected in nature'.[33] But in her view that was the voice of an outmoded, outgrown science; for her, modern science teaches that the natural universe is governed by laws of life-sustaining balance which must be co-operated with, and she believed that our moral universe also has laws, 'but that with these we have not begun to co-operate, nor even to respect'. For her, the moral law had been articulated in the Sermon on the Mount and she made herself very unpopular in the 1920s in certain places by insisting on applying the principles of the Sermon on the Mount to the Austrian children starved by the Allied blockade or to the Russian children not fed by the Allies because Russia was now 'Bolshevik' or to the striking British dockers, or to the Washington Disarmament Conference concerning naval power in the Pacific.[34]

As the 1920s refused to progress, Maude Royden became more and more concerned about the betrayal of the founding principles of the League of Nations. She campaigned in 1925 for conciliation and arbitration to be invoked in practice, and not just in theory, in international conflicts:

> It is really more civilised, and in the end it makes for better justice, if a man is not judge in his own cause, nor executioner . . . We have already given up the right to make war in the case of the individual, the noble, the clan, the city. We must now give it up as between nations.[35]

As early as 1927 she had to deplore the 'reappearance *within* the League of Nations of the idea of preserving peace by a balance of power, as a substitute for which the League of Nations itself actually

[33] Maude Royden, *Can We Set the World in Order?* League of the Church Militant, Westminster, 1921.
[34] See Maude Royden, *Political Christianity*, G. P. Putnam's Sons 1922; and League of Church Militant Supplements, 1923–7.
[35] 'Arbitration: the world's need', League of Church Militant Supplement, 1925.

came into existence'.[36] At certain times, in later years, Maude Royden would blame the failure of the League of Nations on the cynicism of the professional politicians, the practitioners of *Realpolitik*. 'Those who created the League knew what they were about. Had the idealists been left to work out the world's salvation they would have succeeded.'[37] But later still she asked herself what share of responsibility rested with those same idealists who, like herself, had organized and spoken, year in, year out, *for* the League:

> Why did we not make the ideal we worked for sufficiently dear to people of good will to survive all difficulties? We had many excellent meetings in those days – they must have outnumbered even the meetings held for Women's Suffrage. [But it] seems to me that they lacked the thrill of those [suffrage] days, probably because of the presence among us of too many half-hearted people.[38]

The irony was that Maude Royden herself had felt less than 100 per cent whole-hearted about the League of Nations since she had had to compromise her own strict pacifism in working for the League's policy of 'collective security', including possible collective military security. She had made this compromise because of her intense commitment to political relevance. She never believed in saving her own soul, keeping her own hands perfectly spotless, if in so doing she were to be of less help to the world – 'to be turned in upon yourself even from the most religious motives . . . this is death'.[39] But another part of Maude Royden cried out to practise the most uncompromisingly idealistic peace witness possible, even if it led to her own and to others' physical death. Hence her appeal, in 1931, to men and women to join her in forming a 'Peace Army' of unarmed passive resisters who would intervene between the combatants in the world's military confrontations – 'perhaps the most sanguine pacifist initiative of the entire twentieth century'.[40]

[36] 'Peace – our responsibility', League of Church Militant Supplement, 1927.
[37] Essay by Maude Royden in James Marchant (ed.), *If I Had My Time Again*, Odham's Press, 1950.
[38] Royden, 'Bid Me Discourse', ch. 8.
[39] *The Guildhouse Calendar*, Favil Press, London, 1931, quotations from the sermons, speeches and writings of Maude Royden.
[40] M. Ceadel, *Pacifism in Britain*, ch. 6.

Maude Royden had realized that men's readiness to make war is always with us, in every society, and that it is this readiness which is continuously preparing each society in spirit as well as in fact for its next war. 'The soldier is getting ready for war; whether there will ever be another war or not, he is not going to take the risk of being unready when it comes. You can see him in the barracks, in the streets and on the parade ground, the army is ready; the navy is ready.'[41] To counter this constant virile war-preparedness, Maude Royden called on her hearers to constitute themselves an alternative, *un*armed Peace Force, which would need even more courage than that recognized by the Victoria Cross:

> Enrol yourselves! Do not be content to do nothing, to sit and wait until war breaks out in the hope that then you may do some heroic deed . . . as a conscientious objector . . . I would like now to enrol people who would be ready if war should break out to put their bodies unarmed between the contending forces.[42]

At the end of 1931, she, Dr Herbert Gray and the Rev. Dick Sheppard went into retreat to ponder the implications for Christian pacifism (and supporters of the League of Nations) of the Japanese attack upon Shanghai. They emerged with their proposal that an international, unarmed 'Peace Force' should intervene.

> It was an unparalleled opportunity, for the fighting there was not guerrilla warfare nor in the air nor along a vast front of trenches . . . Chinese and Japanese soldiers were facing each other and firing at each other across the streets of Shanghai and even a few thousand unarmed volunteers would have been seen, would have been effective, and could by their acceptance of death without resistance, have stirred the conscience of the human race.[43]

Realizing that their proposal would need to be backed with ships and finance, they forwarded their suggestion to the League of

[41] Maude Royden's Guildhouse Sermon, reprinted in *New World*, organ of the No More War Movement, Nov. 1931.
[42] ibid.
[43] Maude Royden, 'Dick Sheppard, peacemaker', *c*. Nov. 1937, article in Fawcett Archive.

Nations. The Secretary-General replied that he was unable to consider any scheme not originating from the government of a member state – but he did release the proposal to the world press. A thousand volunteers came forward. Maude Royden was profoundly disappointed and even shocked that only a thousand people should have been willing to sacrifice themselves; less idealistic souls might be more amazed that even one person should have been willing to go and get riddled in the cross-fire of two foreign combatants. In any event nothing came of the project and its proposers recognized that a unique opportunity had passed. Maude Royden did, however, still hold protest meetings at the London Docks, *c.*1931, against the sale and shipping of British arms to Japan.

The grim years 1932–7 were mitigated for Maude Royden by her comradeship with her fellow pacifist leader Dick Sheppard. Her obituary article on him declared:

> [The Pacifist Movement] needs the emotional force that can meet and overpower the glamour of war; it needs a leader whose passion is as strong as his intellect is keen. I do not believe that anyone less than such a man can destroy the glamour of war and create the great movement of the heart that alone to-day can save the world from war.
>
> Such a man was Dick Sheppard.
>
> He felt with an intensity beyond the reach of most of us . . . he felt the sorrows of the world, he was moved to compassion, and he acted.[44]

So convinced was Maude Royden by the peace-making power of the man, Dick Sheppard, that she stifled her doubts about the negativism of his policy – a 'Peace Pledge Union' which simply said 'No' to war. Maude Royden had realized from the first that it is not enough to say 'No' to war; we have also to fashion constructive alternatives to war in order to resolve international conflicts. Almost in desperation at the proximity of war in 1938 (and out of a kind of posthumous loyalty to Sheppard), she did finally join the Peace Pledge Union. 'But the moment I came in I felt I was a fish out of water. The

[44] ibid.

PPU seemed far more keen about *opposing rearmament* than supporting a forward policy.'[45]

In October 1939, Maude Royden, by then one of the world's best-known pacifist leaders, publicly repudiated her pacifism. As Sybil Thorndike was to comment after Maude Royden's death: 'Her courage was remarkable when she forsook her pacifist – her complete pacifist – convictions during the war, for I think that must have been very difficult for her.'[46] When this writer asked Maude Royden's secretary, Miss Daisy Dobson, what had made Maude Royden change her mind, she simply replied: 'She could not bear what Hitler was doing to the Jews.' Maude Royden herself said: 'The unbelievable thing had happened – there had come into the world something that was worse than war.'[47] Hitler's *Mein Kampf* (and the implementation of his world-view) had converted her to the reluctant recognition that 'the horror of having our children brought up in the Nazi faith is greater than death.'[48] 'We seek to free Germany no less than ourselves from a horrible cancer.'[49] She still believed that there was an ideally better way of defeating Nazism than by waging war – the way of silent and creative suffering as practised by Gandhi and his followers – but she knew that she and her fellow Britons were not ready for it. Not being ready, they would only fail and in failing they would betray the hopes of all anti-Nazis the world over who depended upon them. Once again Maude Royden could not seek to ensure the safety of her own soul without any reference to the possible consequence to others. She was bitterly attacked by some within the peace movement for her apparent inconsistency, but in her own mind she was not inconsistent. It had been the great shock to her Christian humanism of August 1914 that had first converted her to pacifism and it was the greater outraging of that same humanism by the Nazis which finally compelled her publicly to renounce her pacifism in 1939. She only regretted that she had not done so before.

If Maude Royden herself repudiated her pacifism, what, it may

[45] Letter from Maude Royden in *Peace News*, 13 Oct. 1939.
[46] Report of Service of Thanksgiving and Remembrance for the life and work of Dr Maude Royden, at St Botolph's, 6 Apr. 1957 (in Fawcett Archive).
[47] Royden, 'Bid Me Discourse', ch. 8.
[48] Royden, 'A point of view', 1940 – in Fawcett Archive.
[49] Royden, 'I was a pacifist', *Sunday Despatch*, 16 June 1940.

be asked, is the point of disinterring it now?

Now, at the end of the twentieth century, the world's circumstances have changed once more; yet again global war has become the worst of all possible evils, entailing as it will not only mass incineration and mass torture worthy of an omnipotent Hitler, but also the gradual, irreversible extinction of almost all forms of life on our planet; the cockroach may survive. Given that prospect, there is no doubt in my mind that Maude Royden, were she alive, would once again call upon us urgently to evolve an *effective* Court of International Justice as the only civilized alternative to war, and that she would, once again, call upon women to 'mother' the world before it is too late. She who had worked as a volunteer in a maternity hospital during World War I and who had whole-heartedly supported Eleanor Rathbone in her 30-year campaign (1918–46) for a national income for all mothers,[50] never had any doubts either about the real cost of mothering or about its real value. Maude Royden recognized that mothering is not only the source of all human life but also the original source of the human love of life. 'The love of mothers first raised the human being above the level of the animal.'[51] Thoughtful mothers, she said, are real democrats and real peace-makers, valuing each person in their circle as a unique individual, anticipating conflicts and, when failing to prevent conflict, not happy until reconciliation has once again been achieved.[52] It was her deepest hope that the private, life-centred expertise of ordinary women could be adapted and applied to save the life of the world. She dreamed of a common humanist front that would bond the world's derided idealists with the practical common sense of each nation's women. 'The world was her parish.'

Maude Royden's writings cannot altogether transmit the power

[50] See Eleanor Rathbone, *The Disinherited Family*, E. Arnold and Co., London, 1924, reprinted Falling Wall Press, 1986, and see Suzie Fleming's Introductory Essay, pp. 50–2.

[51] *The Guildhouse Calendar*, entry for 29 Oct. 1931. Maude Royden was not able to be a biological mother but she did become an adoptive parent. When she speaks of 'mothering' she means of course all parental nurturing. The loving co-operation of both sexes is necessary for young human life to be able to flourish, as she pointed out in *Women's Partnership in the New World*, Allen & Unwin, 1941. She stressed the value of women's part in that nurturing simply because it is so often undervalued and taken for granted.

[52] See Royden, *Women's Partnership in the New World*.

that her vibrant voice and personality gave them while she was still alive; nevertheless, as with Kate Courtney, it is impossible not to feel a shock when coming upon her forgotten speeches, articles and sermons and encountering her passionate humanity and her faith in us to do great things. 'How she would blaze out at cruelty and injustice,' Sybil Thorndike remembered. Perhaps the shock of encountering Maude Royden is related to a dim apprehension that if we really were to listen to people like her and Kate Courtney and if we tried to imagine how they would advise us now, we might yet, through a huge collective effort, save ourselves from falling over the edge of darkness.

4

The Wise Fool: Simone Weil (1909–1943)

'Mais elle est folle!'
de Gaulle, c.1942

It is generally agreed that the French philosopher Simone Weil was an extraordinary phenomenon. To the dissident communist Boris Souvarine, in the 1930s, she was 'the only brain that the working-class movement has produced in many years';[1] to the Anglo-Catholic T. S. Eliot, in 1951, she had a 'kind of genius akin to that of the saints';[2] to the humanist Albert Camus, in 1961, she was 'the only great spirit of our time'.[3] Until very recently Simone Weil has been celebrated above all as a religious mystic, but this chapter will concentrate exclusively on her enduring legacy to humanist political thought on the subject of war. The ascetic 'other-worldly' Simone Weil in fact spent the greater part of her last years trying to save *this* world as she struggled to define and articulate an alternative value-system for our world to that favoured by Hitler (and by all his fellow militarists before and since). For war, Simone Weil believed, is *the* affliction of our twentieth century, just as slavery

[1] Simone Pétrement, *Simone Weil: A Life*. Mowbrays, Oxford, 1976, ch. 7, p. 176.
[2] T. S. Eliot, Preface to Simone Weil, *The Need for Roots*, Routledge, 1952.
[3] Quoted by John Hellman, in *Simone Weil: An Introduction to Her Thought*, Wilfred Laurier University Press, 1982, Introduction, p. 1.

(and consequent crucifixion) had been *the* affliction of the Roman Empire.[4]

Simone Weil was a deeply sensitive, hyper-intelligent child of nearly six when she first came into contact with the suffering caused by war. Her doctor father had been sent to Neufchâteau in December 1914 to work in a military typhoid hospital. Against the rules, his family moved there also and Simone and her mother 'went almost every day to the hospitals to bring the patients oranges, crackers and newspapers . . . The hospitals [were] packed to overflowing with sick and wounded'.[5]

Simone became passionately patriotic, learning and declaiming nationalistic verse by heart and at six and a half she 'adopted' a French soldier at the front who had no family, sending him letters and packages. On 29 May 1917, when Simone was eight, this adopted soldier of hers arrived unexpectedly at the Weils' house. 'For Simone it was a great delight, a feast of friendship. Holding hands, the little girl and her big adopted soldier would take walks all through the day. They never saw him again, for soon after his leave he was killed in action.'[6] Dorothy McFarland is surely right in saying: 'It would seem that the war affected her very deeply; it was probably the primary external cause of her obsession with suffering and affliction.'[7] Simone Weil herself was to date her conversion to *anti*-nationalism from the way in which World War I was ended:

> I was ten years old at the time of Versailles, and up to then I had been patriotically thrilled as children are in war-time. But the will to humiliate the defeated enemy which revealed itself so loathsomely everywhere at that time (and in following years) was enough to cure me once and for all of that naive sort of patriotism.[8]

Simone Weil was psychologically well prepared, therefore, to be intensely sympathetic to the teaching of the pacifist moral philosopher Alain, whom she first encountered when she was sixteen and a half

[4] See Simone Weil's letter to Joe Bousquet, 12 May 1942, in Richard Rees (ed.), *Simone Weil: Seventy Letters*, OUP, 1965, p. 137.
[5] Pétrement, *A Life*, ch. 1, pp. 11–12.
[6] ibid., pp. 15–16.
[7] Dorothy McFarland, *Simone Weil*, Frederick Ungar, New York, ch. 1, p. 13.
[8] Letter to Bernanos, in Rees (ed.), *Letters*, p. 109.

Simone Weil

in October 1925. Simone Weil's innate anti-authoritarianism and her passionate fellowship with the victims of society greeted the self-same attitudes in Alain as she whole-heartedly endorsed her professor's implacable opposition to war:

> The First World War had made him an ardent and convinced pacifist, for him the chief goal of political action was the preservation of peace . . . he thought that war makes us into greater slaves than capitalism ever could . . . What is the slavery of a worker when set alongside that of a soldier? His disciples were therefore resolved to be pacifists before all else and to spread the spirit of resistance to war as much as possible.[9]

Simone Weil was taught by Alain for four years and he became a significant, lifelong influence upon her.

Between the ages of 16 and 20, Simone Weil was a typical ardent young peace activist: she addressed envelopes and mailed the monthly newspaper of her pacifist organization, *The Will to Peace*; she leafleted neighbourhoods and put up fly-posters; after the Kellogg Peace Pact 'outlawing war' in August 1928, she circulated a manifesto calling for immediate, total disarmament; in February 1929, her branch of the civil liberties organization, the League for the Rights of Man, voted in favour of urging the French government to accept 'universal and obligatory arbitration', and in international conflicts to initiate genuine disarmament; it also called upon French people to substitute a policy of Franco-German union for their previous policy of intransigent revenge. (Thus, although she did not know them or even of them, the young Simone Weil was in complete agreement with the octogenarian Kate Courtney and the middle-aged Maude Royden, who were campaigning in Britain simultaneously for the same ends.) Also during this period Simone Weil collected signatures protesting against a new policy of the pre-emptive arrest of demonstrators by the police; and in May of 1930 she herself took part in a pacifists' march demonstrating support for Briand. The marchers were charged and truncheoned by the Paris police – Simone Weil herself was knocked down but got up again and carried on marching. In all these activities Simone Weil was a typical radical, anti-militarist student; what was less typical was that her youth

[9] Pétrement, *A Life*, ch. 3, pp. 48–9.

marked not the climacteric of her pacifist radicalism, but merely its beginning. The following years, 1932–9, were to see her continuously pondering the problem of war as the ultimate form of social violence and connecting it with other forms of contemporary social oppression, including the inhumanly efficient technology of industrial mass production and the impersonal, bureaucratic mode of centralized twentieth-century administration.

The freshness and independent-mindedness of Simone Weil's thought on the prevention of war was first seen in an article published on 20 February 1932 in *L'Effort* – the paper of militant unionists in the building trade in Lyons. Perhaps surprisingly, Simone Weil here decisively opposed both collective security through the League of Nations and proposals for civil defence. At the abortive League of Nations' Conference on Disarmament at Geneva, in 1932, France had submitted a memorandum proposing the creation of an international force at the service of the League of Nations. Simone Weil opposed this proposition on the grounds that it was not really serious because everyone knew that there was no chance of its being adopted. Whether she would also have opposed such a proposal, had it been serious, is not clear. Simone Weil also opposed a French proposal that international rules should be established for the protection of the civilian population in case of war. With all-too prophetic insight, Simone Weil argued that civil defence 'only helped to increase the probability of war by guaranteeing the safety of governments and general staffs. She felt that everyone should be in danger if any one person was; the equality of danger was to some extent an assurance against war.'[10]

Although she was now a respectable young probationary teacher of philosophy at a girls' lycée, and expected to behave as such, Simone Weil still took part in street protests that the bourgeois considered to be in deplorable taste. In October 1933, for example, she was hoisted on to a window-sill by her syndicalist/pacifist friends in order to address a demonstration against Lebrun, the French president, who had come to unveil a local war memorial. She took advantage of the occasion to attack the life-and-death powers of the head of state, a man who in this case was also suspected of being in the pocket of the French armaments manufacturers. It was not for

[10] ibid., ch. 5, p. 123.

him to make elegiac speeches at war memorials. Simone Weil followed this up with an anarchist/pacifist article, 'Reflections on War' published in November 1933 in *La Critique Sociale*, the magazine founded by her dissident communist friend Boris Souvarine. Every war, she said, should be evaluated in terms of the means it employs, rather than in terms of the aims it pursues. She took issue with those on the left who were flirting with the idea of a just, revolutionary anti-fascist 'people's war', pointing out that *all* modern wars subordinate 'the combatants to the instruments of combat. In effect then, war is . . . the war of the State apparatus against its own army. In war, as in fascism, the essential "point" is the obliteration of the individual by a state bureaucracy serving a rabid fanaticism.'[11] War *always* strengthens the hand of the state over the people – no matter what ideology that state purports to serve:

> The great error of almost every study on war . . . is to consider war as an episode in foreign policy, when above all it constitutes a fact of domestic policy, and the most atrocious one of all . . . [For] massacre is the most radical form of oppression, and soldiers do not expose themselves to death, they are sent to the slaughter . . . Revolutionary war is the tomb of the revolution . . . Whether the [enemy] is labelled fascism, democracy, or dictatorship of the proletariat, our great adversary remains The Apparatus – the bureaucracy, the police, the military. Not the one facing us across the frontier of the battle lines, which is not so much our enemy as our brothers' enemy, but the one that calls itself our protector and makes us its slaves.[12]

Extraordinarily resonant words for the late twentieth century and anticipating Brecht's poem: 'WENN ES ZUM MARSCHIEREN KOMMT'

> WHEN IT COMES TO MARCHING THERE'S
> PLENTY WHO DON'T KNOW
> That their enemy is marching at their head.

[11] Jacques Cabaud, *Simone Weil: A Fellowship in Love*, Harvill Press, 1964, ch. 3, p. 99.

[12] 'Reflections on war', *La Critique Sociale*, Nov. 1933, quoted by Cabaud, *Fellowship*, p. 100 (and recently translated in full in McFarland and Van Ness, *Formative Writings 1929–1941: Simone Weil*, Routledge, 1987, pp. 237–48).

The voice that's giving the orders
Is their enemy's voice.
For he who talks of enemies
Is himself the enemy.[13]

Simone Weil's conclusion in 1933 was the absolute pacifist one that 'in no matter what circumstances, the worst betrayal is to consent to subordinate oneself to this apparatus and, in its service, to destroy in oneself and in others, all true human values.'[14]

Equally prophetic was Simone Weil's 'Sketch of Contemporary Life' in her *Oppression and Liberty*, written at the end of 1933 and early 1934, and influenced, in its pessimism, both by Hitler's defeat of the German working-class movement and by Stalin's defeat of the Russians. She was appalled by the lack of human scale already visible in every aspect of industrialized society:

> We are living in a world in which nothing is made to man's measure. [Certain] units of measurement are given and have hitherto remained invariable, such as the human body, human life, the year, the day, the average quickness of human thought, [but] present-day life is not organised on the scale of all these things . . . Quantity is changed into quality, as Hegel said, and in particular a mere difference in quantity is sufficient to change what is human into what is unhuman.[15]

The supreme example of inhumanity is war, which is a competition in inhumanity; and in the twentieth century both the scale of warfare and of war preparations and the centralization of bureaucratic administration mean that the 'power and concentration of armaments place all human lives at the mercy of the central authority'.[16] Since the state machine is becoming ever more powerful and since national economies are becoming increasingly subordinate to military interests, the 'pivot around which social life revolves . . . is none other than

[13] 'Deutsche Kriegsfibel 1938', in Bertolt Brecht, *Hundert Gedichte, 1918–1950*, Aufbau Verlag, Berlin, 1959.
[14] Cabaud, *Fellowship*, p. 100.
[15] Simone Weil, 'Sketch of contemporary life', in *Oppression and Liberty*, Routledge, 1958, p. 108. (Simone Weil's own title for this book was *Réflexions sur les causes de la liberté et de l'oppression sociale*.)
[16] ibid., p. 112.

preparation for war'.[17] The economic struggle for power between states can all too easily result in war, whilst the constant preparation for such war only strengthens the centralizing power within each state. Future wars will mean 'a crazy destruction of wealth of all kinds that previous generations have bequeathed us and finally our civilisation will perish'.[18]

It is a remarkable warning from a writer of the pre-nuclear age. Over 50 years ago Simone Weil could already see that 'our present situation . . . resembles that of a party of absolutely ignorant travellers who find themselves in a motor-car launched at full speed and driverless across broken ground.'[19]

Early in 1936, after her year of factory work, 1934–5, Simone Weil was still an absolute pacifist on moral grounds. She criticized the view that war can *never* be a way to avoid having contempt for oneself, since the combatants are compelled to fight, that is, to kill.[20] It was at this same period, April 1936, that she wrote her 'résumé' of *Antigone* for the factory workers at Rosières, and it is significant that it should have been *Antigone* that she chose as essential to popularize then, rather than any other text of world literature. Clearly, she wanted her worker-readers to share her own affirmation of this courageous, proud being's lonely stand against righteous war-hatred in the name of the state. She translated Antigone's defiant credo addressed to Creon: 'Your orders, I believe, have less authority than the unwritten and unrepealable laws of God . . . I was born not to mete out hatred, but love.' Pity for helplessness must take precedence over patriotic moral condemnation.

Only five months later, however, Simone Weil herself was issued with a rifle to fight in a righteous war for which she had volunteered. How could such a volte-face from absolute pacifism have been possible?

Between April and July 1936 it seemed to Simone Weil – as it did to many other youthful radicals the world over – that the Spanish anarcho-syndicalist working class were defending themselves against Franco's fascist invasion in order to create a real 'people's revolution

[17] ibid., pp. 115–16.
[18] ibid., p. 116.
[19] ibid., p. 121.
[20] See Pétrement, *A Life*, ch. 9, p. 262, 'An answer to a question by Alain' (translated and given in full in McFarland and Van Ness, *Formative Writings*).

of self-contained and self-governing communes'.[21] She believed that just for once a war was being fought that was *not* subordinated to the state-machine. Sitting in Paris, reading the news from Spain (as Simone Weil later confessed in a letter to Georges Bernanos), she 'could not prevent [herself] from participating morally in that war – in other words, from hoping all day and every day for the victory of one side and the defeat of the other'. So she left for Spain. Ironically, the commander she enlisted under, the anarchist Durruti, was not only one of the most dedicated, but also one of the most violent of all the war-leaders. Simone Weil comforted herself that she was too short-sighted ever to hit anybody or anything at which she aimed; nevertheless she did point her rifle at Nationalist bombing aeroplanes that were out of range and she did recognize that if she were captured she would deserve to be shot – 'Our troops have spilled a lot of blood. I am morally an accomplice.'[22] Just how much blood, she learned only a few weeks later, after she herself had been invalided out by severe burns. What Simone Weil then had to face was that the genuinely idealistic struggle of the Spanish anarchists had rapidly been betrayed by the ferocity of the means they used to wage it. Pitiless killing had become an acceptable way of life and the 'very purpose of the whole struggle is soon lost in an atmosphere of this sort. For the purpose can only be defined in terms of the public good, of the welfare of men – and men have become valueless'.[23] She had hoped and believed that the Spanish Civil War would be less oppressively 'totalitarian' (that is, involving conscription, the execution of deserters and a pyramidal military command-structure amounting to dictatorship) than were the wars between sovereign states, but instead she had discovered that in anarchist Spain, just as in Bolshevik Russia and revolutionary France, the waging of war dictated totalitarianism even when its original impetus was libertarian. Moreover, in the agony of a civil war, one of the first casualties is law – as opposed, that is, to lynching – as Simone Weil herself was forced to report in her unfinished article, 'Reflections that No One is Going to Like' (October 1936).

[21] James Joll, *The Anarchists*, Methuen, 1979, p. 208, quoted in McFarland, *Simone Weil*, ch. 4, p. 77.
[22] McFarland, *Simone Weil*, ch. 4, p. 81.
[23] Letter to Bernanos, in Rees, *Letters*, p. 108, and see Pétrement's comment, *A Life*, ch. 10, p. 282.

Simone Weil's own brief participation in the Spanish Civil War, from July to September 1936, therefore, actually strengthened rather than weakened her anti-militarism during the subsequent three years. She had experienced, she felt, the self-contradicting, total impossibility of fighting a good, just 'People's War', upon her own pulse. On her return to France she wrote an uncompromisingly pacifist article entitled 'Do We Have to Grease our Combat Boots?' which asked rhetorically: 'Can any war bring to the world more justice, more liberty, more well being?'[24] She was convinced that a general war between nations was the greatest of all evils since it must result in the maximum number of human deaths, and in March 1937 she wrote her great analytical anti-militarist essay 'Ne Recommençons pas la Guerre de Troie' – translated as 'The Power of Words'. This essay is the product of an Olympian mind; Simone Weil's frame of reference ranges easily and authoritatively from Homer's *Iliad* to the contemporary iron industry in Lorraine, from the Moroccan colonial crisis of 1911 to the street-fighting in Berlin in 1932, and from the Roman plebeians to Poincaré in 1917. Her impulse to write the essay came from her premonition that the unreined propaganda-war between Hitler and Stalin would very soon escalate into a second total war. In her insistence that such a war must not be accepted as inevitable, Simone Weil cast doubts on the reality of the alleged ideological gulf between Hitlerism and Stalinism and even on the justifiability of a war between 'democracy' and 'dictatorship'. Furthermore, she tried to demonstrate the irrationality of all national wars and she posed the fundamental questions: Why do nation states prepare for war and wage war upon each other, century after century? Why is it so essential to be able to make war?[25]

Simone Weil's starting-point is that the Trojan War, fought as it was over the phantom of Helen, is a timeless, symbolic expression of the unreality of all warfare. Wars are fought not for a limited, definable object (and we may remember here Jane Addams's vain attempt to persuade the belligerent Great Powers to define *their* war-aims in 1915),[26] but for ideas in the heads of the combatants. And

[24] Quoted in Pétrement, *A Life*, p. 281.
[25] In Richard Rees (ed.), *Simone Weil: Selected Essays 1934–43*, p. 159.
[26] See above, ch. 2 and Anne Wiltsher, *Most Dangerous Women*, Pandora Press, 1986.

these ideas are delusions, unreal abstractions.

> For our contemporaries the role of Helen is played by words with capital letters. If we grasp one of these words, all swollen with blood and tears, and squeeze it, we find it is empty. Words with content and meaning are not murderous . . . but when empty words are given capital letters, then, on the slightest pretext, men will begin shedding blood for them . . . In these conditions the only definition of success is to crush a rival group of men who have a hostile word on their banners; for it is a characteristic of these words that each of them has its complementary antagonist.[27]

Thus 'our political universe is peopled exclusively by myths and monsters' – such absolute and abstract entities as 'Nation', 'Security', 'Capitalism', 'Communism', 'Fascism', 'Democracy' and so forth. The tragedy is that 'Corresponding to each empty abstraction there is an actual human group'[28] and when that group happens to be a nation state, then there is a permanent danger of war:

> In the end, a study of modern history leads to the conclusion that the national interest of every State consists in its capacity to make war . . . What a country calls its vital economic interests are not the things which enable its citizens to live, but the things which enable it to make war; petrol is much more likely than wheat to be a cause of international conflict. Thus when war is waged it is for the purpose of safeguarding or increasing one's capacity to make war.[29]

But, Simone Weil goes on to ask,

> Is it not natural that every State should define the national interest as the capacity to make war, when it is surrounded by States capable of subduing it by arms if it is weak? . . . And, further, a State cannot appear weak in its external relations

27 'The Power of Words', in Rees (ed.), *Simone Weil: Selected Essays 1934–43*, OUP, 1962.
28 ibid., p. 168.
29 ibid., p. 158.

> without the risk of weakening its authority with its own subjects.[30]

Thus every state, or bloc, makes an enemy of its opposite number by threatening to exterminate it; yet it *has* to make such a convincing threat, partly because each state feels threatened by some other state and partly in order to keep control and maintain its own prestige at home. 'Nothing but complete and universal disarmament could resolve this dilemma, and that is hardly conceivable.'[31] In uttering these terrible truths Simone Weil is agreeing with von Treitschke's view that the nation state exists for the pursuance of war (see above, ch. 1) – the vital difference between them being that she abhors what he had enthusiastically affirmed.

To illustrate the irrationality of current ideological conflicts, and hoping that clearer thinking might yet save human lives, Simone Weil pointed out certain vital similarities between Hitlerism and Stalinism:

> In each of them the State seizes control of almost every department of individual and social life; in each there is the same frenzied militarisation, and the same artificial unanimity, obtained by coercion, in favour of a single party which identifies itself with the State . . . and finally there is the same serfdom imposed upon the working masses in place of the ordinary wage system.[32]

In some ways, Simone Weil's essay has much more to say to us 50 years after it was written than it had for her contemporaries. She herself was soon to realize and to acknowledge that she had underrated Hitler's threat to the whole world; but what she said in 1937 about the confrontation between the blocs and about their lethal compulsion to maintain a constant state of military preparedness has a relevance to us that can hardly be exaggerated. Our political universe is at least as much 'peopled exclusively by myths and monsters' as hers. In our day too

[30] ibid., p. 168.
[31] ibid.
[32] ibid., p. 159.

> what is called national prestige consists in behaving always in such a way as to demoralise other nations by giving them the impression that, if it comes to war, one would certainly defeat them; what is called national security is an imaginary state of affairs in which one would retain the capacity to make war while depriving all other countries of it.[33]

It is still 'nearly always believed, with or without reason, by all parties, that the only defence is attack', and 'the swarm of hate-filled abstractions' cause us in our turn to 'forget the value of life'.[34]

Throughout 1938 Simone Weil could not bear to believe in the inevitability of another world war, largely because of her own recent immersion in the reality of war in Spain. She herself had, however briefly, participated in the brutalizing business and she could not allow herself to forget it: 'I was very nearly present at the execution of a priest. In the minutes of suspense I was asking myself whether I should simply look on or whether I should try to intervene and get myself shot as well. I still don't know which I should have done if a lucky chance had not prevented the execution.'[35]

Simone Weil had also had first-hand experience in the field of the corrupting effects of the ideology of 'masculinism' – its identification of virility with ruthlessness. Her male comrades had boasted convivially to her about 'how many priests they had murdered, or how many fascists, the latter being a very elastic term'. She had been forced to come to the grim conclusion that, as she wrote to Bernanos: 'As soon as men know that they can kill without fear of punishment or blame, they kill; or at least they encourage the killers with approving smiles. If anyone happens to feel a slight distaste to begin with, he keeps quiet and he soon begins to suppress it for fear of seeming unmanly.'[36] Given that harsh education in the swift degeneration of even the most idealistic war, it is not surprising that Simone Weil kept up a fierce inner resistance to the realization that yet another, total war would soon have to be fought.

On 25 March 1938, Simone Weil signed a pacifist declaration by French anti-fascists stating that it was essential, in the interests of world peace, to negotiate with Germany. Negotiation and an end to

[33] ibid., pp. 158–9.
[34] ibid., pp. 169–70.
[35] Letter to Bernanos, in Rees (ed.), *Letters*.
[36] ibid.

the deadly armaments race are 'something on which perhaps the entire future of humanity depends'.[37] On 25 April 1938 she was billed, together with Maria Montessori, as a leading pacifist figure to speak on foreign affairs during the following August. Clearly Simone Weil was still closely identified with pacifism in France (and pacifism with her), as was Maude Royden at that time in Britain. Simone Weil, however, was already turning over in her own mind the possibility of armed resistance to a Nazi invasion, a form of resistance that would be at once less 'totalitarian' and more effective than that waged by a 'conventional' national army. Anticipating both the guerrilla tactics of many later anti-colonialist struggles and recent proposals of the 'Alternative Defence Commission' and Ecoropa,[38] Simone Weil defined the problem as 'how to render a possible invasion so difficult that the idea of such an invasion does not constitute a temptation in the neighbouring states'.[39] In an article written early in April 1938 she faced the problem of how to organize a successful revolt in the event of invasion. Her answer was: by decentralizing economic, political and social life, and by decentralizing armed resistance – 'Do not form fronts, do not lay siege to cities; harass the enemy, break up his communications, attack him always where he least expects it, demoralise him, and stimulate the resistance by a series of small but victorious actions.'[40]

Clearly, therefore, Simone Weil was no longer in her own mind a pacifist. But she was still not reconciled to the inevitability of a second world war. She even preferred the thought of a fascist take-over by Daladier in France, although she well knew that that would imperil all her dearest friends on the left, not to mention all French Jews including her own parents and brother. (She recognized that there were already signs of widespread, near-violent, anti-Semitism in France.) How could Simone Weil bear to envisage a fascist France? Her answer was that if that were the only price that could buy peace between France and Germany then 'it would be less murderous of

[37] Quoted in Pétrement, *A Life*, ch. 11, p. 326.
[38] cf. Ecoropa Information Sheet 8 – *Defending Britain Without the Bomb*, Sept. 1982, and The Alternative Defence Commission, *Without the Bomb*, Paladin, 1985, ch. 5, 'National defence, British military options', and ch. 6, 'Strategies against occupation'.
[39] Quoted in Pétrement, *A Life*, ch. 11, p. 328.
[40] ibid.

French youth as a whole'.[41] The 'less murderous' path was now the only one left to opt for, but it was still bitter to have to opt for it – sacrificing the anti-fascist Sudeten Germans, endangering all the other Czechs and humiliating the liberal democracies. After Munich, in September 1938, she wrote: 'We have been humiliated . . . every one of us has been subjected in the very centre of our beings to . . . the abasement of thought before the power of factual reality.'[42] Simone Weil recognized that the Munich Agreement had not averted war, merely postponed it. The rise of fascism and the concomitant near-certainty of war had now destroyed her humanist faith in progress, as is clear in the fragment 'The Distress of our Time': 'The great expectations inherited from the three preceding centuries and above all from the last century, the hope of a progressive spread of knowledge, the hope of general well-being, the hope of democracy, the hope of peace, are all in the process of disintegrating.'[43]

The final stage of the transition in Simone Weil's thinking between her realization that a general war against Hitler would be fought and her recognition that it would *have* to be fought – that it was not merely a political inevitability but also a moral necessity – is found in her first reflections on the brutal duplicity of Republican Rome, published by Richard Rees as 'Three Letters on History' in his edition of her *Selected Essays*. The analogy she drew between Ancient Rome's attempt at world domination and that of Hitler was developed in her 'Réflexions en vue d'un Bilan', translated as 'Cold War Policy in 1939' and written in April 1939 after Britain's introduction of conscription. In this article Simone Weil still clung to one last hope, that the surrounding democracies might yet hold Hitler off from waging unlimited war by means of a combination of tactical concessions and diplomatic resistance, thus buying time in which his regime might grow ever weaker from within. Nevertheless she was beginning to admit to herself that Hitler, like Rome, was not prepared to give his adversaries this option of buying time.

> To find another period when men of every kind, in countries extending over a vast area, were equally disturbed by a political danger one would have to go back to the period when Rome

[41] ibid., p. 326.
[42] ibid., ch. 12, p. 339.
[43] ibid., p. 337. The whole text, 'The distress of our time', is now published in McFarland and Van Ness, *Formative Writings*, pp. 272–3.

> annihilated Carthage and crushed Greece . . . [And] since I believe the Roman conquests, with their atrocious material or spiritual annihilation of entire peoples, to have been history's great disaster, I have no difficulty in accepting the general view that universal domination by Germany would be a catastrophe . . . It is to be feared . . . that the danger is not an illusion . . . [Hitler] governs a country which is strained to full pitch; his will is fiery, unflagging, pitiless, and closed to considerations of humanity; his imagination plays with grandiose historical visions of the future, in a Wagnerian style; and he is a natural gambler.[44]

Once Hitler demonstrated that he was not, in fact, to be restrained, Simone Weil was reluctantly converted, just like Maude Royden, to the moral necessity for fighting World War II; and, again like Maude Royden, she wished she had come round to that conviction earlier:

> Ever since the day I decided, after a very painful inner struggle, that in spite of my pacifist inclinations it had become an overriding obligation in my eyes to work for Hitler's destruction, with or without any chance of success, ever since that day my resolve has not altered; and that day was the one on which Hitler entered Prague – in May 1939, if I remember right. My decision was tardy, perhaps; I left it too late, perhaps, before adopting that position. Indeed, I think so and I bitterly reproach myself for it.[45]

But, Simone Weil insisted, Hitler must be destroyed *not* by outdoing him in brutality, violence and inhumanity, and not even by being just a *little less* brutal, violent and inhumane than he: 'Whoever is only incapable of being as brutal, violent and inhumane as the adversary, yet without exercising the opposite virtues, is inferior to this adversary in both inner strength and prestige; and he will not hold his own against him.'[46] In order to be genuinely, incontrovertibly anti-fascist, argued Simone Weil, the democracies

[44] Rees (ed.), *Essays*, pp. 177, 179.

[45] Letter to Jean Wahl, 1942, in Rees (ed.), *Letters*, p. 158.

[46] Quoted in Pétrement, *A Life*, ch. 13, p. 353. The whole fragment is published in McFarland and Van Ness, *Formative Writings*, pp. 277–8 and ends: 'it is not enough to defend an absence of tyranny. We must be rooted in *armistice* in which every activity is really oriented in the opposite direction from tyranny.'

must first practise the reverse of Hitler's domination and racism themselves. Therefore they must, early on in the hostilities, announce their commitment to renounce their own colonial imperialism in Africa and Asia.

Addressing herself in particular to the situation of France, Simone Weil insistently criticized French colonial policy in Algeria and Indo-China (for example in her 1943 essay 'East and West', now translated in her *Selected Essays*). Nearer home, on the actual war-fronts, Simone Weil argued that the Allies must show themselves to be just as capable of suicidal heroism as the Nazi storm-troopers, only with the motive of saving human life rather than destroying it. Above all, Simone Weil tirelessly reiterated that the one thing that anti-Nazis must *not* do, whether during the war or after its victorious conclusion, was to imitate Hitler. If France, for example, were to take a leaf out of Hitler's book and herself impose a peace of extermination upon the Germans: 'Hitler's system would not disappear; it would simply migrate, with all its characteristic aims and methods, to France . . . for the future of humanity, for civilisation, for freedom, a victory like this would not be much better than defeat.'[47] To clarify this point in her political writing from 1939 to 1943 Simone Weil concentrated on defining what she believed to be the essential evil of Hitler and Hitlerism, seeking out its root in West European history and warning her own people, the Free French, against succumbing in their turn to the temptations of nationalist idolatry, leader-worship and 'false greatness'.

'Analogies,' wrote Simone Weil, 'are deceptive; they must be used with caution, but they are our only guide.'[48] The analogy that she

[47] Simone Weil, 'The Great Beast' (1939–40), in Rees (ed.), *Essays*, cf. George Sand's prophetic letter to Flaubert, Sept. 1871 after the Franco-Prussian war: 'The German triumph is for Germany the first act of her moral dissolution. The tragedy of her fall has begun, and as she works at it with her own hands it will proceed apace. All these great material organisations of humanity are so many idols of clay; it is our duty and our interest to realise it . . . *But the moral downfall of Germany is not the future salvation of France, and if we are fated to do to her as she has done to us, her ruin will not restore us to our life*. It is not in blood that races can renew their youth. Streams of life may yet come from the corpses of France; the corpse of Germany will be a plague centre for all Europe. *There is no resurrection for a nation which has lost sight of the human ideal* [my emphasis]', *George Sand–Gustav Flaubert Letters*, Duckworth, 1922.

[48] Simone Weil, 'Cold War policy in 1939', in Rees (ed.), *Essays*, p. 186.

continued to find most fruitful for an understanding of the essence of Nazism was the history of Rome. Immediately after the outbreak of World War II Simone Weil wrote her 'Reflections on the Origins of Hitlerism', including one section on 'Hitler and Roman Foreign Policy' and another – rejected by the censor in Vichy France – on Hitler and Roman Internal Policy. Simone Weil insisted that the pernicious legacy of Roman values and praxis had not been confined to Nazi Germany (although it was currently seen at its most brutal wherever the Nazis had power):

> Every people which turns itself into a nation by submitting to a centralised, bureaucratic, military State becomes and long remains a scourge to its neighbours and the world. This phenomenon is not connected with Germanic blood . . . The majority of people in Europe obey nothing else than the authority of the State.[49]

And outside itself the authority of the state nowadays encounters no limitation or judge:

> Even the treaties it signs only commit it to its own interpretation of them and no other interpretation can be legitimately imposed on it from outside. Its power is, in fact, limited solely by the power of other sovereign nations, that is to say, by war, or the explicit or implicit threat of war.[50]

It is remarkable that no sooner had World War II begun than Simone Weil was not only seeking out its tap-root two thousand years earlier, but she was also suggesting how the world should reorganize international relations when once the war against Hitler had been won. The League of Nations had been doomed to fail, she wrote, because it had tried to establish a supranational international

[49] 'Europe's colonialism in Africa and Asia'; in Rees (ed.), *Essays*. Simone Weil also made a comparison to Roman Imperialism: 'It would certainly be difficult to deny that we have made and are still making use of methods similar to Rome's in conquering and ruling our colonial empire.' cf. 'God knows that in Africa and Asia there is no shortage of peoples for France to emancipate' – 'A European war over Czechoslovakia' (May 1938), in McFarland and Van Ness, *Formative Writings*, p. 265.

[50] Rees (ed.), *Essays*, pp. 136–7.

order while leaving the dogma of national sovereignty still intact.[51] (Clearly she would have made a similar diagnosis of the failure up till now of the United Nations.) The alternative that she proposed was a federalist world order made up of nations – or rather of ex-nations – that had themselves evolved a great measure of internal decentralization. For the sake of world peace Germany must be dismembered – but so must Germany's conquerors. The victors must:

> accept for themselves the same transformation that they impose upon the vanquished. The victory of those who are armed to defend a just cause is not necessarily a just victory; it is not the cause for which men took up arms that makes a victory more just or less, it is the order that is established when arms have been laid down.[52]

The alternative to such a just, magnanimous peace after World War II, she warned, would be the continued organization of mutual massacres, culminating at last in 'the mutual destruction of all the states'.

Increasingly, Simone Weil had come to see that the fate of the whole world would depend on whether humanity could or could not evolve an alternative value-system to that which upheld the power (and the right) of the stronger to dominate the weaker by military or by economic force. This book began with a presentation of Bismarck's theory and practice of *Realpolitik* – the rationalized Gospel of Force. But *Realpolitik* did not begin with Bismarck; Simone Weil points out that it was familiar to every tyrant – and to his victims – in the Ancient World, and that it first came to full fruition with the almost-global tyranny of Ancient Rome. One of her most profound meditations on the Gospel of Force – and on the alternative to it – is found in her essay on Homer's *Iliad*, written immediately after the French defeat by the Nazi invasion of 1940. On one level the essay is a coded message inspiring the French to recognize the transitoriness of the Nazi conquest, by analogy with the short-lived triumph of Homer's Greeks. On another level it is a

[51] cf. the ideas of Leopold Kohr – *The Over-developed Nations: The Diseconomies of Scale*, C. Davis, 1977.
[52] Rees (ed.), *Essays*, pp. 139–40.

meditation on the perennial threat presented by human awe before the power of the strong. Force, says Simone Weil, 'is that which turns anybody who is subjected to it into a *thing*'.[53] The victims of force are not only those who are defeated in war, but also all those who are defeated socially and economically, powerless slaves the world over, prey to hunger and the will of the powerful. But force, the power to dominate, is itself an illusion – in fact no one really possesses it forever. Rather, the true reality is our universal vulnerability to forces both outside and within us beyond our control. Delusions about total power always bring down nemesis – as the Greek thinkers knew but we have forgotten. 'To the same degree, though in different fashions, those who use force and those who endure it are turned to stone.' Power relations are only transcended in:

> those brief celestial moments in which man possesses his soul . . . The love of the son for the parents, of father for son, of mother for son . . . Conjugal love . . . friendship. These moments of grace are rare in *The Iliad*, but they are enough to make us feel with sharp regret what it is that violence has killed and will kill again.[54]

The alternative to the false gospel that force will always triumph is our human sense of justice. And justice is simply our sense of obligation towards others, rooted in our pity for all who suffer: 'the sense of human misery is a pre-condition of justice and love. He who does not realise to what extent shifting fortune and necessity hold in subjection every human spirit cannot regard as fellow-creatures nor love, as he loves himself, those whom chance separated from him by an abyss.'[55] Simone Weil's essay ends with the heartfelt prayer that the peoples of Europe will yet 'learn that there is no refuge from fate, learn not to admire force, not to hate the enemy, nor to scorn the unfortunate'.

One practical suggestion for how the Allies might live out a humane non-fascist value-system even in wartime was Simone Weil's 'Plan for an Organization of Front-Line Nurses', first thought out

[53] '*The Iliad*, the poem of force', reprinted in Sian Miles, *Simone Weil: An Anthology*, Virago, 1986, p. 183.
[54] ibid., pp. 206–8.
[55] ibid., p. 212.

by her early in 1940 and further worked on in 1941 and 1942.

> This project is concerned with the formation of a special body of front-line nurses. It would be a very mobile organisation and should in principle be always at the points of greatest danger, to give 'first-aid' during battles . . . According to the American Red Cross, by far the greatest proportion of deaths in battle are the result of 'shock', 'exposure', and loss of blood which can only be prevented by immediate treatment.
>
> The American Red Cross has developed a system of plasma injections which can be operated *on the battle field* in cases of shock, burns, and haemorrhage [Simone Weil's emphasis] . . . [These women] would need to offer their lives as a sacrifice . . . and this without being sustained by the offensive spirit but, on the contrary, devoting themselves to the wounded and dying.[56]

The primary importance of such a body of women in the fighting zone would be the saving of human life and the comforting of the wounded and dying on both sides. But there was a still deeper, ideological inspiration behind Simone Weil's proposal:

> Hitler has never lost sight of the essential need to strike everybody's imagination; his own people's, his enemies' and the innumerable spectators . . . For this purpose, one of his most effective instruments has been such special bodies as the SS . . . These men are unmoved by suffering and death, either for themselves or for all the rest of humanity. Their heroism originates from an extreme brutality. We cannot copy these methods of Hitler's, first, because we fight in a different spirit and with different motives; and also because, when it is a question of striking the imagination, copies never succeed. Only the new is striking . . . We ought to create something new. This gift of creation is in itself a sign of moral vitality which will encourage the hopes of those who count upon us, whilst discouraging the enemy's hopes . . . An inspiration is only active when it is expressed, and not in words but in deeds . . .
>
> There could be no better symbol of our inspiration than the

[56] Letter to Maurice Schumann, in Rees (ed.), *Letters*, pp. 144–53.

> corps of women suggested here. The mere persistence of a few humane services in the very centre of the battle, the climax of inhumanity, would be a signal defiance of the inhumanity which the enemy has chosen for himself and which he compels us also to practise. The challenge would be all the more conspicuous because the services would be performed by women and with maternal solicitude . . . Although composed of unarmed women, it would certainly impress the enemy soldiers, in the sense that their presence and their behaviour would be a new and unexpected revelation of the depth of the moral resources and resolution on our side . . . The contrast between this force and the SS would make a more telling argument than any propaganda slogan. It would illustrate with supreme clarity the two roads between which humanity today is forced to choose.[57]

de Gaulle's response to this proposal was said to have been: 'Mais elle est folle!' As Simone Weil noted in her later essay 'On Human Personality', 'In Creon's eyes there was absolutely nothing that was natural in Antigone's behaviour. He thought she was mad.' That Simone Weil, herself a woman, was advocating the founding of a *woman's* organization with which to counter the essence of Hitlerism must have contributed to her craziness in de Gaulle's eyes.

Simone Weil's last testament concerning the spurious 'grandeur' and real mass murderousness of the Gospel of Force is contained in her *The Need for Roots*, written in the last four months of her life. Even though she herself was now a member of the Free French Resistance based in London under de Gaulle, Simone Weil could still perceive all too clearly the danger of idolatry in *all* nationalism, including French nationalism, and its expression in righteous war:

> [when] it is a question of history, morals cease to play any part . . . Everything is done to make children feel . . . that things concerning the country, the nation, the nation's growth have a degree of importance which sets them apart from other things. And it is precisely in regard to [the nation] that justice, consideration for others, strict obligations assigning limits to

[57] ibid., and see Hellman, *Introduction*, p. 82, for Simone Weil's anti-Nietzschean values here.

ambitions and appetites – all that moral teaching one is trying to instil into the lives of little boys – never gets mentioned.[58]

This false assumption of the 'superior' moral claims of the nation places the nation above morality, which in practice means that for reasons of state a nation can, whenever it pleases, have recourse to the immorality of war: 'With morals, properly speaking, thus relegated to a lower plane, no other system is advanced as a substitute, for the superior prestige of the nation is bound up with the exaltation of war.'[59]

Like Maude Royden, Simone Weil identified the fatal contradiction between our personal morality and our public immorality. In personal life it is recognized that:

> limits must be set to egoism and pride. But when it comes to national egoism, national pride, not only is the field unlimited but the highest possible degree of it seems to be imposed by something closely resembling an obligation. Regard for others, recognition of one's own faults, modesty, the voluntary limitation of one's desires – all are now turned into so many crimes, so many sacrileges . . .
>
> Our patriotism comes straight from the Romans. The Romans really were an . . . idolatrous people . . . idolatrous with regard to themselves. It is this idolatry of self which they have bequeathed to us in the form of patriotism.[60]

This absolutist assertion of the validity of national immoralism, which Simone Weil traced back to Rome, she also found in the life-work of the architect of the French state, Cardinal Richelieu, the French equivalent of Prussia's Bismarck. If one asks the Richelieus and the Bismarcks, 'Politics for what?' they answer, 'For the greater glory of the state.' But if one presses on with the next question: 'Why for the greater glory of the state and not for something else?' they have no answer.

> That is the question which mustn't be asked. So-called realist politics [*Realpolitik*] handed down from Richelieu to Maurras [the contemporary French ultra-rightist] . . . only makes sense

[58] Simone Weil, 'Uprootedness and nationhood', in *The Need for Roots*, pp. 131–2.
[59] ibid.
[60] ibid., pp. 133–4.

> if this question is not put. In fact Richelieu's political attitude only makes sense for those who, whether individually or collectively, feel either that they are masters of their country or else capable of becoming so.[61]

In other words, the state is *them*. For power is never really an end in itself; it is always a means. (See the chapter in *The Need for Roots* entitled 'The growing of roots', p. 209.) In practice it has all too often been the means to still more power for those who already have most; but what power *should* be is the means to justice rooted in compassion. That is true anti-fascism – and true patriotism:

> Compassion for our country is the only sentiment which doesn't strike a false note at the present time . . . And this same compassion is able, without hindrance, to cross frontiers, extend itself over all countries in misfortune, over all countries without exception; for all peoples are subjected to the wretchedness of our human condition. Whereas pride in national glory is by its nature exclusive, non-transferable, compassion is by its nature universal.[62]

What hinders us all in creating a civilized world of justice rooted in compassion is 'our false conception of greatness; the degradation of the sentiment of justice and our idolisation of money'.[63] Of these, 'our conception of greatness is the most serious defect of all, and the one concerning which we are least conscious that it is a defect: at least in ourselves; for in our enemies it shocks us'.[64] All our history books foreground the history of conquerors, the champion slayers of humanity, from Alexander to Caesar to Augustus to William the Conqueror to Napoleon – 'No attention is paid to the defeated . . . The defeated disappear.'[65] Official history takes the murderers at their word. This unconscious consensus about the 'greatness' of mass-murdering conquest was, not surprisingly (since it was so general a consensus), also shared by Hitler. The only

[61] ibid., p. 143, and see her 'Three letters on history', in Rees (ed.), *Essays*; '[Richelieu] deliberately and pitilessly fostered the wars in Europe' (p. 85) and 'in my eyes there is grandeur only in gentleness' (p. 79).
[62] ibid., pp. 165–6.
[63] Weil, 'The growing of roots', in *The Need for Roots*, p. 209.
[64] ibid., pp. 209–10.
[65] ibid., p. 212.

difference was that he put these criminal values into practice. Hitler, we are told, modelled himself upon Sulla – that was the model of 'greatness' which Western European history had transmitted to 'that wretched, uprooted youth wandering about in the streets of Vienna'. And it is that same false model of greatness which we must not only refuse to transmit but actually overturn and invert.

> People talk about punishing Hitler. But he cannot be punished. He desired one thing alone, and he has it: to play a part in History . . . Whatever Hitler is made to suffer, that will not stop him from feeling himself to be a superb figure. Above all, it will not stop, in twenty, fifty, a hundred or two hundred years' time, some solitary little dreamer, whether German or otherwise, from seeing in Hitler a superb figure with a superb destiny from beginning to end, and desiring with all his soul to have a similar destiny. In which case, woe betide his contemporaries.
>
> The only punishment capable of punishing Hitler, and deterring little boys thirsting for greatness in coming centuries from following his example, is such a total transformation of the meaning attached to greatness that he should thereby be excluded from it.[66]

But this in turn will demand a total reversal of our own national political values – 'False greatness must first be despised . . . [one must] make a pact with oneself to admire in history only those actions and lives through which shines the spirit of truth, justice and love.'[67]

But Hitler did not simply believe that he had the spirit of human history on his side; he, like Bismarck, also believed that he was acting out the very same laws that govern all the natural sciences. Simone Weil quotes the passage from *Mein Kampf* which articulates Hitler's crude 'scientific' belief in the supremacy of force: 'in a world in which planets and suns follow circular trajectories, moons revolve round planets, and force reigns everywhere and supreme over weakness, which it either compels to serve it docilely or else crushes

[66] ibid., pp. 216–7.
[67] ibid., pp. 224 and 218. cf. 'In order to love France, we must feel that she has a past; but we must not love the historical wrapper of that past. We must love the part which is inarticulate, anonymous, which has vanished' (p. 222).

out of existence, Man cannot be subject to special laws of his own.'[68]

Simone Weil challenges us with an ultimatum: Either we, like Bismarck and Hitler, agree that force is

> the unique and sovereign ruler over human relations [or] we must perceive at work in the universe, alongside force, the intuitive sense of obligation to others[69]. . . We know justice to be real, experientially, in our own hearts. [And the] structure of the human heart is just as much of a reality as any other in this universe, neither more nor less of a reality than the trajectory of a planet.[70]

We all know, in our hearts, that the highest thing we are capable of is the love of our neighbour, intervening to help anyone who has been reduced to 'a little piece of flesh, naked, inert, and bleeding beside a ditch'.[71] Like Kate Courtney (see chapter 2), Simone Weil identified the Gospel of Force as the *Weltanschauung* that would sooner or later destroy the world; like Maude Royden, she drew attention to the grotesque contrast between our personal morality and our collective national immorality; and like Virginia Woolf (see below ch. 5), she mocked the 'false grandeur' of masculinist history, reverencing instead 'the part which is inarticulate, anonymous, which has vanished' (*The Need for Roots*, p. 222).

What part, if any, did the division between the sexes play in Simone Weil's analysis of the phenomenon of war? She pitied men for being victims of the deforming ideology of masculinism; she recognized that ever since they had been small boys they had been brought up to believe that it is heroic to conquer, manly to kill. Her own cherished project for a unit of front-line nurses was explicitly female and maternal, and her heroines from literature and history included Antigone, Electra, Joan of Arc, Teresa of Avila and Rosa Luxemburg. Nevertheless Simone Weil was never a feminist in the (false) sense of claiming that women are morally superior to men. On the contrary, she venerated the creative, humane men throughout

[68] Hitler quoted in Weil, *The Need for Roots*, p. 229.
[69] ibid., p. 230.
[70] ibid., p. 232.
[71] 'Implicit love', in *Waiting on God*, Routledge & Kegan Paul, 1951. As John Hellman pointed out in *Introduction*, Christ's parable of the Good Samaritan is 'the ultimate antithesis to fascism'.

Western history also – Homer, Sophocles, Socrates, Plato, Jesus, Marcus Aurelius, Shakespeare, Racine, Rembrandt and Bach, among others. And, since she held that the only test for virtue is the way that we exercise power, she would have considered the case for women's superior virtue in the political world unproven and improbable. There is no reason to believe that any of Simone Weil's generalizations about 'our' false awe before triumphant brute force, 'our' pernicious dual inheritance from the Judaeo-Christian church and Ancient Rome, and 'our' constant temptation to dominate those weaker than ourselves were addressed exclusively to men. She wrote simply as a human being speaking to other human beings. It is one of the ironies of twentieth-century history that this most audacious of political thinkers, who outlined a radically 'alternative' mode of political praxis and who consistently dared to attack *all* centralized, militarized sovereign nation states, did not herself (because she was a woman, or more particularly, a French woman) ever have a political vote. But far from allowing that specific injustice to distract her, Simone Weil treated it with oblivion and concentrated all the energy of her short life on trying to save the whole world.[72]

Given that Simone Weil, like Maude Royden, was driven by Hitler to renounce her absolute anti-militarist stand, how can we be sure that she would not, today, accept the analogy with Hitler that both blocs now claim to see – the West comparing Soviet communism to Hitler's threat in 1939, the Warsaw Pact likening NATO's war games, and the US's 'Star Wars' plan, to Hitler's *Drang nach Osten* in 1941? And, in that case, might she not also accept, however reluctantly, the stance of 'nuclear deterrence'? Simone Weil did not wish to see totalitarianism of any kind take over the world; nor, incidentally, did she wish to see 'the Americanisation of the whole world'.[73] 'One does not liberate the world by conquering it, on the contrary.'[74] Nevertheless there is clear evidence in her last writings, in my view, that given today's choice between risking possible world domination, even enslavement, and risking possible world extinction, Simone Weil would tell us that it was our moral duty (whichever bloc we

[72] Weil, 'Cold War policy in 1939', in Rees (ed.), *Essays*, p. 192: 'Some of us have thought a great deal about the principles of international policy, in the attempt to find them elsewhere than in violence, hypocrisy, and double-dealing.'
[73] Simone Weil, 'East and West' (1943), in Rees (ed.), *Essays*, pp. 206–7.
[74] Simone Weil, 'Uprootedness and nationhood', in *The Need for Roots*, p. 108.

lived under) to choose the risk of becoming enslaved.

For what Simone Weil termed 'atrocious', 'appalling' in any age, past, present or to come, was mass-murdering cruelty. The massacre of non-combatants, or of slaves, or of prisoners, or of women and children in the course of some 'unlimited' righteous war, was an abomination to her whether that war were waged against the Philistines or against Troy or against Carthage or against heretics or on the Western Front 1914–18.[75] 'The greatest calamity the human race can experience,' she wrote in her essay on *The Iliad*, is 'the destruction of a city'. And Maurice Schumann recalled how, in her last conversation with him, Simone Weil employed, with 'a marvellous and atrocious premonition, [the word] "holocaust". She was troubled by several sections of the Old Testament . . . which seemed to justify genocide. "How can we condemn a holocaust today," she wondered, "if we have not condemned all past holocausts?" '[76]

By the same logic she would have condemned all holocausts to come. Simone Weil's *positive* values are equally relevant to the choice now before us. Whenever she had to weigh the lesser of two current evils in the terrible years 1936–9, she always tried to identify the less murderous one as being the more positive. In her project for front-line nurses she affirmed the supreme value of saving human life, even in the midst of war. And as for non-human life, she loved the precarious, touching beauty of the natural world, seeing in it Christ's smile. Preparing for nuclear extinction would have seemed to her humanity's final blasphemy, its total irreverence towards all Creation and towards all that humans have it in themselves to create. The first part of her last testament, *The Need for Roots*, called 'The Needs of the Soul', spells out a moral alphabet for our time, formulating precisely why we must not even contemplate, let alone risk, the destruction of our world, no matter for what blood-filled word-with-a-capital-letter.

> [We] owe our respect to a collectivity: First because it is food for a certain number of human souls – each of which is unique and if destroyed cannot be replaced.
>
> Secondly, because of its continuity, each collectivity is already

[75] See for example 'The great beast' and especially 'Reflections on barbarism' (fragments), in Rees (ed.), *Essays*, pp. 142–3.
[76] Quoted by Hellman, *Introduction*, p. 73.

> moving forward into the future. It contains food, not only for the souls of the living, but also for the souls of beings yet unborn which are to come into the world during the immediately succeeding centuries.
>
> Lastly, due to this same continuity, a collectivity has its roots in the past. It constitutes the sole agency for preserving the spiritual treasures accumulated by the dead . . . by means of which the dead can speak to the living.[77]

The 'collectivity' to which we in the nuclear age have the most profound obligation is our whole world. Simone Weil's positives were 'the future of humanity, civilization, freedom' – in that order.

But Simone Weil also knew that she was another Cassandra, condemned in her own time to be an impotent prophet, a truth-speaking 'fool' – like *Parsifal der reine Thor durch Mitleid wissend* – Parsifal, the pure-souled fool wise in pity. Finally, haunted by the hunger of those fallen into Nazi hands, Simone Weil either could not, or would not, eat. 'The suffering all over the world obsesses and overwhelms me to the point of annihilating my faculties,' she wrote to Maurice Schumann at the end of July 1942. On 24 August 1943, aged thirty-four, she died. Alain could not believe it. 'When she went into politics I expected much. Much? I expected, quite simply, the answer.'

[77] Simone Weil, 'The needs of the soul', in *The Need for Roots*, pp. 7–8.

5

The Elegiac Artist: Virginia Woolf (1882–1941)

> *Three Guineas* seems to me by far the most penetrating study of the fundamental causes of war that I have ever read . . . I'm quite sure that the time will come when those of us who believe what [Virginia Woolf] taught, must carry on her work.
>
> Shena, Lady Simon, *condolence letter to Leonard Woolf, 1941*[1]

It would be too much to claim that Virginia Woolf had been a convinced pacifist ever since her early childhood. Nevertheless, there is a powerful and very significant passage in her 'Sketch of the Past', written in April 1939, that recalls 'a sudden violent shock' during her happily uneventful summers at St Ives:

> Something happened so violently that I have remembered it all my life . . . I was fighting with Thoby on the lawn. We were pommelling each other with our fists. Just as I raised my fist to hit him, I felt: why hurt another person? I dropped my hand instantly, and stood there, and let him beat me. I remember the feeling. It was a feeling of hopeless sadness. It

[1] Monks House Papers, Documents Section, University of Sussex Library.

> was as if I became aware of something terrible; and of my own powerlessness. I slunk off alone, feeling horribly depressed.[2]

Most normal children periodically get so incensed at some outrageous injustice that they lash out and continue to fight each other until beaten or forcibly separated by a third party. It was a sign of Virginia Woolf's 'abnormality' that her capacity for angry outrage, even as a young child, was less strong than her capacity for horror at what such outrage could make her do to someone else. 'Something terrible' – the fact of righteous human cruelty – had been revealed to her and she had realized simultaneously that she could do nothing at all about it – except let her own fist drop.

Reinforcing her innate revulsion against competitions in hurting were two factors in Virginia Woolf's family background. Her father, Leslie Stephen, who had an immense intellectual influence on her when young, abominated war and 'was willing to let his sons enter any profession with the exception of the Army and Navy'.[3] 'During the Crimean and again in the Boer War he lay awake at night fancying he could hear the guns on the battlefields and he would go out of his way to avoid seeing newspaper posters carrying news of the slaughter.'[4] Secondly, Leslie Stephen's sister, Caroline Stephen, was herself not only a convert to pacifist Quakerism but also the most important English exponent of Quaker thought and vision in the late nineteenth century. Caroline Stephen wrote:

> The most important and the best known of the special testimonies . . . is that which has been steadily borne by our members against all war . . . They have steadfastly refused to take up arms at the bidding of any human authority . . .
>
> [We] regard the opposing of violence by violence as a suicidal and hopeless mode of proceeding . . . Consciences are awakening to the utter incompatability of strife and retaliation and reckless self-aggrandizement with the spirit of brotherhood . . . They

[2] Virginia Woolf, 'A sketch of the past', in Jeanne Schulkind (ed.), *Moments of Being*, Sussex University Press, 1976.

[3] F. W. Maitland, *Life and Letters of Leslie Stephen*, Duckworth, 1906, quoted by Alex Zwerdling, *Virginia Woolf and the Real World*, University of California Press, 1986, ch. 10.

[4] Noel Annan, *Leslie Stephen: The Godless Victorian*, Weidenfeld & Nicolson, 1984, ch. 4, p. 141.

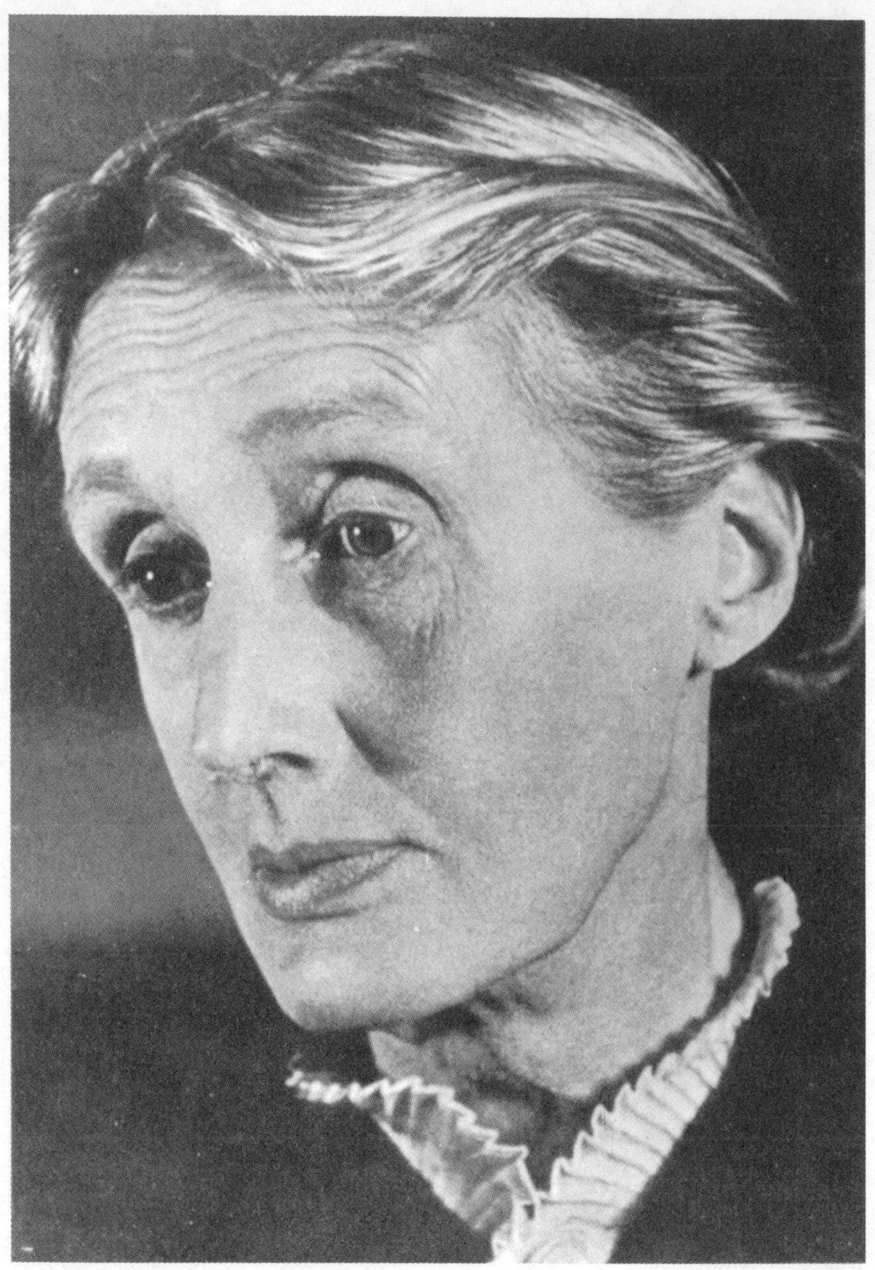

Virginia Woolf

> had need to awake now at the eleventh hour with all Europe making itself ready for war.[5]

Virginia Woolf could be characteristically mocking about this 'nun' aunt of hers but every so often the real seriousness of her influence would break through. After her second nervous breakdown Virginia Woolf stayed with Caroline Stephen in order to help her convalescence in October, November and December 1904. And after another visit, at the end of June 1906, Virginia Woolf wrote: 'I have just come back from a Sunday with my Quaker Aunt . . . We talked for some nine hours . . . She is a kind of modern prophetess . . . The Quaker was charming and wise and humane . . . She is a remarkable woman I always feel when I see her.'[6]

Virginia Woolf's obituary note on this aunt acknowledged:

> Remembering the long hours of talk in her room with the windows opening on to the garden . . . remembering, too, something tender and almost pathetic about her which drew love as well as . . . respect . . . One could not be with her without feeling that after suffering and thought she had come to dwell apart, among the 'things which are unseen and eternal' and that it was her perpetual wish to make others share her peace. But she was no solitary mystic . . . she had a robust common sense and a practical ability . . . with health and opportunity she might have ruled and organised.[7]

Virginia Woolf's very first piece of imaginative writing, *The Journal of Mistress Joan Martyn* (August 1906) contains a portrait of a woman of vision who does rule and organize. *The Journal* purports to be the diary of a young Englishwoman in the late fifteenth century during the onset of the Wars of the Roses. All Joan Martyn's brothers are away in the army, her father is on business in London and it is

[5] Caroline Stephen, *Quaker Strongholds,* Kegan Paul, 1890, ch. 5, 'Spiritual testimonies'.

[6] Letters to Madge Vaughan and Violet Dickinson, July 1906, in Nigel Nicolson (ed.), *The Flight of the Mind: The Letters of Virginia Woolf, 1888–1912*, Hogarth Press, 1975.

[7] Republished in Jane Marcus (ed.), *New Feminist Essays on Virginia Woolf*, Macmillan, 1981, p. 29. I am particularly grateful to Jane Marcus for her essay 'The niece of a nun' in her second collection of essays by various hands, *Virginia Woolf: A Feminist Slant*, University of Nebraska Press, 1984.

her mother who rules the household, ordering the protection of her people within doors. Once the light is out, the old people 'begin talking of the state of the country; and telling dreadful stories of the plots and the battles and the bloody deeds that are going on all round us'.[8] But Joan Martyn's mother has other thoughts to sustain her:

> The fairest prospect in her mind is I believe a broad road running through the land, on which she sees long strings of horsemen, riding at their ease, pilgrims stepping cheerily unarmed, and waggons that pass each other going laden to the coast and returning as heavily laden with goods taken from ships. Then she would dream of certain great houses, lying open to the sight, with their moats filled up and their towers pulled down; and the gate would open freely to any passer-by; and there would be cheer for guest or serving man at the same table with the Lord. And you would ride through fields brimming with corn, and there would be flocks and herds in all the pasture lands and cottages of stone for the poor. As I write this down, I see that it is good; and we should do right to wish it.[9]

That passage was Virginia Woolf's first attempt to evoke what, much later, she was to call 'the life of natural happiness',[10] the real, attainable alternative to perpetual, man-waged war.

Three and a half years later, on 10 February 1910, at the age of twenty-eight, Virginia Woolf testified to her alienation from the whole solemn business of war in a startlingly different way. Bearded, and with blackened face, she participated in the extraordinary *Dreadnought* hoax. She and her brother Adrian and his friends, including Duncan Grant, pretended to be the Emperor of Abyssinia and his entourage, invited by courtesy of the British Foreign Office to inspect the latest, most fearsome British warship, HMS *Dreadnought* – the flagship of the Admiral of the Channel Fleet. It

[8] In *Twentieth Century Literature*, 1977. This was the first publication of *The Journal of Mistress Joan Martyn*, written seventy years earlier.
[9] ibid.
[10] See 'Thoughts on peace in an air-raid', written 2 Sept. 1940, first published in *The Death of the Moth*, Hogarth Press, 1942, and the letter to Shena Simon, 22 Jan. 1940, in Nicolson, *Leave the Letters*.

was as though today one were to breach all the national security regulations of the Ministry of Defence in order to get shown over a top-secret nuclear weapons base, using false credentials. The camouflaged hoaxers were duly greeted with a red carpet and a police barrier to keep the public at bay and the Admiral of the Fleet received his 'royal' visitors wearing ceremonial dress uniform and much gold braid. The party, muttering to each other in Greek owing to their total ignorance of Ethiopian or any other African language, were solemnly conducted over the ship's wireless room and had the big guns' paces shown off by being aimed at different angles especially in their honour.[11] After their irreverent confidence trick had been exposed and embarrassing questions asked in the House of Commons, Adrian and Virginia Woolf's naval cousin stormed into their house demanding, 'Did we realise that we ought to be whipped through the streets, did we realise that if we had been discovered we should have been stripped naked and thrown into the sea? And so on and so on.'[12] Duncan Grant, in fact, did have to be ceremonially struck with a cane in order that the honour of the Navy be avenged, and Virginia Woolf herself never forgot her encounter with a male State Establishment, dressed in gold braid and perfecting the readiness of its latest killing-machine.

It was also at this time, *c.*1910, that Virginia Woolf was engaged in writing her first novel, *The Voyage Out*, in which British warships make a brief but ominous appearance. The passengers sight 'two sinister grey vessels, low in the water, and bald as bone, one closely following the other with the look of eyeless beasts seeking their prey'.[13] Virginia Woolf has her pompous, anti-suffragist Conservative MP Richard Dalloway, and his wife, applaud the spectacle. Richard raises his hat while Clarissa Dalloway asks the young heroine, Rachel, whether the sight doesn't make her glad to be English. 'The warships drew past, casting a curious effect of discipline and sadness upon the waters, and it was not until they were again invisible that people spoke to each other naturally. At lunch the talk was all of valour and death, and the magnificent qualities of British admirals.'[14] Only

[11] Adrian Stephen, *The Dreadnought Hoax*, L. and V. Woolf, London, 1936, reissued 1980.

[12] Quentin Bell, *Virginia Woolf*, vol. 2, Appendix E.

[13] Virginia Woolf, *The Voyage Out*, ch. 4.

[14] ibid.

Rachel's friend, Helen Ambrose, breaks the spell by remarking tactlessly 'that it seemed to her as wrong to keep sailors as to keep a Zoo'.[15] But *The Voyage Out* contains a much more subtle and profound critique of militarism than that.

The struggle against war only matters if every individual life matters. Time and again Virginia Woolf was to testify that our deepest need is for one or two of our dearest people to be allowed to go on living, and already in this, her first novel, she ends with an almost unendurably poignant death. More and more ice is fetched but Rachel's fever will not go down; fresh milk is brought but she cannot swallow it; new doctors are consulted but they are all equally helpless. And the man who loves Rachel

> [could] not get used to his pain, it was a revelation to him. he had never realised before that underneath every action, underneath the life of every day, pain lies, quiescent, but ready to devour; he seemed to be able to see suffering, as if it were a fire, curling up over the edges of all action, eating away the lives of men and women. He thought for the first time with understanding of words which had before seemed to him empty; the struggle of life; the hardness of life. Now he knew for himself that life is hard and full of suffering.[16]

After Rachel's death

> he kept saying to himself, 'This has not happened to me. It is not possible that this has happened to me . . .' As he saw the passage outside the room, and the table with the cups and the plates, it suddenly came over him that here was a world in which he would never see Rachel again. 'Rachel! Rachel!' he shrieked, trying to rush back to her. But they prevented him and pushed him down the passage and into a bedroom far from her room. Downstairs they could hear the thud of his feet on

[15] ibid. cf. Terence Hewet's sympathetic anti-masculinist self-irony in *The Voyage Out*: 'What a miracle the masculine conception of life is – judges, civil servants, army, navy, Houses of Parliament, Lord Mayors – what a world we've made of it!' (ch. 16).
[16] ibid., ch. 25.

the floor, as he struggled to break free; and twice they heard him shout 'Rachel, Rachel!'[17]

Completed in 1913 and finally published in 1915, *The Voyage Out* is a plangent affirmation that every unimportant life is all-important to someone – and in saying that Virginia Woolf is making an implicit but devastating critique of the casualty lists of war.

Ironically, however, Virginia Woolf's own personal response to World War I was detached, to the point of complete alienation, only to be explained by the fact that she had had to spend the first year and a half of that war suffering from intermittent, but very serious, mental illness. Already in July 1913 she had been anorexic and acutely depressed: in September 1913 she had attempted to kill herself with a massively lethal dose of veronal; between September and November 1913 her husband, Leonard, could only save her from being certified insane and compulsorily committed to a mental asylum by himself taking total responsibility for the supervision of her constant nursing care. By April 1914 her condition was again unstable and less than a year later, in February 1915, she suffered a relapse into total insanity, becoming violent, manic, and at one stage in coma – four nurses having to be engaged for her continuous care. It was feared that her mind and indeed her whole personality had suffered serious and irretrievable damage. Very gradually, however, Virginia Woolf did begin to recover and her last nurse was able to leave in November 1915.[18]

In such appalling personal circumstances it is not as surprising as it might otherwise have seemed that Virginia Woolf's very rare comments on World War I in her Diary and letters in the years 1916–19 should have had a curiously unimaginative, even heartless quality, totally unlike that of Kate Courtney, Maude Royden, the child Simone Weil, or, indeed, that of her own earlier or later self. Her hold on the endurability of life was so feeble as she emerged from her private nightmare that she simply could not allow the public nightmare of the war to reach through to her. Hence her brittle attempts at would-be amused detachment. In January 1916, she wrote to Margaret Llewelyn Davies:

[17] ibid.
[18] See Bell, *Virginia Woolf*, vol. 1, Appendix A, 'Chronology'.

> I become steadily more feminist, owing to the Times, which I read at breakfast and wonder how this preposterous masculine fiction [the war] keeps going a day longer – without some vigorous young woman pulling us together and marching through it – Do you see any sense in it? I feel as if I were reading about some curious tribe in Central Africa.[19]

World War I was in many ways 'preposterous' and it was 'masculine' – but 'fiction' it was not. The men really were screaming as they hung bleeding on the barbed wire of no man's land. But that horror could not then be feelingly realized by a Virginia Woolf who was only beginning to allow herself to re-emerge into our terrible world. Similarly, when Leonard's youngest brother Philip was wounded in December 1917 (immediately after the war-death of Philip's most loved brother Cecil), Virginia Woolf visited him, but instead of giving way to impulses of pity or affection she simply recorded in her Diary: 'A feeling of the uselessness of it all, breaking these people and mending them again.'[20] Finally, in a Diary entry in May 1919, there was her notorious lack of felt response to the genocidal attacks on the Armenians – 'How can one mind whether the Armenians number 4,000 or 4 million? The feat is beyond me.' The obvious answer is that it matters a good deal to the Armenians.

It is not, therefore, surprising that the novels that Virginia Woolf wrote during and immediately after World War I were also imaginatively detached from that war. *Night and Day* (written 1917–19) is defiantly pre-war in all its preoccupations and there is not even a hint that war is going to come and sweep its world away. And the novel *Jacob's Room* (written 1919–21), for all that it ends with Jacob's pointless death in the trenches (and Jacob's surname is 'Flanders') is none the less an experiment in the communication of peacetime consciousness. Moreover there are so many fragments of so many different people's inner jottings and scraps of conversation in this novel – Mrs Flanders, Mr Steele, the Rev. Floyd, Captain Barford, Mrs Barford, Mrs Jarvis, Timmy Durrant, Clara Durrant, Bonamy, Florinda, Rose Shaw, Brambourne, Fanny Elmer, Jinny Cruttenden, Sandra Williams, among many others – as well as Jacob,

[19] N. Nicolson (ed.), *The Question of Things Happening: The Letters of Virginia Woolf 1912–1922*, Hogarth Press, 1976.
[20] Virginia Woolf, *Diary*, (ed.) Olivier Bell, Hogarth Press, 1977, vol. 1, p. 92.

that the reader's imaginative attention becomes irritably diffused. And Jacob himself is so lacking in any emotional vulnerability or concern for other people – one feels so little for him when he is alive – that it is impossible to feel any shock of loss at his death. In total contrast, that is, to the impact of the death of Rachel Vinrace in *The Voyage Out*. Virginia Woolf's concentration on capturing the moment in this experimental novel is pursued, I feel, at the expense of a search for meaning; but if there is no attempt at meaning, then there can be no shocked response to meaninglessness; not even to the cruel meaninglessness with which the book ends – the mass extermination of young men in the 1914–18 war.

The only extended reference to war in *Jacob's Room* is a passage that intends to be savagely ironic in its depiction of how 'the other side . . . the men in clubs and Cabinets',[21] perceive the deaths of young men in battle. To them the real thing is no different from a game with tin soldiers:

> The battleships ray out over the North Sea, keeping their stations accurately apart. At a given signal all the guns are trained on a target which (the master gunner counts the seconds, match in hand – at the sixth he looks up) flames into splinters. With equal nonchalance a dozen young men in the prime of life descend with composed faces into the depths of the sea; and there impassively (though with perfect mastery of machinery) suffocate uncomplainingly together. Like blocks of tin soldiers the army covers the cornfields, moves up the hillside, stops, reels slightly this way and that, and falls flat, save that, through field-glasses, it can be seen that one or two pieces still agitate up and down like fragments of broken matchstick.[22]

We are meant to be energized by irony into a fierce rejection of such unfeeling, mass-murderous masculine frivolity, but unfortunately a double irony operates in the context of reading the whole novel in that we ourselves have been made to feel so little, if indeed anything, for Jacob and Timmy (and we never accompany them on to the lethal battlefield) that they are, in the event, little more than distanced

[21] Virginia Woolf, *Jacob's Room*, Hogarth Press, 1922, reprinted Grafton Books, 1986, p. 151.
[22] ibid., pp. 151–2.

matchstick figures for us also – because they have remained so distant from their creator.

But by 1923 all that had changed. Virginia Woolf had recovered her powers of imaginative pity to such an extent that she could now actually fuse her own private nightmare during World War I with that other nightmare endured by the young men in the trenches. Far from the war being just a 'preposterous fiction' to her any longer, she now made tragic fiction out of what the war in fact had done to many of the most sensitive men of their generation, giving her own experience of madness, sometimes in precise detail, to her shell-shocked Septimus Warren Smith. Forcing herself to re-experience all that mental pain was an ordeal – 'Of course the mad part tries me so much, makes my mind squint so badly that I can hardly face spending the next weeks at it';[23] 'that agony – all agony but the end – *Mrs Dalloway*.'[24] But she had to go through with it, she felt, in order to convey what she called 'true reality'.[25] And part of that reality was the realization that whenever humans engage in war they are forced to learn: 'The world has raised its whip; where will it descend?'[26]

The whip descends both on Septimus and on his terrified, tender young wife Rezia. Intermittently throughout his last day alive Septimus relives his war – and his wife has to watch helplessly as Septimus sweats through his tortured haunting: 'There was his hand; there the dead. White things were assembling behind the railings opposite. But he dared not look. Evans was behind the railings! . . . A man in grey was actually walking towards them. It was Evans! But no mud was on him; no wounds; he was not changed.'[27] Evans, Septimus's officer and greatest friend, had been killed just before the Armistice. At the time, 'far from showing any emotion or recognising that here was the end of a friendship, [Septimus] had congratulated himself upon feeling very little and very reasonably. The War had taught him.'[28] In other words the war had desensitized him to the point where he could feel nothing for anyone. Months

[23] Virginia Woolf, *Diary*, 19 June 1923.
[24] ibid., 24 Feb. 1926.
[25] ibid., 19 June 1923.
[26] Virginia Woolf, *Mrs Dalloway*, Hogarth Press, 1925, reprinted 1960, p. 17.
[27] ibid., p. 28 and p. 78.
[28] ibid., p. 96.

later, however, Septimus had begun to panic that he was no longer capable of feeling at all,[29] that he had become dead inside and so would be doomed 'to be alone forever'.[30] 'He had not cared when Evans was killed; that was the worst.'[31] Only a very sensitive man can judge himself unfit to live because he fears that he can no longer feel; it was the most sensitive men that the 'Great War' destroyed in spirit even when they survived in the flesh.

Instead of enabling Septimus to grieve at long last and to curse the war that had wiped out his friend, official medical opinion merely congratulated him on having '"served with great distinction in the War". "The War?" the patient asked. The European War – that little shindy of schoolboys with gunpowder? Had he served with distinction? He really forgot. In the War itself he had failed.'[32] What Septimus and Virginia Woolf meant by 'the War itself', I think, is the life-and-death struggle of each of us to remain real, feeling people, instead of becoming spurious and hollow. 'Out of the struggle with ourselves,' said Yeats, 'we make poetry.' The climax of the horror for Septimus is his war-begotten revelation of human emptiness and cruelty – 'how they tear each other to pieces';[33] 'human nature is remorseless'.[34] *That*, it seems to him, is the truth about human nature. Believing it to be the whole truth and that the cruel ones are in charge of our world, Septimus jumps out of the upstairs window on to the spiked railings below.

Virginia Woolf, however, in her sanity, knew that war and cruelty are not the whole truth about human nature. Another truth about us is that we want other people to have life and to have it more abundantly. Rezia never stops loving and believing in Septimus; ambulances really are a triumph of civilization,[35] and so are Mrs Dalloway's parties in which she offers herself up to testify that we are all members one of another:

> Here was So-and-so in South Kensington; someone up in Bayswater; and somebody else, say, in Mayfair . . . and she felt what a waste; and she felt what a pity; and she felt if only

[29] ibid.
[30] ibid., p. 160.
[31] ibid., p. 101.
[32] ibid., p. 106.
[33] ibid., p. 155.
[34] ibid., p. 108.
[35] ibid., p. 135.

> they could be brought together; so she did it. And it was an offering; to combine, to create; but to whom?[36]

It is her love of life struggling so valiantly against her fear of life – ('Fear no more the heat o' the sun') – that makes Mrs Dalloway give her parties. This love of 'the life of natural happiness' and the sense of human connectedness make up the major-key melodies in the novel that counterpoint and finally triumph over Septimus's tragic discords and his desolate sense of isolation.

Immediately after finishing *Mrs Dalloway*, in 1924–5 Virginia Woolf began writing *To the Lighthouse*, her greatest celebration of happiness in relationship and of the pricelessness of just one imperfect human being. The so-called 'Great War' is allowed only a single sentence in this novel, and that in parenthesis. '(A Shell exploded. Twenty or thirty young men were blown up in France, among them Andrew Ramsay, whose death, mercifully, was instantaneous.)'[37] What is really important, Virginia Woolf is saying, is not these monstrous, mad competitions that wipe out irreplaceable Andrew Ramsays, 20 or 30, 20,000 or 30,000 at a time. No, what is really important is to see feelingly that each man and each woman is an 'I'. For Virginia Woolf's most fundamental preoccupation in *To the Lighthouse* is to try to bring to life the 'I' of Mrs Ramsay. Her conclusion is that it is impossible: 'Fifty pairs of eyes were not enough to get round that one woman with.'[38] And what is true of Mrs Ramsay or of Mrs Dalloway or of Septimus Smith is also, of course, true of the rest of us. What is not so often recognized is that Virginia Woolf's obsession with the irreducible, multi-faceted contradictions and flux of human personality was intimately connected with her implacable opposition to war. For not only did the irreplaceableness of each unique human being make the thought of wholesale extermination intolerable to her, it might also, she believed, if sufficiently acutely imagined, make such competitions in massacre less possible. In one of her very rare attempts to engage with World War I while it was still in progress Virginia Woolf had noted in her Diary on 27 August 1918:

[36] ibid., pp. 134–5.
[37] Virginia Woolf, *To the Lighthouse*, Hogarth Press, 1927, 'Time passes', p. 154.
[38] ibid., 'The lighthouse', p. 229.

> I have half forgotten what I meant to say about the German prisoners . . . I think it was that . . . the existence of life in another human being is as difficult to realise as a play of Shakespeare when the book is shut. This occurred to me when I saw Adrian talking to the tall German prisoner. By rights they should have been killing each other. The reason why it is easy to kill another person must be that one's imagination is too sluggish to conceive of a succession of days which are furled in him and have already been spent.

All of Virginia Woolf's novels of the interior consciousness can be seen – from one point of view – as being her attempt to force our imaginations to become less 'sluggish' and 'to conceive what other people's lives mean to [them] – the infinite possibilities of a succession of days which are furled in [them]'. Her discovery of how 'to dig out beautiful caves behind [her] characters'[39] functions on one level as her antidote to the crudely unimaginative group-hatreds of war.[40]

Many of Virginia Woolf's deepest impulses of antipathy towards war she censored and kept from publication in the early 1930s. Like Simone Weil, she could feel nothing but abhorrence and derision for the masculinist awe at military exploits. On 21 January 1931, for instance, her manuscript notes for her speech 'Professions for Women' contained the passage:

> If I were reviewing books [about the war] now, I would say this was a stupid and violent and hateful and idiotic and trifling and ignoble and mean display. I would say I am bored to death by war books. I detest the masculine point of view. I am bored by his heroism, virtue and honour. I think the best these men can do is not to talk about themselves anymore.[41]

But she decided to delete that outburst. A little later in 1931 she

[39] Virginia Woolf, *Diary*, 30 Aug. 1923.

[40] cf. Freud to Einstein, Sept. 1932: 'All that brings out the significant resemblances between men calls into play the feelings of community, identification . . . and must serve us as war's antidote.' Published in Nathan and Norden (eds), *Einstein on Peace*, Avenel, NY, 1981, p. 199.

[41] Published in Mitchell Leaska (ed.), *The Pargiters by Virginia Woolf*, Hogarth Press, 1978, Appendix, p. 164. Zwerdling, *Virginia Woolf and the Real World*, is puzzled that Virginia Woolf should have expressed such dislike for war memoirs in 1931 since there had so recently been a spate of *anti*-war memoirs, but in fact those she had been reading lately, including John Buchan's *Francis and Riversdale*

began to collect and to paste together notes from her reading relevant to the projected feminist essay that was eventually to become *Three Guineas*. Her first scrapbook (1931) contains on page 38 one very significant passage of personal reflection never published in her lifetime, which demonstrates that her feminism demanded the rejection not only of militarism, but also of party politics and even patriotism:

> Political creed: why should I kill women? Killing women the logical necessity; [that is, if force is the fundamental law behind all life women should feel a drive to kill women as well as men men] but I won't. War not needed by women. – No [political] party possible at present . . . Why should charity cease as the Channel boat starts? What has England done for me: Nothing.
>
> We are all paying now for the manly diversion. Naturally they will have another. Let us get on with the important things.[42]

Between 1932 and 1934 Virginia Woolf's main creative preoccupation was her attempt to write a woman's-eye view of the past 50 years of English history. Unfortunately *The Years*, which was finally a failure in her own eyes, suffered from the same weakness as did *Jacob's Room* – the excessive number of fragmented consciousnesses. One casualty (again as in *Jacob's Room*) is the intended impact of Virginia Woolf's critique of war. War in *The Years* is rendered in terms of the experience of civilians – women and male non-combatants sitting out an air-raid during World War I. But the intended effect of alienation-cum-horror at the monstrosity of having to crouch in a coal cellar while, above one's head, 'other people try to kill each other'[43] is neutralized by the reader's own indifference to Renny, Sara, Nicholas and Maggie, who are doing the crouching. Renny and Nicholas have not even appeared in the novel before the air-raid scene and Sara and Maggie have hardly succeeded in engaging our imaginative sympathy. Only Eleanor Pargiter is felt to embody some degree of sturdy valour, but her (unspoken) poignant question, 'When shall we live adventurously, wholly, not like cripples in a

Grenfell and Lord Lytton's *Antony*, did not question the military ethos.

42 First scrapbook for *Three Guineas*, Monks House Papers, B16f, p. 38.

43 Virginia Woolf, *The Years*, '1917', Hogarth Press, 1937, p. 226.

cave?'[44] is greatly diminished in impact by the excision from earlier drafts of the novel of Eleanor brooding questioningly on her own possible part-responsibility for the war. As Grace Radin's research has revealed:

> In the [cancelled section of the] proofs we find Eleanor asking herself what she might have done to prevent a young sailor from being drowned, and realising that the question is absurd. There seems to be nothing she could have done. The original holograph mss. of this episode provides an additional gloss on this passage. There . . . she wonders 'if she as a girl had always read the papers; if she had followed the course of politics; if she had twenty years ago formed a society and headed a procession and gone to Whitehall and said, if you don't stop what you're doing.' . . . But she realised she had had no education; all her energies had been absorbed in caring for her father and building houses for the poor.[45]

Yet even that limited area of social intervention, Eleanor realized – in the cancelled episode in the proofs – might have revolutionized life in the slums had England not squandered her treasure on war – 'if I'd had a quarter of a millionth part of that money . . . I could have . . . But what's the use of thinking? she thought.'[46] However, all those passages that deepen the reader's understanding and respect for Eleanor's social concern in contrast to the futile slaughter of World War I were cut in the final revision and the 'Raid chapter' was weakened accordingly.

On 2 October 1935 Virginia Woolf attended the Labour Party Conference at Brighton and that experience at last 'broke the dam' between her and her long-projected new essay on feminism. 'Tears came to my eyes as [the pacifist] Lansbury spoke' (Diary, 2 Oct. 1935). She now felt that she must call her essay 'The Next War',[47] which reveals just how far she had had to move both from alienated, detached contemplation of the last war and from an exclusive concern

[44] ibid., p. 227.
[45] Bulletin of the New York Public Library, Virginia Woolf issue, vol. 80, no. 2, 1977, pp. 234–5.
[46] *The Years*, p. 233.
[47] Virginia Woolf, *Diary*, 15 Oct. 1935. See note to *Diary* 20 Jan 1931.

for women's access to education and the professions – her original starting-point for the essay.

It is possible, from a close scrutiny of Virginia Woolf's quarry for *Three Guineas*, her second and third scrapbooks of newspaper cuttings and typewritten quotations (dated 12 August 1935 to 6 February 1937, and 11 June 1937 to 20 December 1937) to detect how her mind was now bridging the two subjects of feminism and anti-militarism. By 1935 she had come to realize that she must connect her essay on women's contribution to civilization and her thoughts on how to prevent war by focusing on the nature of fascism. Since, for Virginia Woolf, feminism meant the application to women of the humanist values of creative self-realization for all, the anti-feminism of the fascists was not marginal to their anti-humanism but an integral part of it. Fascist anti-feminism was simply fascist anti-humanism, only applied to women. For this reason Virginia Woolf could not attack Hitler as evil while at the same time leaving out of discussion his attacks on women.[48] Her newspaper cuttings about contemporary Nazism constantly underline the fusion of Hitler's masculinism, his militarism and his anti-feminism: for instance, on page 22 of her second scrapbook, she pasted from the *Sunday Times* of 13 September 1936 the paragraph headed: 'Praise for Women'. On their part in the 'Nazi Triumph', Hitler is quoted:

> 'So long as we have a strong male sex in Germany – and we Nazis will see to it that we have – we will have no female hand-grenade-throwing squads in our country' . . . He attacked foreign critics who contend that women do not enjoy equal rights in Germany, and emphasised that women are most useful to the nation when they bring up large families . . . 'There are two worlds in the life of the nation, the world of men and the world of women. Nature has done well to entrust the man with the care of his family and the nation. The woman's world is, if she is happy in her family, her husband, her children and her home.'

On 3 February 1937, Virginia Woolf pasted in an entry on Nazi

[48] e.g. when Princess Bibesco invited Virginia Woolf to join the Committee of the Anti-Fascist Exhibition, Virginia Woolf asked why the woman question was ignored (*Diary*, 6 Jan. 1935).

education – 'Nazi "Blood and Race" theory to be taught to picked boys.' The boys were to be taught that Germans were Nordic and that 'Too much dancing, feminine art and the like does them harm.' The boys' teachers were to be men who had taken part in the last war. Most chilling of all was her cutting from *The Times* of 16 December 1937 (which she juxtaposed with news of more attractive uniforms for the British Army!) headed 'Life in Modern Germany. Dr Woermann on the State's Aims. Status of Women'.

> Dr E. Woermann, Counsellor of the German Embassy, gave a lecture on present-day Germany at the Royal United Service Institution yesterday.
>
> . . . History had taught them that the cowards and the weak were the targets of aggression from other people. Only the brave and the strong could subsist, and only strong nations could maintain the peace of the world . . .
>
> In some foreign countries fantastic ideas were current about the position of women in Germany today. Nothing could be more ridiculous and stupid than the assertion that National Socialism looked on women only as breeding machines . . . It was the aim of National Socialism to let man's work be done by men and not by women. To believe that woman's principal work was family life and bringing up the young generation was simply to return to natural and eternal law. . . . Regarding concentration camps, he said there were two types in Germany, one for unsocial elements, several times convicted of certain crimes, the other for political offenders. He assured them that the treatment of these political offenders was reasonable . . .
>
> The Chairman (General Sir Felix Ready), thanking Dr Woermann for his lecture, said in this country there had always been a great admiration for the powers of organisation of the German people and for their great thoroughness with which they dealt with their social problems. After what they had heard they would agree that this admiration had not been misplaced.

Not only the Nazi lies but also the British Establishment's gullibility and temptation to emulate Germany are made all too clear in the above passage. Virginia Woolf also made a point of cutting out news items and correspondence testifying to Nazi persecution of women. She pasted into her third, late 1937, scrapbook, a letter she had received two years earlier (7 June 1935) from Monica Whately of the feminist Six Point Group:[49]

> Every step is being taken by the German Government to close all avenues to women. She [*sic*] is being deprived of her right to higher education, of entering into the Trades and Professions – ruthlessly she is to be forced back into the home, the unpaid servant of her husband, but not the legal guardian of her own children.
>
> What is perhaps even more serious, is the fate of those women held as prisoners . . . for the alleged misdemeanours of their menfolk . . .
>
> The degrading of women in Germany lowers the status of women all over the world, and is bound to react against a better understanding between the Nations.

Finally, and most graphically, Virginia Woolf juxtaposed (see opposite) Hitler's definition of maleness as combat-readiness ('A Nation of men') with a photograph of Mussolini's son-in-law, Count Ciano, smiling above his death's-head emblem and, above Ciano, a cutting about the persecution of Frau Pommer of Essen ('The Thorn of Hatred') – for speaking out against anti-Jewish hatred in Germany. She was arrested for 'slandering the State'.[50] Frau Pommer became a twentieth-century Antigone-figure for Virginia Woolf in notes 39 and 40 of chapter 2 of *Three Guineas*. 'Antigone's crime was of much the same nature and was punished in much the same way . . . The fine words of Antigone are: " 'Tis not my nature to join in

[49] The Vice-Presidents of the Six Point Group included Vera Brittain, Lady Violet Bonham-Carter, Winifred Holtby, Viscountess Rhondda, Elizabeth Robins, and Virginia Woolf's friend, Dame Ethel Smyth. Monica Whately, the Six Point Group Secretary, had recently published a leaflet, 'Women behind Nazi bars', 1935.

[50] See p. 20 of the second scrapbook. Although almost all of this scrapbook's entries are from 1937 sources, this particular page is dated 12 Aug. 1935, which suggests that Virginia Woolf had made a special point of preserving these items.

Opposite, Fascism equals anti-feminism. Page 20 from Virginia Woolf's second scrapbook for *Three Guineas*.

difference. 12' Aug. 1935 - Times

"THE THORN OF HATRED"

OUTSPOKEN ESSEN WOMAN ARRESTED

FROM OUR OWN CORRESPONDENT

BERLIN, Aug. 11

Frau Pommer, the wife of a Prussian mines official at Essen, has been arrested and is to be tried on a charge of insulting and slandering the State and the Nazi movement.

Frau Pommer told the girl behind the counter of a confectioner's shop that if her favourite brand of chocolate was not in stock she would have to go to another shop which she mentioned. The girl replied, with some pertness, it may be imagined, that the other shop was "pure Jewish." Frau Pommer is then alleged to have said: —

> I and my husband are and remain German Nationalists; but as long as one does not cohabit with a Jew one can safely buy from him. The thorn of hatred has been driven deep enough into the people by the religious conflicts and it is high time that the men of to-day disappeared.

Count Ciano in flying kit.

12' Aug 1935

THE TIME

"A NATION OF MEN"

THE FÜHRER'S BOAST

SPEECH TO NAZI OLD GUARD

FROM OUR OWN CORRESPONDENT

BERLIN, Aug. 11

Herr Hitler made an unexpected appearance and speech to-day at the celebration of the fifteenth anniversary of the Rosenheim branch of the National-Socialist Party, the second oldest in Germany. Addressing the assembled "old guard," Herr Hitler recalled his first speech in the town 15 years ago—15 years "filled with a wonderful struggle, such as had never before been waged for the heart and the soul of the German nation." In apparent reference to opponents at home, Herr Hitler said: —

> In battle we have won the German Reich, and in battle we shall maintain and guard it. Those who are against us need not deceive themselves. We have never shrunk from the combat. If they want it they can have it. We shall crush them in such a way that they will abandon for the next 14 years all idea of continuing the struggle.

Recalling "the heavy trials of the movement in the last 15 years," Herr Hitler said: —

> If fate is to put it to the test again, we should be really hardened by the hammer-blows of Providence. The years since 1918 have taught us: "Woe to the people which is unprepared to take its liberty and independence under its own protection." Nobody will deny that in the last two and a half years Germany has attained a different position in the world. I am convinced that nobody in the world can attack our Reich again. We want peace and reconstruction, but just as we want peace so the other nations ought to want peace. He who wishes to disturb our peace will no longer fight against a nation of pacifists but against a nation of men. This fact alone will contribute more to peace than all the speeches.

HEROIC

hating, but in loving." '[51] Just as anti-humanist fascism was essentially anti-feminist and militaristic, so true feminism for Virginia Woolf had to be humanistic and anti-militaristic – 'Let us substitute for feminist the word "humane"[?] to signify we who believe that we hbs [human beings] though now shreds and patches can be brought to a state of greater completeness.'[52]

Three Guineas is addressed to an anonymous, anti-fascist young Englishman. It is probable that Virginia Woolf had in mind men like the poet Stephen Spender and her nephew Julian Bell, both of whom went out to Spain's Civil War where Bell was almost immediately killed. Before enlisting, Bell had written a long, prolix Open Letter to E. M. Forster on 'War and Peace' in which he attempted to justify his participation in war. It is a confused piece of writing (as Forster's reply makes clear) but it does hit some political bull's-eyes and it is also much more psychologically revealing than Bell himself had possibly realized. The unanswerable portion of the essay is Bell's confrontation with the immediate political situation in Europe in 1936: 'Somehow or other, we have to cope with a world half full of dangerous and armed lunatics . . . The only thing to do is to adopt such finite and limited objectives as will in fact curb the mischief, and then devise means for obtaining them with a minimum of pain and destruction.'[53]

What is a lot less convincing is Bell's attempt to justify warfare and its concomitant, male soldiering, in general. Although Bell cannot see it, the reader, including Bell's aunt, cannot help but hear the quasi-fascist noises now coming from the pleasant and cultivated left-wing Englishman:

> I have always been grateful for being made, as a child, to look at a stag having its throat cut, and that I have reached the stage of contemplating a corpse in the road without a Baudelairian extravaganza of horror . . . I think the militarists are right in

[51] cf. Simone Weil above. Sophocles' *Antigone* had been the foundation text for Virginia Woolf's resistance to state militarism ever since she had been introduced to its lasting relevance by her Greek teacher, Janet Case, in 1901.

[52] Monks House Papers B16b. I think Brenda Silver mistakenly inserts the word 'women' for the initials 'h.b.' (i.e. human beings) in this admittedly difficult-to-decipher MSS passage (see '*Three Guineas* before and after', in Marcus, *Virginia Woolf: A Feminist Slant*).

[53] Julian Bell, 'War and peace, a letter to E. M. Forster', in Quentin Bell (ed.), *Julian Bell, Essays, Poems and Letters*, Hogarth Press, 1938, p. 386.

insisting on men being disciplined, 'blooded' and inured to horror. For such repulsions are, when all is said and done, mere weakness of flesh . . .

To kill men is to prevent good, and to kill some men may be to prevent very great good . . . But considering that in most human lives evil and indifferent states of mind predominate, I cannot feel that their loss is too heavy to outweigh some possible gains. [No acute imagining of the succession of days furled in another human being here.] I do not see how you can doubt that some men enjoy fighting, just as they enjoy other dangerous and violent sports, and for such men fighting – and killing – mean good states of mind and approved acts . . .

If gas is extensively used on large cities, the aged and the invalid should suffer more than the young and healthy – a change greatly for the better . . .

The type I seek to define is above all that of the republican soldier, the public servant in arms . . . if I were pressed for a contemporary example I should say . . . that Pétain and perhaps Lyautey come nearest to this type . . .

To most of the human race the mere physical courage of the fighting soldier is stirring and heartening as no saint in his virtues ever can be . . .

The essential attraction of war and of the military character lies in the submission of the intelligence to facts and of facts to the resources of intelligence . . . The strength of the revolutionary attitude lies partly . . . in the admission of force as the foundation of politics . . .

prolonged and violent activity . . . may well dull and impoverish. But I doubt if it brutalises quite as horribly as does idealism.[54]

With that hard shield of 'the military attitude', Bell hoped to 'preserve what can still be preserved of liberal civilisation'. By his own account, there would not seem very much left to save.

Already in April 1935 Virginia Woolf had been exposed to Julian's exuberant, one-eyed masculinism:

[54] ibid., pp. 364–88. When Bell actually arrived in the Spanish Civil War zone he responded to the boyishness of war with a zest reminiscent of August 1914: 'It's really rather fun and all's boy-scouts in the highest', ibid., pp. 188–9.

> Conversation: whether one can give people a substitute for war. Must have the danger emotion: must climb mountains, fight bulls . . . Lust and danger. Can't cut them out at once. Must divert them on to some harmless object. But what? Some fantasy must be provided. I say many people have found life exciting without war and bull-fighting . . . Obviously, Julian's quite unaware of some of his own motives.

She ends that Diary entry: 'What is the use of trying to preach when human nature is so crippled?' It was dismaying indeed to have to recognize that young 'progressive' men, including her own sister's son, were once again rationalizing their will to fight and kill. She did not agree, of course, with Julian's letter on 'War and Peace', feeling very irritated that he could 'never force himself to think to the bottom of his idea' (Diary, 2 Sept. 1937) and feeling, 'Lord, how I wish I could argue the whole thing with him' (*Letters*, 8 Sept. 1937).

Three Guineas is, on one level, her attempt to argue with Julian, inviting him to recognize and analyse the would-be dominant fighting male within himself. Why fight? she asks. She sees the perpetual recourse to competitions in violence as an almost universal male problem. Men have been socialized by every society into believing that it is better to kill than to be killed and that their virility depends upon their success in dominating – in both the private and the public worlds. And the mass of women in every society, who are economically and therefore also ideologically dependent upon men, endorse these masculinist views. What, then, is to be done?

Virginia Woolf's conclusion is that war, in the long term, can only be abolished if both men and women can rid themselves of their subconscious need to dominate and to be dominated. To this end she advocates a radically different education programme – in the first place for women but also, by implication, for men – one that would teach not 'the arts of dominating other people, not the arts of ruling, of killing, of acquiring land and capital but . . . medicine, mathematics, music, painting and literature . . . the arts of human intercourse; the art of understanding other people's lives and minds.'[55] She advocates a radically different code of practising the professions,

[55] Virginia Woolf, *Three Guineas*, Hogarth Press, 1938, ch. 1, pp. 39–40.

one of open access to 'all properly qualified people, of whatever sex, class or colour,'[56] which would not be motivated by greed or hierarchical ambition, both so inimical to peace. She advocates state payment for mothers not only that women may be economically (and ideologically) independent of men but also that men may be freed from the work-slavery of sole-earnerdom. Through sharing in the nurture of the young, 'the half-man might become whole'.[57] She urges all independent-minded women henceforth to 'refuse in the event of war to make munitions or nurse the wounded' and to maintain an attitude of unconvinced indifference if their brothers 'insist on fighting for their country', saying instead: 'As a woman I have no country. As a woman I want no country. As a woman my country is the whole world.'[58] It is noteworthy that whereas Julian Bell's Letter on 'War and Peace' talked as though there were but one sex on earth – his only reference to women being 'the pleasures of an underdone beefsteak and a pretty girl' – Virginia Woolf's answer to Bell and his friends insistently reminds them that there are in fact two sexes, and that women may well evolve a very different approach to saving the world from that traditionally chosen by the warrior male.

It is, in her view, the warrior male himself, in whatever uniform or costume, who constitutes the problem, and who, through the ages, has shut women away from his counsels – the Creons 'in no wise suffering a woman to worst' them. Having outlined more or less tentatively how independent-minded 'Outsider' women might contribute in both practical and intellectual ways to the eventual abolition of 'the inhumanity, beastliness, the horror, the folly of war',[59] Virginia Woolf turns in her last 20 pages of *Three Guineas* to analyse the psychopathology of masculinism. *Why* do men have such a centuries-old fear of women that no woman may be initiated into their priesthoods? *Why* should a Victorian middle-class father have felt quite so outraged at his daughter's capacity to earn an income not emanating from himself? *Why* should men in power, from Creon to twentieth-century Whitehall civil servants and fascist

[56] ibid., ch. 2, p. 92.
[57] ibid., ch. 3, p. 128.
[58] ibid., ch. 2, p. 96. cf. Ernst Toller in 1938, 'Meine Heimat ist die Erde, die Welt mein Vaterland' and see Helen Keller, ch. 8 below.
[59] Woolf, *Three Guineas*, ch. 2, p. 96.

militarists have insisted so consistently and destructively that 'there are two worlds, one for women, the other for men'? Why, in short, should domination be deemed essential to virility? Her tentative answer, reiterated on every page, is 'infantile fixation', the irrational sex-phobia that subconsciously makes men fear they will be castrated – like women – if they do not preserve their mastery of the world by force.[60] Millennia of dominance and of acquiescence in dominance have finally produced the saluting uniformed Führer, his hand upon his sword. 'Some say, others deny, that he is Man himself.' Men and women between them have produced that figure, but men and women together can also 'change that figure'.[61] Virginia Woolf's penultimate footnote is worth quoting at length:

> The nature of manhood and the nature of womanhood are frequently defined both by Italian and German dictators. Both repeatedly insist that it is the nature of man and indeed the essence of manhood to fight. Hitler, for example, draws a distinction between 'a nation of pacifists and a nation of men'. Both repeatedly insist that it is the nature of womanhood to heal the wounds of the fighter. Nevertheless a very strong movement is on foot towards emancipating man from the old 'natural and eternal law' that man is essentially a fighter: witness the growth of pacifism among the male sex today.
> . . . 'it is not true to say that every boy at heart longs for war. It is only other people who teach it us by giving us swords and guns, soldiers and uniforms to play with' (*Conquest of the Past*, by Prince Hubertus Loewenstein, p. 215). It is possible that the Fascist States by revealing to the younger generation at least the need for emancipation from the old conception of virility are doing for the male sex what the Crimean and the European wars did for their sisters. Professor Huxley, however, warns us that 'any considerable alteration of the hereditary constitution is an affair of millennia, not of decades.' On the other hand, as science also assures us that our life on earth is

[60] cf. Klaus Theweleit on the irrational, pathological fear of castration expressed in novels about *Freikorps* officers by Thor Goote, in *Male Fantasies*, Polity Press, Minnesota, 1987, vol. 1, p. 74.
[61] ibid., p. 163.

'an affair of millennia, not of decades', some alteration in the hereditary constitution may be worth attempting.

If 'male' could come to mean private nurturer and if 'female' could come to mean humane political decision-maker, then, Virginia Woolf suggests, there might still be hope. Antigone would not be shut away by Creon for trying to follow her inner light, nor one brother fight the other until the end – 'the human spirit [would] overflow boundaries and make unity out of multiplicity, [realizing] the dream of peace, the dream of freedom.'[62]

But Virginia Woolf's millennial vision was irrelevant to the Europe of 1938. In the short term Julian Bell was right – there was no longer any way to be both anti-fascist *and* anti-war by then. Slowly and painfully, like Maude Royden and Simone Weil, Virginia Woolf had to renounce her pacifism.[63] Finally she could no longer say with her character Kitty in *The Years*: 'Force is always wrong – don't you agree with me? – always wrong?' As early as April 1933 Bruno Walter had warned the Woolfs that all anti-Nazis 'must band together' (Diary, 29 Apr. 1933). Two years later: 'Toller says we are on the brink of war. Wants the allies to declare war on Hitler' (Diary, 20 Apr. 1935). But it was only at the time of the Sudetenland crisis (10 Sept. 1938) that Virginia Woolf saw the British politicians face to face with Hitler 'like grown ups staring incredulously at a child's sand castle which for some inexplicable reason has become a real vast castle, needing gunpowder and dynamite to destroy it'. She still felt unwilling to accept that necessity, saying that it would be 'a hopeless war this – when we know winning means nothing' (Diary, 14 Sept. 1938). Although feeling anger and shame at the Munich Agreement, she recorded it as 'soberly and truly life after death . . . No slaughter of the young beneath us' (Diary, 30 Sept. 1938). Simone Weil and Maude Royden had also welcomed, albeit uneasily, the temporary reprieve of Munich. In May 1939, however, Simone Weil renounced her pacifism, in the face of Hitler's occupation of Prague. It took Virginia Woolf, like Maude Royden, a little longer. By 25 August 1939, she was more fatalistic but still full of the

62 ibid.

63 See Zwerdling, *Virginia Woolf and the Real World*, ch. 9. for a close discussion of Virginia Woolf's reluctant renunciation of pacifism. In my view Zwerdling slightly overstates her hopelessness in 1939–40.

uttermost horror at the prospect of 'young men torn to bits: mothers like Nessa 2 years ago'. On 31 August 1939, she was *still* hoping against hope that war might be averted; but by 6 September, war having been declared, Virginia Woolf wrote not only: 'Lord, this is the worst of all my life's experiences,' but also 'One merely feels that the killing machine *has* to be set in action' (my emphasis). She could no longer even hope for an alternative. By 29 October she was writing to Edward Sackville-West: 'My only comfort lies in the obvious horror we all feel for war: but then with a solid block of unbaked barbarians in Germany, what's the good of our being comparatively civilised?' Hitler had to be resisted; and when Nazi invasion seemed imminent during the Battle of Britain, Virginia Woolf wrote: 'When the 12 planes went over, out to sea, to fight, last evening, I had I think an individual, not communal BBC dictated feeling. I almost instinctively wished them luck' (Diary, 26 July 1940).

Thinking was Virginia Woolf's way of fighting, as she noted in her Diary 15 May 1940, and one subject about which she had been continually thinking at least since September 1939 was: How may humanity ultimately succeed in abolishing war? She was taking into account the views of several critical woman readers about the hypotheses she had outlined in *Three Guineas*,[64] and she was also enlisting the help of Shena, Lady Simon, for an article for America about women and war. Lady Simon, who, as Virginia Woolf knew, was one of the Englishwomen closest in spirit to the thinking behind *Three Guineas*, sent her her thoughts on war on 8 January 1940. Although Shena Simon supported armed resistance to Hitler, she had no wish at all to glorify the British men then engaged in killing Germans:

> It seems as if we lose all sense of the importance of individual life when we engage in war . . . It is this universal acceptance of force as the final sanction that I find so depressing . . . I feel that we ought to admit that that fact is a disgrace that all of us must share, and that no plans will be successful for avoiding war until we recognise it as 'murder' . . . with malice aforethought . . .

[64] See Brenda Silver in Jane Marcus, *Virginia Woolf: A Feminist Slant*.

> Somehow or other surely we must discredit force . . . get it across that war is not merely 'a hideous evil' but something like cannibalism.[65]

To this end Lady Simon made what would still be considered an outrageous suggestion today:

> I am more and more convinced that we shall never abolish war until the so called 'Womanly Virtues' are inculcated in boys all through their school life and I would begin by insisting that all boys should be taught by women teachers – provided the women would treat them as if they were girls [that is, not tolerate physical fighting]. After some generations of feminine upbringing it would probably be safe for the boys to be educated in mixed schools with mixed staffs.[66]

Virginia Woolf replied on 22 January 1940:

> I shall work on from your paper when the time comes. Meanwhile, do cast your mind further that way: about sharing life after the war: about pooling men's and women's work: about the possibility, if disarmament comes, of removing men's disabilities. Can one change sex characteristics? How far is the women's movement a remarkable experiment in that transformation? Mustn't our next task be the emancipation of man?[67] How can we alter the crest and the spur of the fighting cock? That's the one hope in this war: his soberer hues, and the unreality (so I feel and I think he feels) of glory. No talk of white feathers anyhow . . . So it looks as if the sexes can adapt themselves: and here (that's our work) we can, or the young women can, bring immense influence to bear. So many of the men, could they get prestige and admiration, would give

[65] Letter to Virginia Woolf on women and war, Monks House Papers.
[66] ibid. Lady Simon ends by envisaging that 'if Germany is defeated, the women of that country will get the chance of making common cause with us.'
[67] cf. Virginia Woolf's holograph Reading Notes, vol. 21, annotating Freud: 'In the present war . . . we are fighting for liberty. But we can only get it if we destroy the male attributes. Thus the woman's part is to achieve the emancipation of the man. In that lies the only hope of permanent peace.' Quoted by Brenda Silver (see n. 52 above).

> up glory and develop what's now so stunted – I mean the life of natural happiness. (*Letters*, vol. VI)

Virginia Woolf's essay 'Thoughts on peace in an air-raid' finally got written at the beginning of September 1940 despite the most unpropitious circumstances imaginable. The British were having to live with the prospect of an imminent Nazi invasion, in which event the Woolfs planned to commit immediate joint suicide. The hospital trains bearing British wounded back home from defeated France were travelling slowly past Virginia Woolf on her walks across the marsh. And, at the end of June, the German air-raids on south-east England began. 'Every day we have our raids: at night the bloodhounds are out' (Diary, 12 July 1940). It was no comfort surviving a bomb attack: 'If it doesn't kill me it's killing someone else.'[68] 'We're almost daily shot at – it's not what they call a healthy neighbourhood.'[69] On 16 August the Woolfs had to lie under trees in their garden as a German bomber sawed the air just above them – 'We lay flat on our faces, hands behind head. Don't close your teeth said L.' Twelve days later they narrowly missed being shot by a German plane while playing bowls. Finally, on 10 September they learned that there was an unexploded bomb in the front garden of their London home which was soon to bring all the ceilings down.

Yet it was in the midst of these same most battering weeks of the whole war that Virginia Woolf produced her 'Thoughts on peace'. Indeed she felt compelled to try to think about peace just then: 'Unless we can think peace into existence we – not this one body in this one bed but millions of bodies yet to be born – will lie in the same darkness and hear the same death rattle overhead.'[70] Therefore she had to 'fight with the mind' in order to 'help the young Englishman who is fighting up in the sky . . . to protect freedom'.[71] But the paradox was that 'Mental fight means thinking against the current, not with it.'[72] And so once Virginia Woolf began to think, she was compelled to say, however heretically: 'It

[68] Letter to Benedict Nicolson, 13 Aug. 1940 in Nicolson (ed.), *Leave the Letters*.
[69] Letter to Sybil Colefax, 14 Aug. 1940 in Nicolson, ibid.
[70] Virginia Woolf, 'Thoughts on peace in an air-raid', in *The Death of the Moth*.
[71] ibid.
[72] ibid.

is not true that we [English] are free. We are both prisoners tonight – he boxed up in his machine with a gun handy; we lying in the dark with a gas mask handy!'[73] War-fighting, even when it is 'freedom-fighting', is incompatible with freedom. What then has inflicted this freedom-less freedom-fight upon humanity? 'Hitler! the loudspeakers cry with one voice. Who is Hitler? What is he? Aggressiveness, tyranny, the insane love of power made manifest, they reply.'[74]

But Virginia Woolf was then compelled to utter her second heresy. Hitlerism was not the exclusive property of the Germans; 'subconscious Hitlerism – the desire for aggression; the desire to dominate and enslave' was also alive and well inside Britain.[75] We might think we are in the familiar territory of *Three Guineas* – *cherchez l'homme*. However, Virginia Woolf's thinking about the fundamental causes of war had been modified since *Three Guineas* by some of her women readers' comments and by friends like Lady Simon. One Quaker woman had criticized Virginia Woolf for not recognizing women's role in constructing the false ideology of strong, aggressive masculinism – 'are not we mothers as well as fathers responsible in a very large measure for that [infantile] fixation?'[76] And Lady Simon had written to her about the 'universal acceptance of force' being a disgraceful fact that 'all of us must share'. Therefore, unlike *The Journal of Mistress Joan Martyn, Mrs Dalloway* and *Three Guineas*, Virginia Woolf's 'Thoughts on peace in an air-raid' are no longer satisfied with indicting men as being primarily responsible for 'the manly diversion'. Now she sees the 'subconscious Hitlerism' made visible first of all in the behaviour of self-consciously 'feminine' women: 'We can see shop windows blazing; and women gazing; painted women; dressed-up women; women with crimson lips and crimson fingernails. They are slaves who are trying to enslave. If we could free ourselves from slavery we should free men from tyranny. Hitlers are bred by slaves.'[77] Men fight for domination in the public arena, in part at least, because women enslave in private. Sexually stereotyped

[73] ibid.
[74] ibid.
[75] ibid.
[76] Quoted by Brenda Silver (see n. 52 above).
[77] Woolf, 'Thoughts on peace in an air-raid'.

enslaved and enslaving women breed Hitlers large and small. Women must take partial responsibility for the socialization of men in the past and therefore for a vastly different, pacific socialization of men in the future.

Addressing women, Virginia Woolf writes: 'We must compensate the man for the loss of his gun . . . and free him from the machine.'[78] This will only be accomplished, she suggests, if both women and men are allowed many more outlets for their creative feelings and creative power. Music, beauty, nature, friendship – each of these can heal and revive, making up the 'life of natural happiness . . . that's now so stunted'.[79] When once the guns stop firing, 'The natural darkness of a summer's night returns. The innocent sounds of the country are heard again. An apple thuds to the ground. An owl hoots, winging its way from tree to tree.'[80] The planet can live again.

On 20 September 1940, Virginia Woolf read a version of that essay to eight members of the Rodmell Labour Party in which she enlarged on her ideas about the future pooling of men's work and women's work in a disarmed, peaceable world. Her hearers were not impressed: 'Mrs West prefers not to have money, a woman should stay at home . . . Fears [the postman] admitted: the wage earner keeps a perk for himself' (Diary, 21 Sept. 1940). Virginia Woolf reported dispiritedly to Lady Simon several months later:

> No, I don't see what's to be done about war. Its manliness; and manliness breeds womanliness – both so hateful. I tried to put this to our local labour party: but was scowled at as a prostitute. They said if women had as much money as men, they'd enjoy themselves: and then what about the children?[81]

Notwithstanding her deepening sense that she would not be understood, Virginia Woolf continued throughout the period November 1940 to February 1941 to revise her final novel, putting into it all her last intuitions about our potential to transcend what separates us and to become both one and whole. For while Virginia

[78] ibid. cf. Christa Wolf, ch. 7 below.
[79] Letter to Shena Simon, 22 Jan. 1940 in Nicolson, *Leave the Letters*.
[80] Woolf, 'Thoughts on peace in an air-raid'.
[81] Letter, 25 Jan. 1941 in Nicolson, *Leave the Letters*.

Woolf was finishing her first draft of *Between the Acts* and enduring the Blitz, she had experienced a quite unexpected rebirth of faith in humanity:

> Bombs were dropping round Sissinghurst, and [Vita] had to stay, as she drives an ambulance. Rose Macaulay is doing the same in London. I admire that very much . . . We had a fête: also a village play. The sirens sounded in the middle. All the mothers sat stolid. I also admired that very much . . .
>
> Bomb in Meck[lenburgh] Square still unexploded, everyone evacuated . . . Yet the clerks seemed as tough as leather . . . What touched and indeed raked what I call my heart in London was the grimy old woman at the lodging house at the back, all dirty after the raid, and preparing to sit out another . . .
>
> The other day we drove through an air-raid. London like a dead city. We took shelter at Wimbledon in a gun emplacement with an East End family whose house had been bombed. There they were as cheerful as grigs with a rug, a kettle and a spirit lamp: had been there for 3 nights: wind blowing through gun holes . . .
>
> What I'm finding odd and agreeable and unwonted is the admiration this war creates – for every sort of person: chars, shopkeepers, even much more remarkably, for politicians – Winston at least, and the tweed-wearing sterling dull women here, with their grim good sense: organising First-aid, putting out bombs for practice, and jumping out of windows to show us how . . . I'd almost lost faith in human beings . . . Now hope revives again.[82]

That hope animates *Between the Acts*. No one is idealized, but no one is irredeemable. Old Bart Oliver does frighten and despise his little grandson, but he can also growl a tacit apology to his devoted, elderly sister, Mrs Swithin; the miserable furtive homosexual William Dodge can respond to Isa and to Mrs Swithin

[82] Letters to Ethel Smyth, 11, 12, 20 and 25 Sept. 1940.

and feel totally accepted by them; Mrs Manresa, dressed to kill in her pursuit of man after man, also has a core of unexpected genuineness – loving the countryside and country life – she can yodel among the hollyhocks and cry over music; the wooden young stockbroker, Giles Oliver, unfaithful and oppressive within his family, is still the only person at the pageant appalled by the news 'that sixteen men had been shot just over there [on the Continent]'; he feels that he had been 'manacled to a rock . . . and forced passively to behold indescribable horror. His face showed it.'[83] Virginia Woolf expresses her own revulsion at being compelled to compete with the Nazis and even to outdo them in violence through her episode of the snake and the toad:

> There, crouched in the grass, curled in an olive green ring, was a snake. Dead? No, choked with a toad in its mouth. The snake was unable to swallow; the toad was unable to die. A spasm made the ribs contract; blood oozed. It was birth the wrong way round – a monstrous inversion. So, raising his foot [Giles] stamped on them. The mass crushed and slithered. The white canvas on his tennis shoes was bloodstained and sticky. But it was action. Action relieved him.[84]

To kill the predatory snake one had to get blood on one's shoes – and destroy the victim toad as well.

The impressionistic village pageant, created by the 'Outsider', Miss La Trobe, is an attempt to make not just the audience but also the reader share in a vision of human interrelatedness, despite all the barriers of sex, class, place and time: 'Toutes les existences sont solidaires les unes des autres.'[85] Or, as the Vicar puts it in *Between the Acts* 'We are members one of another. Each is part of the whole . . . Surely we should unite?'[86] Unity, however, is not going to be possible during the immediate lifetime even of a 'unifier' like old

[83] Virginia Woolf, *Between the Acts*, Hogarth Press, 1941, repr. Penguin, 1953, pp. 37 and 46.
[84] ibid., pp. 72–3.
[85] George Sand, *Histoire de ma vie*, pp. 240–1, quoted by Virginia Woolf at the end of her final footnote to *Three Guineas*.
[86] *Between the Acts*, pp. 133–4.

Mrs Swithin, for the fighter planes are already flying over the village on that June afternoon in 1939. But a vision has for a moment been imparted that might yet help to save us, if not from World War II then from World War III. For just as in *Mrs Dalloway* the suicidal insanity of war-damaged Septimus Smith had been counterpointed by a radiant love of life, so, in this final novel, there is a continuous musical dialogue between the motifs of destruction and brutality and the contrasting motifs of beauty, creativity and human fellowship. There is a new gentleness transfiguring this work, a tenderness for all that lives – swallows, beetles, a stray bitch and her puppies in the barn, a bluebottle, a butterfly, cows, the fish in the lily pool, flowers, trees and sky. At the novel's opening a little boy has the experience Virginia Woolf had had as a small child – he perceives root, flower, tree and grass as constituting one whole.[87] And at the end of the novel yet another child may be conceived. Despite all that has always separated and all that will continue to separate warring humans from one another – 'greed, sexual jealousy, the love of power, the privacy of fantasy and need'[88] – nevertheless we must still hand on both our disparate visions of life and life itself to the millions of human beings yet unborn:

> But how's this wall, the great wall, which we call, perhaps miscall, civilisation, to be built by . . . orts, scraps, and fragments like ourselves? . . . listen to the gramophone affirming . . . Was it Bach, Handel, Beethoven, Mozart, or nobody famous, but merely a traditional tune? . . . Like quicksilver sliding, filings magnetised, the distracted united. The tune began; the first note meant a second; the second a third . . . On different levels ourselves went forward; flower gathering some on the surface; others descending to wrestle with the meaning; but all comprehending; all enlisted . . . Was that voice ourselves? Scraps, orts and fragments, are we also, that?[89]

It was Virginia Woolf's ultimate vision of truth 'that we – I mean all human beings – are connected . . . that the whole world is a work of art . . . we are the words; we are the music; we are the

[87] See 'A sketch of the past', in Schulkind, *Moments of Being*, p. 71.
[88] Zwerdling, *Virginia Woolf and the Real World*, ch. 10.
[89] *Between the Acts*, pp. 131–2.

thing itself.'[90] If only both sexes could be granted time to evolve into more complete, creative and humane human beings, we would finally be capable of saying: 'As human beings we have no country; as human beings we want no country; as human beings our country is the whole world.'

[90] 'A Sketch of the Past', in Schulkind, *Moments of Being*, p. 72.

6

Germany's Antigone: Sophie Scholl, 1921–1943

> It seems ridiculous for a girl to care seriously about politics.
>
> Sophie Scholl (*28 June 1940*)

Whereas Maude Royden, Simone Weil and Virginia Woolf were all converted by the fact of Hitler to a reluctant renunciation of their pacifism, Sophie Scholl was converted by Hitler to a total commitment to anti-militarism. The decisive difference in her situation, of course, was that she was a German. In many ways Sophie Scholl's task of total resistance to the Nazis' 'New Order' was more audacious and demanding than that of any other woman discussed in this book because she had to resist what almost everyone outside her immediate family believed to be the vital national good. 'It is perhaps more difficult to stand up for a worthy cause when . . . one risks one's life on one's own and in lonely isolation.'[1] Or, as Jane Addams had written 20 years earlier: 'Even to appear to differ from those she loves in the hour of their affliction has ever been the supreme test of a woman's conscience.'[2]

When Hitler became Chancellor, in January 1933, Sophie Scholl

[1] Inge Scholl, *Students Against Tyranny: The Resistance of the White Rose, Munich, 1942–43*, Wesleyan University Press, 1970, p. 4.
[2] Quoted in Alice Hamilton, Jane Addams and Emily Balch, *Women at The Hague*, Macmillan, 1915, ch. 7, p. 125.

was eleven and a half years old, the youngest daughter and the fourth of Robert and Magdalena Scholl's five children. Her father had been one of the few Germans who had refused to fight in World War I and he had met his wife, a Protestant deaconess/nurse, while they were both caring for wounded soldiers in a military hospital. Sophie was a reflective, introverted child, expressing herself most often in her drawing and solitary play in the woods and streams, but occasionally she would burst out into a spontaneous protest at some injustice. At first, like her elder brother and sisters, Sophie took all Hitler's idealistic promises at face value:

> We heard much oratory about the Fatherland, comradeship, unity of the Volk, and love of our land . . . And Hitler – so we heard on all sides – Hitler would help our Fatherland achieve greatness, fortune and prosperity. He would see to it that everyone had work and bread. He would not rest until every German was independent, free and happy . . . There was something else that drew us with mysterious power and swept us along: the closed ranks of marching youth with banners waving, eyes fixed straight ahead, keeping time to drum-beat and song . . . All of us, Hans and Sophie and the others, joined the Hitler youth. We entered into it with body and soul.[3]

Only their father dissented. He tried to warn his children that Hitler's 'economic miracle' was achieved by preparing for another war and that Hitler was another Pied Piper, leading the children to destruction. But at first they had no ears to hear. Sophie wholeheartedly enjoyed the hiking and camping, the singing by the torchlit fires with the *Jungmädel*, among whom she soon became a leader. Right from the first, however, she could not accept the anti-Jewish paranoia. It made absolutely no sense to her and she insisted on keeping up her friendship with one of the few Jewish girls in her class, Anneliese Wallersteiner. It was only after the Nüremberg rally of 1936, when Sophie was 15, that she began to share her elder brother Hans's first misgivings about other aspects of Nazi Party ideology and praxis – above all its relentless emphasis on militarism, its authoritarianism and promotion of 'Deutschland über alles'. Now that they too had begun to question aspects of Nazism, the Scholl

[3] Scholl, *Students Against Tyranny*, p. 6.

Sophie Scholl

children could draw close to their father again. They asked him what a 'concentration camp' was and he told them what he knew and what he suspected, adding, 'That is war. War in the midst of peace, within our own people. War against the defenceless individual . . . It is a frightful crime.'[4] He urged his children to try to remain 'upright and free' no matter what.

As well as belonging to the Hitler Jugend, Hans had belonged to an alternative, secret, boys' group, 'Deutsche Jungenschaft vom 1 November', which read banned poetry, swapped postcards by proscribed artists and sang Russian, Scandinavian and Gipsy songs that were all taboo; and Sophie, although only on the fringe, as a non-boy, had also quietly absorbed much of this alternative, forbidden culture. Early one November morning in 1937 the Gestapo arrived to arrest Inge (18), Sophie (16) and Werner (15) as part of a national crackdown on such subversive pastimes. Hans (19), was arrested in his barracks. Sophie had been arrested by mistake; they had thought her trousers and short-cropped hair meant that she was a boy; clearly no young girl could have had anything to do with forbidden 'Resistance' activities. Sophie regarded this first attack upon her family by the Secret State Police as a mark of distinction, refusing to apologize for it in any way; and she incurred further odium within the Bund Deutscher Mädel by naively recommending Heine as a poet for special study. Everyone was aghast, while Sophie muttered: 'If you don't know Heine you don't know German literature.'

Between the ages of 16 and 18 Sophie was kept to the normal academic grind of the German Gymnasium as she prepared for her *Abitur*. But school life was increasingly remote from her real self, which brooded over her private reading, or escaped into her usual refuge of nature or art. All the family took it for granted that Sophie would be an artist when she grew up, and the quality of her surviving drawings and sketches gives real substance to that assumption. The pictures taken of her at this time by her younger brother show a finely modelled, sensitive face sometimes quietly thoughtful, sometimes frowning over a book or else laughing with the sheer joy of being alive in sea and sun. Paula Modersohn-Becker was her heroine then – the independent-eyed woman artist, conforming to no one else's vision. Her reading included Shaw (most probably *Saint Joan*),

[4] ibid., p. 11.

Maritain's *Anti-moderne*, Socrates' *Apology*, Claudel and Thomas Mann, as well as introductions to comparative religion, including Buddhism and the Bhagavad Gita. All such foreign and forbidden books were passed from hand to hand within Sophie Scholl's circle of friends and served to strengthen their inner resistance to the life and thought of Nazi Germany.

But Sophie, like her family and friends, knew that merely reading alternative thoughts was not enough; one has also to try to live what one has read. Therefore, when Hitler initiated World War II on 1 September 1939, Sophie, now 18, felt driven to make an impossible demand of all the young men in her immediate circle, including the man for whom she cared most and who loved her, a professional army officer, Fritz Hartnagel. She asked them to promise not to kill. She wrote to Hartnagel on 5 September 1939: 'Now of course, there'll be more than enough for you lot to do. I just can't grasp that people are going to be under constant threat from other people from now on. I'll never grasp it and I find it quite horrific. Don't say it's for the Fatherland.'[5]

It is clear that already in the early months of World War II Sophie Scholl was stiffening her resolve to resist Hitlerism, though precisely how she was to do so was not yet clear to her. Subconsciously she had already got as far as anticipating imprisonment, 'I dreamed recently that I was in a prison cell, kept there for the whole duration of the war. I had a thick iron ring around my neck – that was the most unpleasant bit' (letter to Hartnagel 6 Oct. 1939). She warned Hartnagel against turning into an arrogant, uncaring army lieutenant. 'It's so easy to become callous and indifferent. And I think that would be terrible' (Apr. 1940). Hartnagel was at that time part of the German operation overrunning the Netherlands and Sophie's most fervent hope for him was that he would manage to survive the war and 'these times' without becoming their creature. 'We all have inner standards of behaviour within us, only we search them out too rarely. Perhaps because they are the most difficult standards of all to live up to' (16 May 1940). She was struggling at this time to

[5] Quotations from letters throughout this chapter from Inge Jens (ed.), *Hans Scholl, Sophie Scholl; Briefe und Aufzeichnungen*, Fischer, 1984, translated as *At the Heart of the White Rose; Letters and Diaries of Hans and Sophie Scholl*, Harper & Row, 1987. I have used this translation, making occasional idiomatic changes.

define the standard according to which she herself must live:

> Even if I don't understand much about politics and have no ambition to do so, nevertheless I still have some idea of right and wrong, because that has nothing to do with politics or nationality. And I could weep at how mean and small-minded people are even in the area of high level politics, and how they betray their fellow-creatures just on the off-chance of gaining personal advantage . . .
>
> Sometimes I'm tempted to look on humanity as a skin disease on the earth's surface. But only sometimes, when I'm very tired, and people who are worse than animals loom large in front of me. But basically all that matters is whether or not we can pull through, stand fast against the majority who are only after their own interests and who think any means justified to gain their own ends. This mass-pressure is so overpowering that one must be bad to survive at all. There has probably only ever been one human being who has managed to walk an absolutely straight road to God.
>
> But who even looks for it now? . . . At any rate I believe that the individual, whatever befalls, must stay morally awake and especially now when it is hard to do so . . . Precisely here and now fate has offered us a shining opportunity to prove ourselves and perhaps we shouldn't underrate that.
>
> We heard today that France is laying down her arms. It made me shudder unspeakably before writing to you. I too am inclined at times to lay down my arms. But 'Defying all the powers that be',[6] I shall try not to be satisfied just with dreams, with high culture and noble gestures. One cannot allow oneself to be too faint-hearted these days. (letters to Hartnagel, May–June 1940)

What might have sounded in any other context like a typical 19-year-old's naïve idealism is here a very untypical 19-year-old's desperate effort to hold on to a basic humane ethic, while almost all

[6] 'Defying all powers that be, never going under, proving oneself strong in spirit, calls up the power of the Divine' – favourite lines from Goethe that were a motto for the Scholl family; Hans Scholl inscribed them on his cell wall before standing trial.

those around her were rationalizing mass murder. It was vital for Sophie Scholl that Fritz Hartnagel, above all people, should become one in spirit with her on this fundamental moral issue of Nazi aggression. Therefore many of her letters to him during 1940 wrestle for his soul:

> I'm perfectly prepared to believe that you simply argue with me for argument's sake when we get onto ideological and political subjects. Personally, though, I've never argued for argument's sake, as you may secretly believe . . .
>
> I can't imagine two people living together when they differ on these questions in their views, or at least in their activities.
>
> People shouldn't be ambivalent themselves just because everything else is, yet one constantly meets the view that, because we've been born into a world of contradictions, we must defer to it. That doesn't mean I would range myself on the side of those who are single-hearted in the true sense. Scarcely an hour passes without one of my thoughts flying off at a tangent, and very few of my actions correspond to what I consider right. I'm so often scared of those actions, which loom over me like dark mountains, that all I want to do is cease to exist . . . Don't think I'm good, that's all I ask, because I'm bad. Don't do it for my sake, so I needn't be always afraid of disillusioning you someday. (letter to Hartnagel, 22 June 1940)

After the surrender of France to the Nazis in June 1940, Sophie wrote to Hartnagel, who was part of the invading German Army there, aware that her objectivity about politics and her moral seriousness could sound 'unwomanly':

> I'd have been more impressed if the French had defended Paris to the last bullet . . . even if it had been hopeless, as it certainly was, in the immediate situation anyway. But self-interest is all that counts today, there is no meaning anymore. Nor honor. All that matters is just saving one's own skin . . . If I didn't know that I'll probably survive many older people than myself, I could have the horrors sometimes thinking what kind of spirit dictates history today. I'm sure you find it unwomanly, the way I write to you. It seems ridiculous for a girl to care seriously about politics. She's supposed to let her feminine emotions rule

> her thoughts, compassion, above all. But I find that thoughts take precedence, and that emotions often lead you astray because you can't see big things for the little things that may concern you more directly – personally perhaps.

Two months later Sophie answered Hartnagel's attempt to defend the calling of the professional soldier. Like Julian Bell, Hartnagel tried to insist that the decent, self-disciplined soldier could fulfil an honourable role in the scheme of things. Sophie tried to show him that this was cant by concentrating on the heart of the matter – the amorality of the soldier's 'obeying orders', no matter what those orders are. She was, thus, already in 1940, anticipating the moral basis of the 1946 Judgement at Nuremberg:

> I think you got me wrong about what concerns me in your profession. Or rather I think that the soldier's calling today is quite other than how you described it. A soldier has an oath to keep; his job is to carry out his government's orders. Tomorrow he might have to obey precisely the opposite viewpoint from that of yesterday. His calling is to obey. The soldier's attitude is in fact no 'profession' at all . . . How can a soldier have an honest attitude, as you put it, when he's compelled to lie? Or isn't it lying when you have to swear one oath to the government one day and another the next? You have to allow for that situation and it's already arisen before now. You weren't so very much in favour of a war, to the best of my knowledge, yet you spend all your time training people for it. You surely don't believe it's the job of the armed forces to teach people an honest, moderate, sincere attitude. If a soldier's commandment is to be loyal, sincere, moderate and honest, he certainly can't obey it, because if he receives an order, he has to carry it out, whether he considers it right or wrong. Otherwise, he gets court-martialled, right? (letter to Hartnagel, 19 Aug. 1940)

Hartnagel then tried to justify soldiering by reference to the needs of one's people. Sophie replied:

> You ask me to tell you how I see the concept of 'Volk' . . . I see the position of a soldier in relation to his people as roughly that of a son who swears to stand by his father and his family

come what may. If the father wrongs another family and thereby gets into trouble, the son is then supposed to stand by his father no matter what. But such commitment to one's 'kith and kin' is beyond me. I think justice, what is right, *must* always take precedence over every other, often just sentimental, attachment. And it would surely be better if people engaged in a conflict could take the side they consider right.

Similarly I consider it just as wrong when a German or a Frenchman, or whatever, stubbornly defends his own nation just because it is *his* nation. Feelings often lead one astray. Whenever I see soldiers marching in the street, especially when there's music playing, then I too am stirred – I even used to have to ward off tears whenever I heard military marches. But those are feelings for sentimental little old ladies. It'd be ridiculous to let oneself be governed by them. (letter to Hartnagel, 23 Sept. 1940)

Towards the end of 1940 Sophie began to doubt whether she should continue the correspondence with Hartnagel; he still seemed far apart from her in his thinking and she could not yet commit herself to him emotionally as he wished:

I've already been asking myself whether I ought not to give up hearing from you since it's for selfish reasons that I keep on writing to you. But I don't think it is necessary. Perhaps it's not even right. For in my view (which doesn't have to coincide with yours), you find yourself in an atmosphere completely at odds with that to which I want to win you over.

And at the bottom you're already half on my side and will never feel wholly comfortable on that other side again. It's the same struggle that I'm having to wage myself, which you've got, not to go under to mere creature comforts and easy Philistinism. Isn't it a prop and consolation to know that one isn't all alone? Or rather feel it.

But you obviously feel very deserted. Here I can't help you. I may not help you – even though it hurts me so much. You know that . . .

Dear Fritz, don't think me uncaring. It's much harder standing firm than turning weak . . .

Do you still want to write to me? (10 Nov. 1940)

Hartnagel did want to go on writing to her and did in fact come over to her side. Forty years later he testified:

> As to politics, Sophie was the one that set the trend. We often argued and at first were far from being of one mind on all issues. Only hesitantly and reluctantly did I become ready to follow her way of thinking. It meant a huge leap for me, in the midst of the war, to say: 'I'm against this war,' or: 'Germany must lose this war.'[7]

Finally, during his service in Russia, in 1941, Hartnagel heard his fellow officers referring to the mass shooting of Jews as though it were the most natural thing to do in the world. At last he could hide from himself no longer the truth of Sophie's accusation – that he was serving a criminal regime. Even so he could still be shocked by the lengths to which Sophie would go in her absolute opposition to Hitler's war. In the winter of 1941–2 the German people were called upon to send warm coats, blankets, gloves, socks etc. to the German troops freezing outside Leningrad and Moscow. Sophie refused. She did not deny that it was as bad for a German to freeze to death as for a Russian but she insisted that the one thing that mattered was for Germany to lose the war as quickly as possible – woollen socks for German troops could only prolong it. At last, after fierce arguments with her – in person, not by letter – Hartnagel had to agree that either one was for Hitler or against him and if one were against him the only thing to bring him down and give the Germans back their freedom was military defeat.

Sophie had hoped to begin studying for her degree in biology and philosophy at Munich University in May 1940. Instead, she was compelled by the regime to do six months of *Reichsarbeitsdienst* – national work service. In order to try to avoid that, Sophie had undertaken a year-long training as a kindergarten teacher at the Froebel Institute, a training which was at first accepted as a substitute for work service. No sooner had she qualified as a teacher, however, than the rules were changed and she had to do six months' national work service none the less, stationed in a barracks and wearing uniform. It was gall to her spirit: 'her convictions forced her into a

[7] Hermann Vinke, *Das kurze Leben der Sophie Scholl*, Otto Maier Verlag, Ravensburg, 1980, p. 71. Translated by Hedwig Pachter as *The Short Life of Sophie Scholl*, Harper & Row, 1984.

state of continuous resistance. Wasn't it an unforgivable sign of weak character if she gave the least bit of service to a state founded on lies, hatred and bondage?'[8]

Once those hateful six months were over, the regime imposed yet another six months' compulsory service on all girl would-be university students. Refusal would have meant instant imprisonment, of course. 'So I've got to spend another half year in the strait jacket,' Sophie reported furiously to her brother Hans: 'The time I've already spent has quite sufficed to ripen my loathing and contempt for the whole business. But, strangely enough, only now for the first time do I feel that nothing will have power over me. I have a marvellous feeling of inner strength sometimes' (letter to Hans, 7 Sept. 1941). She was now a female 'compulsory-war-service-auxiliary' – 'the name is as ghastly as everything else about it' (letter to Hans, 20 Nov. 1941). The only things that supported her spirit during this whole period, in addition to the lifeline of letters and books, were music and nature.

Sophie Scholl was capable of a quite exceptional intensity of response to the natural world, partly perhaps because she was so gifted artistically, and partly because of her reverence for life. Her letters and diary entries are as full of ecstatic, sensitively precise 'nature notes' as were those of Kate Courtney (see above, ch. 2):

> As we lay in the grass, the pale green beech twigs and white cobwebbed sky above us, it was as though war and worry could find no room in such beauty. The meadow by the brook was pink with campion and there were lovely juicy marsh marigolds. (letter to Hartnagel, 16 May 1940)
>
> Best of all I lay on the ground so that I could be near all the little creatures and a part of them all. The ants and beetles looked on me simply as a piece of wood, and I quite liked it when they tickled and crawled right over me. (letter to Hartnagel, 8 Aug. 1940)
>
> We leaned against the wind, hair streaming out like witches, while the leaves kept whirling over us as though scattered down by some strong hand. And the little leaves on the ground tumbled about in droves as though they simply had to keep

[8] Scholl, *Students Against Tyranny*, p. 23.

> moving faster and faster. How we laughed. (letter to Hartnagel, 4 Nov. 1940)
>
> I spent half an hour in the park this evening, and just as you were able to pick snowdrops in yours some months back, so I now find innumerable cowslips in mine. And in my park the clumps of trees looked so lovely in the evening light that I walked home backwards so as to prolong the sight of them. Clouds were floating high above like the slender white feathers of some strange bird, and the spring sky and the lower-lying clouds were tinged all over with orange by the setting sun. (20 Apr. 1941)

Finally, in her Diary of 12 December 1941: 'Only Nature gives me any nourishment now, sky and stars and the quiet earth.' They were the innocent, beautiful, life-giving reality with which to counter the death's-head reality of the Nazis' scorching of the earth. For music, her other life-giver, Sophie had to depend during her national work service period on being allowed to play Handel or Bach on the organ of some nearby village church. In addition there were precious recitals of classical music on the wireless – 'It is music that can best and most quickly stir my dull heart to tumultuous feeling. And that is so necessary, the precondition for everything else' (letter to Lisa Remppis, 14 Jan. 1942). Sophie's private motto at this period was from Maritain: 'It is necessary to have a tough spirit and a tender heart.' It is music, she wrote in her Diary, in January 1942, that 'makes the heart tender: brings order to its wild confusion, loosens its crampedness and prepares the soul for the influence of the spirit that had been knocking at its firmly closed doors in vain. Yes, quite quietly, and without forcing its way, music opens the doors of the soul.'[9]

In the spring of 1942 the Scholls read some secretly distributed extracts from a recent sermon by the Catholic Bishop of Munster, Count von Galen. Von Galen saw that Hitler was attempting to root out Christianity in Germany and he denounced the latest Nazi policy of 'mercy-killing' for the incurable, the handicapped and the insane. Von Galen alleged that 'the officials follow the precept that it is

[9] cf. Jens, *At the Heart of the White Rose*, p. 190. Sophie's last letter was an overflowing of joy at Schubert's 'Trout' Quintet.

permissible to destroy life which does not deserve to live.'[10] His rousing peroration, which was circulated secretly throughout Germany and cost many distributors their lives, ran:

> Grow strong. Stand firm. Remain steadfast. Like the anvil under the blows of the hammer. It may be that obedience to God and loyalty to conscience will cost you or me our lives, our freedom or our home. But let us rather die than sin. May the mercy of God without which we can do nothing give us that strength.[11]

Hans Scholl's reaction was: 'At last a man has had the courage to speak out. We really ought to have a duplicating machine.'[12]

It is possible that Bishop von Galen's sermons may have helped Sophie to gain a new respect for organized Christianity – compromised as it had been in Germany ever since 1933 by the deafening silence of both Churches concerning Hitler. Her sister Inge has written that religion, to Sophie, was an intensive search for meaning both in her own life and in history. 'God' demanded not only that she be true to her most authentic self – which was also what she meant by freedom – but also that she find some way of acting out such authenticity in the world. 'But be ye doers of the word, and not hearers only' was a decisive life-motto for her.[13] She found it very difficult to gain any sense of a personal God, however, and could only pray to be enabled to pray. Nevertheless, the New Testament constituted an increasingly powerful 'forbidden book' under a brutish dictatorship that was trying to instil pitilessness as the national German consciousness: 'Hate is Our Prayer – and Victory Our Reward . . . We will March on, though everything Break into Fragments' was an approved Nazi daily newspaper headline then.[14] In reaction against such a Gospel of Hate Sophie found herself becoming more and more of a would-be Christian, which is perhaps the only real kind of Christian.

[10] Quoted in Scholl, *Students Against Tyranny*, p. 19.
[11] Quoted in Annedore Leber, *Conscience in Revolt: 64 Stories of Resistance in Germany, 1933–45*, Vallentine, London, 1957, p. 188. Marie Terwiel was one of those executed for distributing von Galen's sermon, see Leber, p. 123.
[12] Scholl, *Students Against Tyranny*, p. 20.
[13] The Epistle of James 1: 22.
[14] Quoted in Scholl, *Students Against Tyranny*, p. 45.

This then was the ardent, serious and very impatient 21-year-old who arrived in Munich in May 1942, complete with home-baked birthday cake and bottle of wine, in order to start out on life as a university student at last. What she possibly did not realize, however, was that Munich was also the secret uncrowned capital of Nazism and Munich University one of the most fanatical in Germany – its very Chancellor being a high-ranking member of the SS.

It is not certain precisely when Sophie joined the activities of Hans's White Rose Resistance Group. Certainly she was introduced by Hans to his closest friends Probst, Schmorell and Graf the moment she arrived, about 1 May.[15] Fritz Hartnagel has testified that as early as May she asked him, without giving a reason, whether he could get her a duplicating machine. And in a letter to her friend Lisa Remppis, dated 30 May 1942, Sophie reports a three-hour non-stop philosophical discussion by her brother and a friend, adding: 'Actually I feel more of a need to be on my own because I've an urge to act on what I've hitherto only theoretically recognized as being right.' Whether Sophie had any part at all in preparing the first Resistance leaflet, which appeared six weeks after her arrival in Munich, or whether, the moment she discovered that leaflet and that Hans had written it, she then immediately insisted on becoming part of the Resistance group, we shall never know. What is certain is that Hans could never have kept his youngest sister safely out of the protest action indefinitely, even had he hoped to do so. Ever since Hitler had begun his attack on Poland, the Netherlands and France, Sophie Scholl had been a secret resister in spirit to this war. She had been yearning for some active way to testify to her opposition to Nazi militarism, and from the moment that she discovered her brother's involvement, her own independently evolved humane credo, as well as her love for him, impelled her to be one with Hans to the end. Both in putting 'the Law' before 'the laws' and in choosing to join in loving rather than in hating her outlaw 'traitor' brother, Sophie Scholl was Germany's Antigone.

The first three leaflets were written in May, June and July. There is no way of identifying specific contributions by Sophie but there is not a word that she did not endorse and the clear, passionately

[15] Probst, Schmorell and Graf were all medical students (like Hans Scholl), committed to anti-Nazism in the name of humanism; they were all executed.

uncompromising tone of urgent, youthful pleading is one that had already been present in her letters to Hartnagel two years earlier.

> If everyone waits until the other man makes a start, the messengers of avenging Nemesis will come steadily closer; offer passive resistance – *resistance* – wherever you may be, forestall the spread of this atheistic war machine before it is too late, before the last cities, like Cologne, have been reduced to rubble, and before the nation's last young man has given his blood on some battlefield for the *hubris* of a sub-human.[16]

That first leaflet ends with a very apt quotation from Schiller's essay comparing 'The Lawgiving of Lycurgus and Solon':

> Anything may be sacrificed to the good of the state except that end for which the state serves as a means. The state is never an end in itself; it is important only as a condition under which the purpose of humanity can be attained, and this purpose is none other than the development of all of man's powers, his progress and improvement . . .
>
> At the price of all moral feeling a political system was set up in Sparta and the resources of the state were mobilised to that end . . .
>
> In the Spartan code of law the dangerous principle was promulgated that men are to be looked upon as means and not as ends – and the foundations of natural law and of morality were destroyed by that law.[17]

For Sophie, as for Antigone and Simone Weil, the state was not the ultimate political authority; every state exists only to serve a humane moral end. The citizen's conscience regarding his or her fellows must be enabled to grow – rather than be suppressed 'for the good of the state' – and the citizen's conscience, therefore, must be his or her ultimate authority and reality.

The second leaflet, which was distributed in June, began as an appeal by intellectuals to other intellectuals in Germany, demoralized and isolated from each other though they were:

[16] The first leaflet, published fully in Scholl, *Students Against Tyranny*, pp. 73–6.
[17] ibid.

> Now it is our task to find one another again, to spread information from person to person, to keep a steady purpose and to allow ourselves no rest until the last man is persuaded of the urgent need of his struggle against this system. When thus a wave of unrest goes through the land, when 'it is in the air', when many join the cause, then in a great final effort this system can be shaken off. After all an end in terror is preferable to terror without end.[18]

'An end in terror' – clearly the Scholls were prepared to go under themselves rather than do nothing while Europe went under. But they overestimated most people's readiness for martyrdom, much as Maude Royden had overestimated it in her call for a Peace Army to volunteer for death to stop the Sino-Japanese war. The second leaflet goes on to spell out what the group had learned so far about Nazi atrocities both in Poland and towards Jews and the leaflet indicts the Germans for knowing about the barbarities but simply shrugging them off as a fact of life:

> Since the conquest of Poland three hundred thousand Jews have been murdered in this country in the most bestial way. Here we see the most frightful crime against human dignity – a crime that is unparalleled in the whole of history. For Jews, too, are human beings . . . Is it a sign that the Germans are brutalised in their simplest human feelings, that no chord within them cries out at the sight of such deeds, that they have sunk into a fatal conciencelessness from which they will never, never awake?[19]

Germans must rouse themselves from their stupor and show not only sympathy for these hundreds and thousands of victims but also an awareness of their own complicity in the guilt. German apathy is what has allowed the Nazis to act as they do:

[18] ibid., pp. 77–80.
[19] ibid.

> Each German wants to be exonerated of a guilt of this kind, each one continues on his way with the most placid, the calmest conscience. But he cannot be exonerated; he is *guilty, guilty, guilty*![20]

One could almost swear that it was Sophie's desperation and moral passion which gave those words their italics and exclamation mark. The leaflet ends with a definition of true patriotism for Germans now:

> Up until the outbreak of the war the larger part of the German people was blinded; the Nazis did not show themselves in their true aspect. But now, now that we have recognised them for what they are, it must be the sole and first duty, the holiest duty of every German to destroy these beasts.[21]

The third leaflet reiterates the group's libertarian and ethical definition of the state and then spells out how Hitler's tyrannical and criminal system must be resisted and military defeat for the Nazis brought nearer:

> Every individual human being has a claim to a useful and just state, a state which secures the freedom of the individual as well as the good of the whole . . . But our present 'state' is the dictatorship of evil . . . Many, perhaps most, of the readers of these leaflets do not see clearly how they can practise an effective opposition . . . The only means available is *passive resistance* . . .We must . . . bring this monster of a state to an end. A victory of fascist Germany in this war would have immeasurable, frightful consequences. The military victory over Bolshevism dare not become the primary concern of the Germans. The defeat of the Nazis must *unconditionally* be the first order of business . . .
>
> *Sabotage* in armament plants and war industries, sabotage at all gatherings, rallies, public ceremonies, and organisations of the National Socialist Party. Obstruction of the smooth functioning of the war machine (a machine for war that goes on solely to shore up and perpetuate the National Socialist

[20] ibid.
[21] ibid.

Party and its dictatorship). *Sabotage* in all the areas of science and scholarship which further the continuation of the war – whether in universities, technical schools, laboratories, research institutes, or technical bureaus. *Sabotage* in all cultural institutions which could potentially enhance the 'prestige' of the fascists among the people. *Sabotage* in all branches of the arts which have even the slightest dependence on National Socialism or render it service. *Sabotage* in all publications, all newspapers, that are in the pay of the 'government' and that defend its ideology and aid in disseminating the brown lie. Do not give a penny to public drives (even when they are conducted under the pretence of charity). For this is only a disguise. In reality the proceeds aid neither the Red Cross nor the needy. The government does not need this money; it is not financially interested in these money drives. After all the presses run continuously to manufacture any desired amount of paper currency. But the populace must be kept constantly under tension, the pressure of the bit must not be allowed to slacken! Do not contribute to the collections of metal, textiles, and the like. Try to convince all your acquaintances, including those in the lower social classes, of the senselessness of continuing, of the hopelessness of this war.[22]

That third leaflet, the last for several months, ends with the warning from Aristotle's *Politics*: 'the tyrant is inclined constantly to foment wars.'

After that quotation came the plea: 'Please duplicate and distribute.' Sophie herself did much of the duplicating and distribution. Thousands of copies of the three leaflets had to be printed off secretly at night and then packed in suitcases and rucksacks and taken by train to Frankfurt, Stuttgart, Freiburg, Saarbrücken, Mannheim and Karlsruhe – all the major cities of southern Germany. Once there, the leaflets had to be posted from different boxes, using addresses arbitrarily selected from the local telephone directory; and all this under the continuous minute-by-minute fear of discovery. Only the conviction that what she and the others were trying to communicate to their fellow Germans *had* to be said could have sustained them.

[22] ibid., pp. 81–4.

In addition, the White Rose Group, including Sophie,

> collected dried white bread to send via go-betweens to concentration camp prisoners; they helped support the families of those prisoners; they refused to prolong Hitler's war by donating to the Nazi 'Winter Aid' clothing drive that was to benefit German soldiers in Russia; they showed human understanding for prisoners of war and foreign workers. Examples of small-scale resistance, practical and tangible, and potentially contagious.[23]

It is very possible that Sophie and Hans were borne up by their new acquaintance with Christian Existentialism mediated to them by their 75-year-old mentor in Munich, Carl Muth.[24] It was Muth who introduced the Scholls to his friend, the Catholic philosopher Theodore Haecker, the rediscoverer of Kierkegaard, and the Scholls may well have felt inspired by Haecker's resonant re-statement of Kierkegaard's insistence that *everyone* in this world has a mission:

> God did not create one soul uselessly and without a place in the scheme of salvation . . . it is true whether a man is conscious of his mission or not, whether he fulfils it with all his strength or only half-heartedly or even fights against it; it is true whether he is victorious or succumbs, whether it brings him happiness or misery and persecution; it is true whether great or small; but the more important it is, the more conscious of it will the man be who has to fulfil it.[25]

There now had to be an interval in the Resistance work in the summer and autumn since Hans and the others were all dispatched to a tour of military duty in the Soviet Union, where they narrowly escaped court martial for opposing Nazi brutalities towards the Russians. Sophie, meanwhile, was conscripted, bitterly against her will, to do several months' work in an Ulm armaments factory. Nothing could have been more abhorrent. Now she made Simone Weil's discovery of the intolerable slavery inherent in servicing a machine on a conveyor belt hour after hour, and all in aid of a

[23] Vinke, *Short Life*, p. 98.
[24] Carl Muth (1867–1944), editor of the liberal and progressive Catholic periodical *Hochland* until 1941, when it was banned by the Nazis. See Jens, *At the Heart of the White Rose*, pp. 260–2.
[25] T. Haecker, *Soren Kierkegaard*, OUP, 1937, p. 56.

purpose that was anathema to her. It seems probable that she did not refuse this war-work and incur imprisonment because that would only have meant the end of her active participation in the resistance work of the White Rose.

The one positive aspect of her factory experience was that she found herself working beside a Russian slave-worker and so was able to live out her total rejection of 'the enemy concept'. Sophie Scholl would have endorsed Kate Courtney's statement to *The Times* 27 years earlier that those we call 'the enemy' are really nothing other than 'the most unfortunate, because most hated people':

> Working next to me is a Russian girl, a child in her guileless, touching trustfulness – even towards the German foreman whose fist-shaking and brutal shouts she counters with just an uncomprehending, almost merry smile. These people probably strike her as funny and she takes their threats for jokes. I'm glad that she's working beside me and I do my best to correct her picture of the Germans a little. But many of the other German women workers also make a point of being friendly and helpful, astonished to find human beings even amongst Russians, especially such uneducated ones, and without an ounce of mistrust in their nature. (letter to Hartnagel, Aug. 1942)

Between July and October 1942 Hans wrote home from Poland and Russia. He had seen with his own eyes the cities ruined by the German attack; the half-starved children whimpering for bread in the streets, the walled-off Warsaw ghetto, the proud, defeated Poles refusing to exchange a word with their conquerors, the man-made gigantic suffering of Russia where, as he wrote, Christ was being crucified a thousand times each hour.[26] All this, of course, was passed on immediately to Sophie. Nothing other than renewed total resistance to the Nazi war-lords would be possible for them both from now on, cost what it would. Sophie's long letter to Hartnagel at this time shows how she was girding up her own spirit for such resistance, as well as standing by him in his attempt to resist the corrupting pressures from his fellow officers in Russia:

[26] See Hans Scholl's letters to his parents, in Jens, *At the Heart of the White Rose*, pp. 83–6.

> I wish I could stand by you with all that I know and am, in the arguments which you're often compelled to have with your brother officers. It strikes me as absolutely terrible and either degenerate or else totally insensitive that their whole inner being does not rise up against this 'natural law' of the victory of the strong over the weak. Even a child is filled with horror when forced to witness the defeat and destruction of a weaker animal by a strong one. I was always deeply moved and saddened by that inescapable fact, not only as a child but later on as well, and I racked my brains for some way of remaining aloof from this universal state of affairs. The sight of an innocent little mouse in a trap always brought tears to my eyes, and I can only attribute my regained and continuing happiness to forgetfulness, which is no solution. Nor can there be any solution here on earth. In the Epistle to the Romans it says that the suffering of creation has to wait – to be delivered into the glorious liberty of the children of God. (28 Oct. 1942)

Sophie entreated Hartnagel to read the whole of that chapter, which contains the great words of spiritual inspiration that can withstand death:

> If God be for us, who can be against us? . . . Who shall separate us from the love of Christ? Shall tribulation, or distress, or persecution, or famine, or nakedness, or peril, or sword? . . . For I am persuaded, that neither death, nor life, nor angels, nor principalities, nor powers, nor things present, nor things to come, nor height, nor depth, nor any other creature, shall be able to separate us from the love of God, which is in Christ Jesus our Lord.[27]

Sophie then returned to Hartnagel's struggle with his Nazi fellow officers and their arrogant faith in *Machtpolitik* as constituting ultimate reality:

> And if they put their faith in the triumph of force believing that might must prevail, ask them whether they think that man is nothing more than an animal or whether he can reach beyond that and partake of the world of the spirit . . . And then ask

[27] Romans 8: 31, 35 and 38–9.

> them whether a physical victory of brute strength is not an insult to the world of the spirit, or whether in that world different laws count from those in this world of the flesh, whether perhaps a sick inventor, or, to get away from the dubious realm of technology, a sick poet or philosopher doesn't have more weight than a stupid athlete, a Hölderlin more than the boxer Schemeling . . . Yes, we too believe in the victory of the stronger, but the stronger in spirit. And that this victory will perhaps have force in another world than our limited one . . . that doesn't make it any less worth striving after. I shall never ever believe that a human being can consider it good when a weak country, overrun by a mighty army, goes under . . . The triumph of brute strength must always mean the defeat or at least the obscuring into invisibility of the spirit. Is that what they want, those who argue with you? . . . Life can only come out of life, or have they seen a dead mother give birth to a child? Or a stone manage to reproduce itself and increase? They still haven't pondered the absurdity of the [Nazi] saying: 'Only out of death comes life.' (letter to Hartnagel, 28 Oct. 1942)

Sophie's appeal to the laws of the spirit that differ vitally from the laws of the powerful in this world echoes Antigone's appeal to Creon to remember the Law rather than the laws. And Sophie's insistence that this Law teaches us the sanctity of life, out of which alone more life can come, echoes the life-centred values (focusing on the life-needs of others) that were shared by all the women in the other chapters of this book.

Once Sophie and Hans returned to Munich in November 1942, ostensibly just to begin the new academic year, they redoubled their efforts at resistance. First Sophie obtained money from Hartnagel 'for a good cause' with which to buy a new duplicating machine, typewriters and paper. Next the Resistance group was expanded to include the Philosophy Professor Kurt Huber and others, who in turn made contact with the Italian Resistance, and with student Resistance cells in Hamburg and Freiburg. Hans himself went to a secret meeting with Falk Harnack, the brother of the communist resister Professor Arvid Harnack, then already imprisoned on a charge of treason; and Falk Harnack, in turn, promised to arrange a meeting in February 1943 between Hans Scholl and Dietrich

Bonhoeffer. Thus the White Rose Group was rapidly making connections both with intellectuals and with communists and learning of the existence of other dedicated political, religious and even military opponents of Hitler. Sophie worked night after night duplicating the leaflets and then taking them by day to post in Stuttgart, Ulm and Augsburg. 'Soon the White Rose leaflets appeared in many other German cities: Frankfurt, Berlin, Hamburg, Saarbrücken, even in Salzburg and Vienna. A few copies even reached Norway, England and Sweden. The Munich Gestapo was in a state of extreme alarm.'[28] On one of her trips to Stuttgart Sophie said to a woman friend: 'If Hitler were to come toward me right now and I had a gun I would shoot him. If the men won't do it, well, then a woman will have to . . . One has to do something – or else be guilty.'[29]

The fourth leaflet, in December 1942, began by stressing the mass-killer role of the apparently successful Hitler:

> In the past weeks Hitler has chalked up successes in Africa and in Russia . . .
>
> This apparent success has been purchased at the most horrible expense of human life . . .
>
> Neither Hitler nor Goebbels can have counted the dead. In Russia thousands are lost daily . . . Yet Hitler feeds with lies those people whose most precious belongings he has stolen and whom he has driven to a meaningless death.
>
> Every word that comes from Hitler's mouth is a lie. When he says peace, he means war, and when he blasphemously uses the name of the Almighty, he means the power of evil, the fallen angel, Satan . . .
>
> We *must* attack evil where it is strongest, and it is strongest in the power of Hitler.[30]

The leaflet concluded by insisting that the White Rose Group was not in the pay of any foreign power but was attempting to achieve a spiritual renewal within Germany:

[28] Vinke, *Short Life*, pp. 123–4.
[29] ibid., pp. 122–3.
[30] Scholl, *Students Against Tyranny*, pp. 85–8.

> This rebirth must be preceded, however, by the clear recognition of all the guilt with which the German people have burdened themselves, and by an uncompromising battle against Hitler and his all too many minions, party members, Quislings, and the like . . . for Hitler and his followers there is no punishment on this earth commensurate with their crimes. But out of love for coming generations we must make an example after the conclusion of the war, so that no-one will ever again have the slightest urge to try a similar action. And do not forget the petty scoundrels of this regime; note their names, so that none will go free! They should not find it possible, having had their part in these abominable crimes, at the last minute to rally to another flag and then act as if nothing had happened! . . . We will not be silent. We are your bad conscience. The White Rose will not leave you in peace![31]

On 3 January 1943, Sophie wrote to Hartnagel, who was still in the midst of the horrors of the Russian campaign:

> Oh, I can well believe that hardship desensitises, but remember: Un esprit dur, du coeur *tendre*! I'm often wretched that I cannot be a vehicle for universal suffering, so that I could take away at least a part of my guilt towards those who, undeservedly, have to suffer so much more than I.

Ten days later on 13 January 1943, the city *Gauleiter*, Giesel, very nearly caused a riot at Munich University by a speech to the students in which he urged the women there to present the Führer with a child instead of completing their education. He could offer a few of the prettier girls the services of one of his own adjutants. Several women students got up and walked out of the hall in protest, only to be instantly arrested, whereupon male students rose in their defence and took a leading Nazi Party official hostage. The authorities appeared to climb down, releasing the women from custody after a few days. The Scholls felt immensely heartened by this evidence that there clearly was some spirit of resistance (waiting to be tapped) among their Munich contemporaries. The Gestapo, however, secretly intensified their efforts to identify the anti-Nazis responsible for the White Rose leafleting.

[31] ibid.

In mid-January the group issued their fifth leaflet, headed 'Leaflet of the Resistance – A Call to All Germans'. Two and a half years before World War II ended, the White Rose tried to convince the Germans of their inevitable defeat:

> The war is approaching its destined end . . . in the East the armies are constantly in retreat and invasion is imminent in the West. Mobilisation in the United States has not yet reached its climax, but already it exceeds anything that the world has ever seen. It has become a mathematical certainty that Hitler is leading the German people into the abyss. *Hitler cannot win the war; he can only prolong it* . . . Germans! Do you and your children want to suffer the same fate that befell the Jews? Do you want to be judged by the same standards as your traducers? Are we to be forever the nation which is hated and rejected by all mankind? No. Dissociate yourselves from National Socialist gangsterism . . . A war of liberation is about to begin . . . Do not believe the National Socialist propaganda which has driven the fear of Bolshevism into your bones.[32]

That entreaty not to identify Germany's survival with an anti-communist 'crusade' indicates the new influence upon the group of their recent left-wing Resistance contacts in Germany. This fifth leaflet is much more politically constructive than the earlier, idealist writings. Decentralization, as with Simone Weil, is now seen to be essential to democratic liberty, but economic liberation of the workers and the poor, not only in Germany, is called for as well. Above all, the pernicious legacy of Prussian militarism with its ideology of force would have to be buried and buried for all time, if there were ever to be the co-operative reconstruction of a peaceful, federal Europe. (The existentialist Haecker, in his unpublished war diary from which he read extracts to the Scholls in Munich at this very time, also indicted the heritage of Prussianism for having taken away Germany's 'heart of flesh and substituting one made of iron and paper'.)[33] Haecker had also written in his diary (13 Sept. 1941) that the Germans had crucified Christ a second time by crucifying the Jewish

[32] ibid., pp. 89–90.

[33] Diary entry, 2 June 1940, quoted in Jens, *At the Heart of the White Rose*, p. 266.

people and that they would have to wear the badge of anti-Christ for that terrible guilt.[34]

On the 3 February 1943, the German Army surrendered at Stalingrad. The final White Rose leaflet, drafted by Professor Huber and addressed to 'Men and Women of the Resistance!' began:

> Shaken and broken, our people behold the loss of the men of Stalingrad. Three hundred and thirty thousand German men have been senselessly and irresponsibly driven to death and destruction by the inspired strategy of our World War I Private First Class. Führer, we thank you! For us there is but one slogan: fight against the party! Get out of the party organisations, which are used to keep our mouths sealed and hold us in political bondage! Get out of the lecture room of the SS corporals and sergeants and the party bootlickers! We want genuine learning and real freedom of opinion. No threat can terrorise us, not even the shutting down of the institutions of higher learning. This is the struggle of each and every one of us for our future, our freedom, and our honour . . .
>
> Freedom and honour! For ten long years Hitler and his coadjutors have manhandled, squeezed, twisted, and debased these two splendid German words to the point of nausea, as only dilettantes can . . . They have sufficiently demonstrated in the ten years of destruction of all material and intellectual freedom, of all moral substance among the German people, what they understood by freedom and honour. The frightful bloodbath has opened the eyes of even the stupidest German – it is a slaughter which they arranged in the name of 'freedom and honour of the German nation' throughout Europe, and which they daily start anew. The name of Germany is dishonoured for all time if German youth does not finally rise, take revenge and atone, smash its tormentors and set up a new Europe of the spirit.
>
> The dead of Stalingrad implore us to take action 'Up, up, my people, let smoke and flame be our sign!'[35]

That leaflet was intended by Professor Huber principally for the students of Munich University and Hans and Sophie Scholl

[34] ibid., p. 263.
[35] Scholl, *Students Against Tyranny*, pp. 91–3.

volunteered for the dangerous task of its distribution inside the main lecture hall before anyone arrived for classes. They were caught in the act of distribution on the morning of 18 February 1943.

During the four subsequent days of their separate interrogations both the Scholls said that their one motive had been their hope that by building up public opinion in Germany against the war they would contribute to shortening it and thus save hundreds of thousands of lives by sacrificing their own. Sophie's interrogator lectured her on the principles of National Socialism, the importance of the Führer, Germany's honour and the damage that the Scholls had inflicted on Germany's fighting morale. It was self-evident to him that his was the only right-thinking, realistic, patriotic stance and he pressed her to acknowledge that if only she had taken all those things into account she would never have allowed herself to be seduced into Resistance activities. Sophie answered: 'You are deluding yourself, I would do exactly the same all over again; it is you, not I, who hold the wrong world-view.'[36]

On the third day she was confronted with the official charge of 'preparation to commit treason' which carried the mandatory death penalty. For a moment she blanched.

That night Sophie dreamed she was carrying a child, dressed in long white robes, to be baptized. The path to the church went up a steep mountainside, but she was holding the child very securely. All of a sudden a crevasse gaped open in front of her and she only just had time to place the child in safety before she herself plunged down into the abyss. Sophie interpreted the dream next day to her cell-mate:

> The child in the white robe is our ideal which will triumph despite all obstacles. We were permitted to prepare the way for it, but first we have to die for it.[37]

The fourth day after her arrest, 22 February, was the day of her sham trial before Freisler. Her father attempted to intercede for his children but both parents were ordered out of court. The death sentence, for 'preparing to commit treason and . . . [give] aid to the enemy' was then read out. The parents saw Hans and Sophie one

[36] Testimony of Sophie Scholl's cell-mate, Else Gebel, quoted in Vinke, *Short Life*, p. 155.
[37] ibid.

last time. Sophie had been deeply afraid that her mother would not be able to bear the loss of two of her children at once, but when she saw her mother standing staunchly by her side she felt immeasurably relieved and strengthened – released from guilt and fear.

'Gelt, Sophie, Jesus,' said her mother.

'Ja, aber du auch,' Sophie replied.

Like Hans, Sophie read Psalm 90 aloud with the prison chaplain:

> Lord, thou hast been our dwelling place in all generations. Before the mountains were brought forth, or ever thou hadst formed the earth and the world, even from everlasting to everlasting, thou art God. Thou turnest man to destruction and sayest: Return ye children of men. For a thousand years in thy sight are but as yesterday when it is past and as a watch in the night. Thou carriest them away as with a flood; they are as a sleep: in the morning they are like grass which groweth up. In the morning it flourisheth, and groweth up; in the evening it is cut down, and withereth . . .
>
> Return, O Lord, how long? and let it repent thee concerning thy servants. O satisfy us early with thy mercy: that we may rejoice and be glad all our days. Make us glad according to the days wherein thou hast afflicted us and the years wherein we have seen evil. Let thy work appear unto thy servants, and thy glory unto their children, and let the beauty of the Lord our God be upon us; and establish thou the work of our hands upon us; yea, the work of our hands establish thou it.

Then she was manacled to two warders and taken to the execution hut, where they beheaded her.

Aftermath

> As for those who want to . . . transpose into pure political action all that inspires their mind and heart – they can only perish murdered, forsaken even by their own people, vilified after their death.
>
> Simone Weil, 'Obedience and Liberty' (1937) published in *Oppression and Liberty*

Sophie had believed that the students would rise up against Hitler after her and Hans's execution, but in fact that same evening several thousand Munich University students roared out their condemnation of the two Scholls, and no member of faculty or student protested against the summary 'justice'. The 'impact of their deaths was undermined by abuse or icy silence'.[38] The *Münchener Neueste Nachrichten* commented:

> Typical outsiders, the condemned persons shamelessly committed offences against the armed security of the nation and the will to fight of the German Volk by defacing houses with slogans attacking the state and by distributing treasonous leaflets. At this time of heroic struggle on the part of the German people these despicable criminals deserve a speedy and dishonourable death.[39]

Underground, however, the work of Resistance went on. The news of the Scholls' death reached the Resistance in Norway, and then neutral Sweden and Switzerland, enabling Thomas Mann to broadcast to the Allies that there was a Germany within Germany other than that of the Nazi state.[40] The Soviet Union broadcast news of the heroism of the Scholls back to Germany on their 'Deutsche Freiheitssender' wavelength, and news of the Resistance leaflets even got through to the concentration camps, including Auschwitz.

The most direct and immediate legacy of the Scholls, however, was to their counterparts, who called themselves 'Candidates of Humanity', in Hamburg. The medical students Grethe Rothe, Albert Suhr and Frederick Geussenmaier, the bookshop assistant Hannelore Willbrandt, the chemistry students Hans Leipelt and Marie Luise

[38] Eberhard Zeller, *The Flame of Freedom: the German Struggle Against Hitler*, Wolff, London, 1967, ch. 8, p. 166.

[39] Scholl, *Students Against Tyranny*, p. 148.

[40] ibid., p. 152. See also Hanser, *A Noble Treason: The Revolt of the Munich Students against Hitler*, Putnam, 1979; William Bayles (ed.), *Seven Were Hanged*, Gollancz, 1945, which told the story of the Scholls and in which Eleanor Rathbone, MP, put the question to the British public: 'Ask yourself what *you* would have done, were you a German'; and Ricarda Huch, 'Hans and Sophie Scholl', in *Gesammelte Werke*, vol. 5, Kiepenheuer & Witsch, 1951. '"These young people did what we should have done and did not dare to do" – was how thousands reacted to the secret news of their resistance and execution in Spring 1943,' wrote 80-year-old Ricarda Huch in 1946, shortly before her own death.

Jahn, and the philosophy students Heinz Kucharski and Reinhold Meyer banded together with other like-minded people to continue the work of the Scholls. Fired rather than deterred by the execution of Hans and Sophie, they duplicated the Munich students' leaflets with the epigraph: 'Their spirit lives on in spite of all' and circulated the wavelength of the Russian 'Deutsche Freiheitssender' with its motto 'Against Hitler and War' in countless public places. In making forbidden friendly contact with a Yugoslav slave-doctor, Margarethe Rothe and Hannelore Willbrandt explicitly invoked the great affirmation of Antigone: 'My way is fellowship in love, not hate.'[41] The Hamburg branch of the White Rose was dedicated, like the Scholls, to the recreation of a humanistic Germany and Europe after the war, but, also like the Scholls, they were destroyed by the Nazis before the war was over. Betrayed by *agents provocateurs*, 30 of the 50 'Candidates of Humanity' in Hamburg were delivered into the hands of the Gestapo between October 1943 and February 1944; they were all imprisoned and interrogated and eight of them met their deaths.

'Was it' – in Yeats's words – 'needless death after all?'[42] Not if one believes in the redemptive power of martyrdom endured for the sake of others – martyrdom for the very principle of *humanitas* itself. Sophie Scholl, like her brother, their friends and their later counterparts in Hamburg, gave her life to testify to the reality of another, greater power within human beings than the power to hurt and kill. Reality, for her, was the reality of everyday life rather than the infliction of death, and the ultimate, greatest power on earth, for her, was our power to transmit life, both physical and spiritual, to others. Whether drawing or writing or making music or caring for babies and small children or arguing passionately with Hartnagel or laughing for joy in the mountains, *life* was what Sophie Scholl cherished and what she wanted for others as much as she wanted it for herself. In the event she wanted it so much for others that she gave her own life away in order to resist the Nazi death-bringers. She is, therefore, a lasting challenge to all those politicians and

[41] Ursel Hochmuth and Ilse Jakob, 'Weisse Rose Hamburg', in *Streiflichter aus dem Hamburger Widerstand 1933–45*, (Roderberg, Frankfurt, 1969), pp. 387–421. See p. 393 for the 'Antigone' episode – and note that the identical speech of Antigone was quoted both by Simone Weil and by Virginia Woolf.

[42] W. B. Yeats, 'Easter 1916'.

military thinkers, Creons and Bismarcks under whatever system, who have continued ever since the end of World War II to assert that they alone are the realists in their belief that strength has to mean *armed* strength – *Machtpolitik* – and that there is no final reality on earth other than destructive force. Preparedness to incinerate other people's children could never have been Sophie Scholl's conception of the only way to maintain international peace for the foreseeable future:

> And if they put their faith in the triumph of force, ask them whether they think that man is exactly like an animal or whether he can reach beyond that and partake of the world of the spirit . . . Life can only come out of life. (letter to Hartnagel, 28 Oct. 1942)

7

Communism's Cassandra: Christa Wolf 1929—

You can tell when a war starts, but when does the prewar start?

Christa Wolf, *Cassandra*

Christa Wolf is the spiritual heir of Simone Weil, Virginia Woolf and Sophie Scholl. Like Simone Weil, she has perceived the critical twentieth-century interconnections between highly technical modern industrialism, the centralized authoritarian state and nationalistic militarism. Like Virginia Woolf, she sees the woman artist as a pacifist 'Outsider', forced to try to find her own words with which to address the social and psychological causes of war. And, like Sophie Scholl, she is the possessor of an uneasy, introverted, self-critical political conscience.[1] Christa Wolf has been derided recently in certain eminent literary quarters on account of her lack of humour.[2] And it is perfectly true that she is incapable of seeing the funny side

[1] Christa Wolf was awarded the Scholl Prize in Munich, in November 1987, in recognition of the moral courage of her book *Störfall*, published in 1987, by Luchterhand, Darmstadt, and by Aufbau, Berlin.

[2] See Uwe Wittstock, 'Christa Wolf und der fremde, unbekannte Gott', *Frankfurter Allgemeine Zeitung*, 14 Apr. 1987, Marcel Reich-Rainicki 'Macht Verfolgung Kreativ?', also in the *Frankfurter Allgemeine Zeitung*, 1987, and Horst Krüger, 'Der Hang zum Allgemeinen', *Frankfurter Allgemeine Zeitung*, 4 Oct. 1988. What West German critics would really seem unable to forgive is Christa Wolf's continued resolve to stay in East Germany.

of Auschwitz or of Hiroshima and Nagasaki. For if ever there were a writer trapped in a double *connected* nightmare that she cannot shake off – the nightmare of Nazism and the nightmare of an atomic or chemical World War III, that writer is Christa Wolf. What makes it quite impossible for her to shield herself behind distancing irony or humour is her recognition that she herself is not above the horrors and stupidity and ineffectuality of our late twentieth-century political scene, but is in fact a participant, perhaps even a colluder.

Any discussion of Christa Wolf's thinking on war has to begin with her autobiographical novel *Kindheitsmuster* (1976) (translated, ironically, as *A Model Childhood*, Virago, 1981). In 1933 Christa Wolf was four years old, precisely the right age to receive a 'model' Nazi militarist education up to the age of sixteen. Indeed this extraordinary book is still the only one to emerge from either Germany, to the best of my knowlege, that documents in any depth what it really meant to have been a good young Nazi, experiencing a 'normal' childhood next to Adolf Hitlerstrasse. What countless other Germans have succeeded in forgetting for their sanity's sake, Christa Wolf insists on forcing herself to remember – however unbearable it is for her to connect that 'tiny word "I" with the word "Auschwitz". "I" in the past conditional: I could have. I might have. I would have done it. Obeyed orders.'[3] The crucial question behind her whole book is: 'What kind of circumstances are those that cause a collective loss of conscience?'[4] And conscience, as defined by Christa Wolf, is grounded in 'sensitivity to people who do not belong to one's own narrow circle'.[5] Her mother was the only adult in their circle to have this sensitivity. The three circumstances that Christa Wolf considers decisive in a 'collective loss of conscience' – including that of herself as child and adolescent – are deception, seduction, and, it goes without saying, terror. She, like so many others, including her own immediate family, had been at the receiving end of quite a terrifying police state dictatorship; but she and they had also been the unquestioning dupes of Goebbels's cynical appropriation of patriotism, communalism and heroism. She too had grown up a

[3] Christa Wolf, *A Model Childhood*, Virago, 1981, ch. 10.
[4] ibid., ch. 15.
[5] ibid. cf. Simone Weil on justice being grounded in pity for human misery in her essay on *The Iliad*.

Christa Wolf

fervent German nationalist quite unable to see who it was who was really destroying everything of true worth in Germany; she too had never thought of questioning the assumption that non-Germans were a lesser form of life (Ukrainian slave-workers deserved no meat), and that if she were to love Germany she had to hate all the vile and alien forces (Jews and Reds) allegedly threatening her Fatherland; she too had believed between the ages of five and sixteen that the Führer was Germany's saviour. But, in addition to being duped into believing that evil was good, Christa Wolf also shows that she had been seduced into that fatal delusion. How she had revelled in the tuneful Nazi songs by the campfire, in the throbbing, addictive excitement of German war-newsreels retailing victory after victory, and in the opportunity to be a champion athlete and youth leader of the *Hitlermädel*, swastika emblazoned on her gym shirt. At a still deeper level of commitment, Christa Wolf had even given her first love to a Nazi – her very able woman teacher of history and German literature – who had loved her in return. In the deeply painful awakening to reality of the book's last chapter, young Christa Wolf – or Nelly as she is called in the novel – has to discover that love itself is no excuse for blindness to cruelty. Even though her teacher had not personally committed any atrocity, she had allowed her German Nationalism to block out any rational or moral self-questioning and in this way she had corrupted the young people under her – and propped up a totally criminal regime. Finally, this teacher's beloved star pupil, 16-year-old Nelly, has to face the realization that there can be no hiding-place in a private devotion that is incompatible with basic fundamental morality. The book ends in 1946 with the girl tempted never to love or even commit herself again – 'why should I get involved?' – but finding that she *has* to respond to a five-year-old refugee child dying in her sanatorium. Kindness is truth.

Kindheitsmuster is a *Muster* – or – 'Monstrous' demonstration and pattern for post-Nazi generations also. Righteous mass hatred, torturing oppression and war are not finished with yet, and Christa Wolf attacks herself for failing to intervene to any effect in the present: 'You remain seated at your typewriter, absorbed in your own affairs, while the fighting continues with unabated violence.' But at least in this immensely complex and honest autobiographical novel Christa Wolf has managed to unmask some of the deceptions, the seductiveness and the terror of the one example of militarism which almost everyone on earth agrees to abhor. She leaves it to us to identify any parallel deceptions, seductions and terror, East or West, in the competing patriotic militarisms that are alive and well today.

Christa Wolf's next attempt to engage with war and the war mentality, centres on her absorption in the myth of Cassandra. Let us remind ourselves of that grim story. The myth tells how Cassandra, the daughter of Priam and Hecuba, King and Queen of Troy, was passionately desired by the god Apollo who promised to grant her whatever she wished if only she would give herself to him. Cassandra asked for the power of foreseeing the future – but as soon as she had received this gift, she refused to fulfil her promise and spurned the god. He punished her by ensuring that none of her prophecies would ever be believed. When she desperately tried to warn her fellow Trojans that Troy was doomed, they merely thought her mad and locked her away. Once Troy was finally taken by the Greeks, Cassandra fled for sanctuary to the temple of Minerva, but she was discovered there by Ajax who raped her. She was then allotted to Agamemnon as part of his war booty; he took her back with him to Mycenae despite her warnings of what would befall them. Just as Cassandra predicted, Agamemnon's wife, Clytemnestra, butchered them both in the Palace of Argos.

In the spring of 1980, Christa Wolf relates that Cassandra 'took me captive'.[6] She implies, though she never quite states, that she identifies very closely indeed with that 'first professional working woman in literature who defined herself as a non-murderer'.[7] For, as Christa Wolf points out drily, Cassandra's 'message would apply to more than one city'[8] – East Berlin, West Berlin, Moscow, London, Washington, Warsaw, Paris, Budapest, Munich. Which, or all? the reader is prompted to wonder. The 'human slaughterhouse', alias the House of Atreus, before which Aeschylus' Cassandra lets out her last terrible shriek, is juxtaposed, in Christa Wolf's third Frankfurt

[6] Christa Wolf, *Cassandra – Conditions of a Narrative*, Virago, 1984, Lecture 1, p. 143. In these Frankfurt Lectures on Poetics, Christa Wolf records the gestation of her novella *Cassandra*, her preparatory reading and thinking, as well as her journey to Mycenae.
[7] ibid., pp. 176 and 179.
[8] ibid., p. 161.

Lecture on *Cassandra*, written in May 1980, with the contemporary nuclear strategy meetings being held just then by the respective High Commands of NATO and the Warsaw Pact. As a late twentieth-century Cassandra, Christa Wolf utters *her* prophetic cry: '*Europe cannot be defended against an atomic war.*' Then come the sentences that Christa Wolf was made to delete from the first East German edition of her lectures in order to get them published there at all:

> *Meteln, July 8, 1980* . . . Armed with nothing but the intractable desire to allow my children and grandchildren to live, I conclude that the sensible course may be the one that holds out absolutely no hope: unilateral disarmament. I hesitate: in spite of the Reagan Administration? Yes, since I see no other way out: in spite of it! By choosing this course, we place the other side under the moral pressure of the world public; we render superfluous the USSR's extortionary policy of arming itself to death; we renounce the atomic first-strike capability, and we devote all our efforts to the most effective defence measures. Assuming that this involves some risk, how much greater is the risk of further atomic arms, which every day increase the risk of atomic annihilation, by accident, if nothing else?[9]

Seven years before Gorbachev's own fresh thinking about the nuclear arms menace to the world, it was not possible to publish such heretical thoughts in Eastern Europe – but it was possible to think them. Now, however, it is possible to publish them – a complete, unabridged edition of the Lectures has recently been brought out in the German Democratic Republic.

In October 1980, Christa Wolf interrupted the writing of these lectures on the gestation of *Cassandra* in order to give the Büchner Prize Lecture in West Germany. In her acceptance speech, entitled 'Citadel of Reason', Christa Wolf took as her starting-point the words of a doomed man of power, Danton in Büchner's *Dantons Tod*: 'I will retreat into the citadel of reason.' She collocated that statement from a leader of the 1790s with the perverted military applications of reason and science by men who have the power to determine our 1990s. To her, the vaunted 'rationality' of an unbridled profit motive

[9] ibid., Lecture 3, pp. 229–30. cf. Maude Royden's advocacy of unilateral disarmament – too late in 1915.

coupled with an uncontrolled drive towards technological 'perfection' are in truth *pseudo*-rationalism, because what these two drives have led to is something quite insane – the capacity for global self-destruction. What has been lost en route is an extermination-inhibiting sensitivity to the vulnerable and the human, including that which is vulnerable and human in the very selves of those at the top of the pyramid of scientific and political power:

> The natural scientists have managed with the help of scientific jargon to protect their inventions from their own feelings; apparently logical linguistic constructions support the politicians' idée fixe that the salvation of humanity lies in the possibility of its multiple destruction.[10]

It is to women, excluded for so long from the citadel of men's 'reason', and to imaginative writers of both sexes, that Christa Wolf looks for help in assisting the world to recover its sanity. The real language of feeling human beings has to be recovered – 'peace', instead of 'nuclear stalemate'; 'moon', instead of 'earth satellite'; 'city', instead of 'settled conurbation'; 'meadow', instead of 'fertile area'; and so forth. 'Literature today must be peace research.'[11] Christa Wolf's alternative realism to the pseudo-realism of military research and development is the emotionally resonant realism of the imaginative writer:

> Every place and landscape, everything about human relationships which literature has described minutely, exactly and partisanly, painfully, critically, devotedly and fearfully and joyfully, ironically, rebelliously and lovingly, should be erased from [the nuclear strategists'] map of death . . . It is conceivable that a military command really would find it harder to mark out for destruction a city described in precise and intimate detail than one which no-one knows very well, or one which affected no-one so deeply that they had felt compelled to describe it as the place [where] they grew up, the place where they had been humiliated or first fallen in love.[12]

'She's stark raving mad, you say.' Christa Wolf admits in her Büchner

[10] Christa Wolf, 'Citadel of reason', 1980 lecture translated by Barbara Einhorn in *Socialist Register*, 1982.
[11] ibid.
[12] ibid.

Prize Lecture that she has assumed the Cassandra role, but insists defiantly that it seems to her that Cassandra 'must have loved Troy more than she loved herself when she dared to prophesy the downfall of their city to her fellow citizens'.[13]

Returning to her lectures on *Cassandra* in East Germany, in December 1980, Christa Wolf asserts her conviction that 'The people of Troy were no different from us. Their gods were our gods, the false gods.' In order to help avert a Trojan fate for Europe, she says she wants 'to gather together all the things that make me, that make us, into accomplices of self-destruction; and that enable me, enable us, to resist it'.[14] And in order to strengthen that resistance, the curiously humourless Christa Wolf forces herself to be a 'seer' of the unbearable:

> Several times a day, if only for a few seconds, I try to picture what annihilation would 'look like', how it would feel – how it *will* feel. Why only for a few seconds? Because the inner images are unbearable? That's one reason. But above all, because a deep-rooted dread prohibits me from 'bringing on' the misfortune by imagining it too intensively, too exactly.[15]

If the two Germanies do immolate each other – and the rest of Europe – then indeed Hitler will have had his 'Final Victory' and caught up with us. And that is not an amusing thought.

Christa Wolf was now almost ready to start the actual writing of her novella *Cassandra*, a Cassandra for our times, faced with our version of the human slaughterhouse. Her novella would focus on her intuition that our version of imminent reciprocal extermination is intimately related to the exclusion of the Cassandras – the women who define themselves as non-murderers – from the counsels of powerful men. *Cassandra* would not, however, be a simplistic, feminist text asserting that men are the evil destroyers and women the only life-savers. She would tell the tale of the Fall of Troy from a woman's viewpoint, but she would not render it as a reductive, separatist, mystically 'female' vision of the world:

[13] ibid.
[14] Wolf, *Conditions of a Narrative*, Lecture 3 – a Work Diary: 28 Apr. 1981.
[15] ibid.

> Why do I feel uneasy when I read so many publications – even in the field of archaeology, ancient history – which go under the title of 'women's literature'? Not just because I know by experience the dead end into which sectarian thinking – thinking that rules out any point of view not sanctioned by one's own group – invariably leads. Above all, it is because I feel a genuine horror at that critique of rationalism which itself ends in reckless irrationalism. It is not merely a dreadful, shameful, and scandalous fact for women that women were allowed to contribute virtually nothing to the culture we live in, officially and directly, for thousands of years. No, it is, strictly speaking, the weak point of culture, which leads to its becoming self-destructive – namely its inability to grow up. But it does not make it any easier to achieve maturity if a masculinity mania is replaced by a femininity mania, and if women throw over the achievements of rational thought simply because men produced them, in order to substitute an idealisation of prerational stages in human history . . . There is no way to bypass the need for personality development, for rational models of the resolution of conflict and thus also for confrontation and cooperation with people of dissident opinions and, it goes without saying, people of different sex.[16]

The novella *Cassandra* (first published in both Germanies in 1983), is in my view the greatest piece of imaginative writing by a woman on the subject of war – its multiple preconditions and devastating consequences – since Simone Weil wrote her essay on *The Iliad* in 1940. It begins after the Trojan War is over; the enslaved Cassandra, now prisoner of Agamemnon, has been brought with his other spoils before the stone lion gates of the Palace of Atreus. She knows what is about to happen to her – Clytemnestra will cut her throat. Now, in her last minutes, Cassandra's restless, reflective intelligence darts backwards and forwards among the memories, affections, self-searchings and griefs of her whole life but concentrating especially on her own and her city's last ten years.

The Trojan War – that first 'Total War' in Europe's collective conscious, is thus recreated in fragments from the perspective of an

[16] ibid., 7 May 1981.

outsider, a non-combatant woman. But Cassandra is far from being a representative 'Trojan Woman'; she is exceptional in being political-minded – as 'unwomanly', in fact, as Sophie Scholl. Her version of the Trojan War moreover, is untypical in another way: she cannot foreground that war's deluded, touching heroism as a male 'veteran's' version might have done – the killing sanctified by sacrificial dying, male friend for male friend. Instead, we have here nothing of war but its nauseous sequence of exterminations. Cassandra has had to see, either literally or with her inner eye, every member of her family, and almost every friend, die an unbelievably horrible death, beginning with Achilles strangling her 17-year-old brother Troilus and ending with the ritual human sacrifice of her younger sister Polyxena. As for her oldest brother Hector, he is reduced to a chunk of raw meat while their mother shrieks and their father howls. The wind carries the smell of charred human flesh back to the bereaved city. A comparable worst fate could happen to us also, Cassandra/Christa Wolf would seem to be saying, because the worst has already happened, time out of mind, to other people and we *still* have not learned to see the truth about ourselves: that we must stop preparing to inflict the worst in our power on others if there is to be hope for anyone; 'Like ants we walk into every fire. Every water. Every river of blood. Simply in order not to see. To see what, then? Ourselves (p. 42).

On another level of interpretation Troy can be seen as the beleaguered German Democratic Republic, threatened by the more powerful West, with Christa Wolf as its not always popular, and not always heroic, critic in their midst. The first casualties of a 'Cold War', she suggests, are openness and trust among the besieged themselves. The dictates of 'security' turn every citizen into a suspect 'security risk'; Troy, the beloved city, changes into Paris under Marat, Moscow under Beria, East Berlin under ? – as Eumelos, the head of the Palace guard, demands and obtains ever wider powers:

> Eumelos's people were at work. They had won disciples among the palace scribes and the servants in the temple. We must be armed mentally, too, if the Greeks attacked us, they said . . . We prepared for war in all innocence and with an easy conscience. The first sign of war: we were letting the enemy govern our behaviour. (p. 64)

The consequences of mental domination by a totally evil 'enemy' is that, in order to save ourselves, we believe we have to become more like him, but in becoming like him we lose our own soul.[17] Troy becomes a locked citadel, an armed camp, almost exactly like the Greek armed camp, with Eumelos justifying every new oppressive regulation by reference to the danger from the hated Achilles. Eumelos needs Achilles, Achilles Eumelos. Finally both sides, Troy and Greece, degenerate into rival 'macho' brutalisms. And all allegedly for the sake of Helen. Helen, for Christa Wolf as for Simone Weil in her essay 'The Power of Words', symbolizes the abstract values for which a society tells itself that it is willing to die. However, by being willing not only to die but also to destroy and kill for some abstraction – whether 'Socialism' or 'Freedom' we gradually destroy the value itself, and the less we have of it, the more destructive and self-deceived we become. 'In the Helen we had invented, we were defending everything that we no longer had. And the more it faded, the more real we had to say it was' (p. 85). 'Troy' can be read, not just as walled East Berlin but as West Berlin also. And that is Cassandra's most shocking discovery: 'They are like us!' (p. 13).

There is a third alternative both to Cold War and to Total War in this novella – the women's counter-culture that comes into evidence outside the citadel of Troy in caves below Mount Ida where the River Scamander flows. It is one of the many strengths of the work that Christa Wolf manages to bring to life the whole secluded female world of Troy – not just Queen Hecuba and her royal daughters, but Cassandra's nurse Parthena and her daughter Marpessa who nurses Cassandra's children and who will die with her; Myrine, the companion-in-arms of Penthesilea; Briseis, doomed daughter of Calchas; beautiful Oenone of the healing hands; slave-women; Greek camp followers; old midwives; old mothers – all of them worshippers of Cybele. In contrast to Penthesilea, the man-killer, who represents 'the doomed line of matriarchy',[18] these women testify to the fact that 'between killing and dying there is a third alternative: living' (p. 18). For two last summers and two last winters the women grow food and make things of cloth and wood and clay; they create a

[17] cf. Kate Courtney, Maude Royden and Simone Weil on the categorical imperative *not* to imitate the very Prussianism or Hitlerism we claim to abhor.
[18] *Conditions of a Narrative*, Lecture 4 – 16 June 1981, p. 263.

human world of shared knowledge and stories, showing one another trust and kindness. They can even enjoy jokes and songs, although most know that they are doomed. Christa Wolf is not saying, however, that all women, or that only women, are capable of making a truly human world. Most women, like most men, remain *inside* the citadel; some women – Clytemnestra, Penthesilea, the wardresses who torment Cassandra in her prison – can be as deadly as any men; and some men, including Cassandra's lover Aeneas and his father Anchises, affirm and support the dissident women's counter-culture, coming over to it themselves.

It is, in fact, ironic, humane Anchises who emerges as the most surprising character in the whole novella, its real hero. Now for the first time, 2,000 years after Virgil, we can really understand wherein Aeneas' famous 'pietas' lay in carrying his old father safely on his back away from the flames of Troy. For Anchises is the polar opposite of brutal Eumelos/Achilles. Little by little, Cassandra (and thus the reader) pieces together this marvel of a genuine human being – a *Mensch*, as the Germans say. Now captive at Mycenae in what are almost her last moments alive Cassandra thinks:

> Anchises. If only Anchises were here. If he were with me I could bear anything. He did not allow you to fear that anything could be unbearable, no matter what happened. Yes, the unbearable did exist. But why fear it long before it arrives! Why not simply live, if possible serenely? Serenity, that is the word for him. Gradually I saw where he got it from: he saw through people, above all himself, but he did not feel disgusted by what he saw . . . he enjoyed it . . .
>
> Oenone, who loved him like a father, used to say: 'His mouth is laughing, but his forehead is sad.' You could not help but look at his hands, which were almost always working a piece of wood . . . He never had a tree chopped down without first conferring with it at length, without first removing from it a seed or twig which he could plant in the earth to ensure its continued existence . . . And the figures he carved and gave away to people became a sign by which we could recognise each other. He knew people . . . he would talk with everyone, he did not turn away from anyone who wanted to visit him . . . 'What does it cost you? . . . One shouldn't give up on

> anyone until he's dead . . .' As far as I could see, he had no dealings with the Gods. But he believed in people. Yes, Anchises made everything easier. (pp. 91–4)

> Anchises, I believe, loved our life in the caves wholeheartedly . . . He was fulfilling a dream of his and was teaching us younger ones how one can still dream with both feet on the ground. (pp. 134–5)

Throughout this extraordinary work there is a constant implicit two-way connection being made between Cassandra's version of the tale of Troy and our own world predicament at the end of the twentieth century. With the benefit of knowing the last 60-odd years of European history, Christa Wolf is enabled to create a very convincing pre-war and wartime society in Troy, and by setting her study of war in age-old, legendary Troy, the analogies with our present time take on a quite prophetic insight. The echoes between then and now are resonant with the folly and pain of all the many intervening generations. Examples of such insights, at once historically resonant and prophetic, are the thoughts that Christa Wolf gives Cassandra – for it is her calling to be a witness 'even if there is no longer a single human being left to demand my testimony' (p. 22).

> Mental armament consisted in defamation of the enemy (people were already talking about the 'enemy' before a single Greek had boarded ship). (p. 63)

> You can tell when a war starts, but when does the prewar start? (p. 66)

> I interpreted for the king a dream he told at table. Two dragons were fighting. One wore a hammered-gold breast-plate, the other carried a sharp, polished spear. Thus the one was invulnerable but unarmed; the other, though armed and hate-filled, was vulnerable. (pp. 65–6)

> Protest begins with a silence in which more than one takes part. (p. 91)

> We must not become like Achilles, just to save ourselves . . . Isn't it more important to live in our own way, than just to live? (p. 102)

> The duty to kill our worst enemy ate up the right. (p. 129)

> Everything suffering gives rise to falls back on the heads of those who caused the suffering. (p. 121)

In December 1983, Christa Wolf was questioned about her attitude to women's values versus 'patriarchy' in an interview with Jacqueline Grenz in Paris. Asked whether she believed in innate female qualities, Christa Wolf declared: 'I am far removed from biologism . . . I am far from idealizing 'women' or 'the female principle' . . . As a Marxist, I am not to be persuaded that oppression can be beneficial or useful – and that goes for men's oppression of women too.' On being asked how she saw her figure of Penthesilea in *Cassandra*, Christa Wolf answered:

> I wanted to show the way in which a femaleness-mania can take the wrong turning. She embodies a sectarian tendency which is repugnant to me, like everything else that flows from pure distancing and enmity towards otherness – for all that I can also understand the Penthesilea-stance. More than in Penthesilea, I am interested in those women who put themselves in question and who do not simply plunge into an absolute struggle against men and the world of men: their position is more productive than that of the separatists since they do not tear apart the links with the rest of society as a whole.[19]

Christa Wolf's humanistic feminism is absolutely central to her most recent work, her autobiographical essay triggered by the disastrous nuclear accident at Chernobyl. *Störfall (A Disturbing Case)* was written in the summer and early autumn of 1986 and published in both Germanies in 1987. What distinguishes it from all the other commentaries on the dangers of low-level radiation accompanying nuclear technology is its focus on the vulnerability of just one human being. *Störfall* is a double-meditation that alternates between the ecological implications of the reactor-disaster many hundreds of miles, and even years, away – and the immediate personal crisis of the narrator's brother, who is undergoing an operation for a malignant brain tumour – not very many miles away and lasting an eternity of just a few hours, the day after Chernobyl. Page by page the focus changes as Chernobyl (or Livermore, the

[19] Christa Wolf, *Die Dimension des Autors*, vol. 2: *Essays und Aufsätze, Reden und Gespräche, 1959–1985*, Aufbau, Berlin, 1986, p. 468.

American SDI laboratory) swaps places with the author's personal suspense in her East German country home. It is in fact her brother's desperate plight that engages most of Christa Wolf's emotional and intellectual energy. The two poles of concern are not totally distinct, however, any more than are radiation and radium-treatment. In fact they are even more intimately interconnected, for her brother is himself a male 'scientific type' like those at Chernobyl and Livermore, delighted with his computer and defensive about the achievements of modern technology. And now both his own life and personality are totally dependent on miraculous medical science – the benign face of a brilliant technology that can also, as at Chernobyl or Livermore, encompass mega-death.

Störfall is not only centred on Christa Wolf's brother, her *Gegenteil* or opposite; it is also addressed *to* him. He is her 'Du', her 'lieber' with whom she has sparred verbally ever since she can remember; but he is also of all human beings, one of the closest to her, and one who affectionately accepts her as she is. Thus her critique of 'male' science gone mad in the service of paranoid militarism is qualified by an immense tenderness for the men in her private world – not just this stricken younger brother, but also her own husband and two sensitive little grandsons. 'Bruder' is not a dirty word to Christa Wolf. The climax of the book, to which the whole meditation leads, is Christa Wolf's half-joking, half-serious appeal to her brother to remember how they had once acted out Grimm's fairy-tale' *Brüderchen und Schwesterchen*, under the kitchen table. That story tells of another vulnerable, stricken brother who needed his sister to save him from the consequences of another unappeasable, forbidden thirst. The sister cannot stop her brother from drinking the bewitched water, but she does not desert him, despite his consequent metamorphosis – 'Was macht mein Kind / Was macht mein Reh?' – the fawn-brother is still as beloved as her own child. An infinite vulnerability is matched by an infinite, redemptive gentleness and wish for the other to live.

At the end of Christa Wolf's essay we learn that the brain operation has been successful and so the last accent can fall on continued hope – both planet and brother are still alive, despite their dual *Störfall*. 'How hard it would be, brother, to say goodbye to this world.'[20]

[20] The ending of *Störfall*.

Some women readers have been irritated, but I found it very moving that the most recent, plangent meditation written by a woman on the endangered state of our earth should fuse her *Angst* for the planet with her loving anxiety for an irreplaceable brother.

> I try to write against the current instances of crazy destructiveness and contempt for people, which threaten, in my more despairing moments, to seem quite overpowering . . . Cautiously yet undeflected, one should work within one's own society for those changes that are essential if our earth is to be habitable for another thousand years. I look upon my book [*Störfall*] as just one voice within a much broader dialogue which has to be continued, whatever our doubts and despondencies . . . Do we not all yearn to relate to one another in a humane way?[21]

[21] From Christa Wolf's acceptance speech on receipt of the Scholl Prize for her book *Störfall*, Munich, 25 Nov. 1987.

8

American Visionaries: Helen Keller, and the poets Muriel Rukeyser, Denise Levertov and Sharon Olds

What do we see? What do we not see?
Muriel Rukeyser, 1973

Wars Unseen

Unlike European women, American women anti-militarists this century have never had to operate within an immediate war-zone – they have not been shot at by fighter-planes as were Virginia Woolf and Christa Wolf, nor been stoned by a patriotic mob as was Maude Royden in 1915, nor bombed like Simone Weil during the Blitz, let alone beheaded like Sophie Scholl for the public denunciation of her country's militarism. Nevertheless, American women peace-thinkers have still needed great moral and physical courage in order to withstand political hostility, police intimidation, arrest and imprisonment – and even violence on occasion from American National Guardsmen; but on the whole theirs has been a spiritual struggle to engage with the problem of wars fought always outside America, even when fought by Americans. Images 'of levelled cities, refugees clogging highways, starvation and disease are snapshots from another place for Americans'.[1]

> where no bombs ever
> have screamed down smashing
> the buildings, shredding the people's bodies,
> tossing the fields of Kansas or Vermont or Maryland into the air
> to land wrong way up, a gash of earth-guts . . .
> (Denise Levertov, 'Fragrance of Life, Odor of Death' from *The Freezing of the Dust*, 1975)

For that very reason the American public can regard war as something distant and unreal, while American anti-militarists have needed correspondingly greater reserves of moral energy and imaginative vision, in order to reach their public.

Helen Keller 1880–1968

One American woman who did possess such reserves in abundance was Helen Keller. Until Joseph Lash's monumental biography, *Helen and Teacher* (1980), the political radicalism and pacifism of Helen Keller had largely been passed over as something of an embarrassment in a great American folk-heroine.[2] But in fact her lifelong peace-witness lay at the very heart of Helen Keller's inner vision. For no one who has ever lived has understood more profoundly than she did that there *is* an alternative to the iron fist – our own hand of flesh reaching out to answer someone else's need or trying to express our own.

When Helen Keller was 19 months old she was struck down by an acute illness that left her blind, deaf and therefore unable to talk. By the time she was six she had grown, in her own words, 'into a wild destructive little animal' who did not know the difference between day and night, who pulled the food off other people's plates at every meal and who erupted into more and more frequent violent, frenzied rages over her frustrated drive to communicate. Without access to language 'nothing was part of anything', as Helen Keller was later to write in her book *Teacher*. It was only when that same

[1] Jean Bethke Elshtain, *Women and War*. Basic Books, 1987, Part II, ch. 5.
[2] One other recent writer who has not overlooked Helen Keller's radical political thought but concentrated on it is Philip S. Foner in his anthology: *Helen Keller: Her Socialist Years*, International Publishers, 1967.

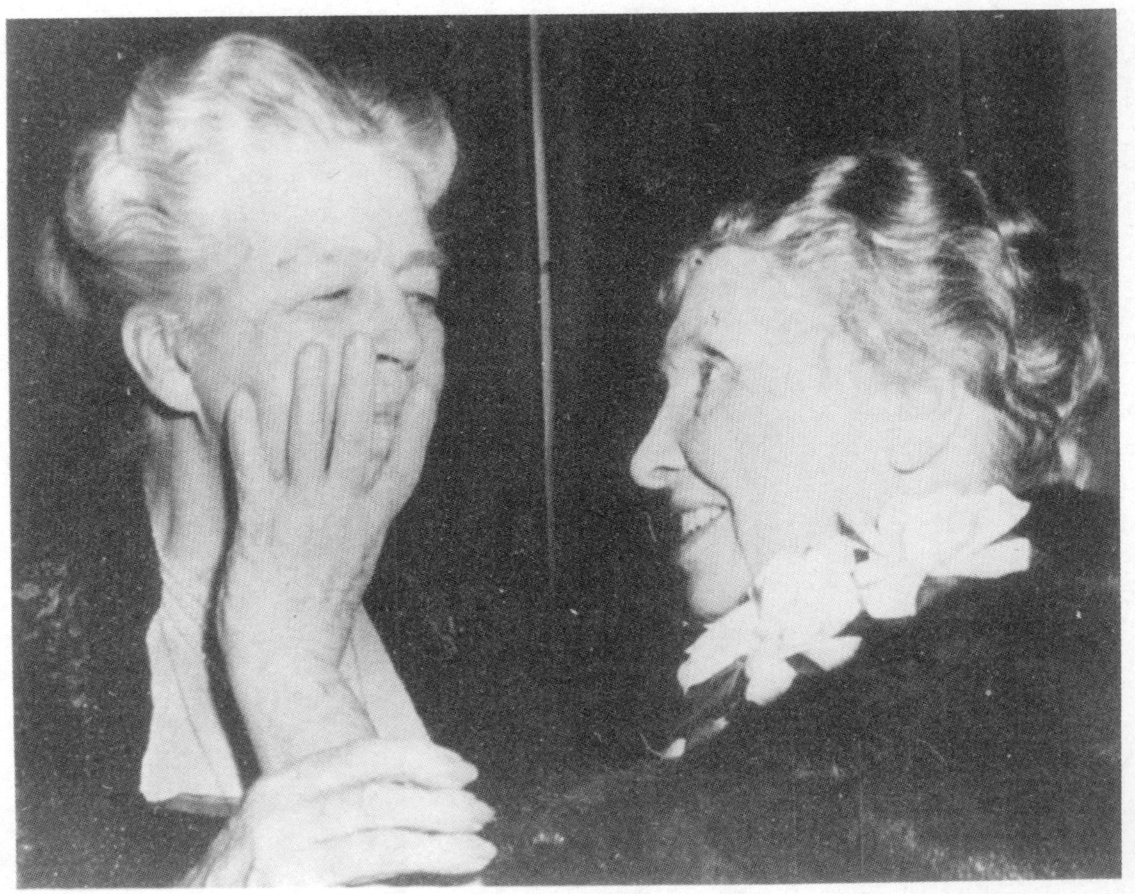

In place of the iron fist – Helen Keller's hand reaches out to Eleanor Roosevelt, 1955.

teacher, 21-year-old Annie Sullivan, first finger-spelled W–A–T–E–R over and over again into one of Helen Keller's hands while holding her other hand under the flow from a pump that the child first grasped that for everything on earth there is a word, a word which she could understand and then communicate back. From that moment she could not rest or let her teacher rest – she had to know, through her hand, the name for everything. Words had given birth to her mind. Although she would still be confined for the next 80 years in her 'steel cell of total silence and absolute darkness',[3] Helen Keller would henceforth possess a means of communication. In later years, using the halting, handicapped speech that she had slowly and painfully forced herself to acquire, Helen Keller would publicly define her own liberation into humanity through the touch of the caring human hand as being symbolic of the way to reciprocal liberation for all human beings: 'I was dumb; now I speak, I owe this to the hands and hearts of others . . . Don't you see what it means? We live by each other and for each other. Alone we can do so little.'[4] 'The meaning of the word "hand", she said, filled eight pages of her dictionary.'[5]

When the anarchist Emma Goldman met Helen Keller during World War I she instantly understood how human spirit could, in spite of every barrier, reach out to human spirit: 'The marvellous woman, bereft of the most vital human senses, could nevertheless, by her psychic strength, see and hear and articulate. The electric current of her vibrant fingers on my lips and her sensitised hand over mine spoke more than mere tongue. It eliminated physical barriers and held one in the spell of her inner world.'[6] When her great teacher and friend Anne Sullivan Macy died, after having spent almost every day under the same roof with her for fifty years, Helen Keller mourned:

> Every hour I long for the thousand bright signals from her vital, beautiful hand. That was life! The hand that with a little word touched the darkness of my mind, and I awoke to happiness and love . . .
>
> After fifty years I continue to feel her dear, communicative

[3] Joseph Lash, *Helen and Teacher*, Penguin, 1981, ch. 27, quoting Will Cressy.
[4] ibid., ch. 25.
[5] Van Wyck Brooks, *Helen Keller*, Dent, 1956, ch. 4.
[6] Emma Goldman, *Living My Life*, Pluto Press, 1987, vol. 2, ch. 47. cf. the photo of Helen Keller with Eleanor Roosevelt.

> hand's warmth and urge in mine . . . Look as I will, it is not there.[7]

Every morning Helen Keller would ask to have the world's news spelled out into her fingers. 'All her life she grieved over the catastrophes that filled the news – dust storms in the Middle West, floods in Mississippi – and she instinctively hated the unjust and the cruel.'[8] Hostile American political columnists mocked Helen Keller's response to world events as invalidated by her handicaps and by her assumed dependence upon the opinions of those few who could spell into her hand. But, as Helen Keller pointed out with some spirit, there are other kinds of blindness and deafness than the physical – the morally imaginative blindness and deafness to the remediable suffering of others. Moreover, she and Teacher did not, in fact, agree on politics for many years. Annie Sullivan was, at first, a convinced pessimistic conservative on all issues – 'The more we talked, the less we thought alike' – and yet she was eventually converted to a more radical critique of the world. She was converted in part by Helen herself, rather than the other way around. 'I can read,' Helen Keller pointed out; and read she did, in Braille, in many languages expressing many conflicting views. Her ardent, idealistic response to the world thus revealed was her own.

The first public expression of Helen Keller's approach to politics was published when she was 24 and newly graduated from Radcliffe College. In 'My Future as I See it' she committed herself to work as a social interventionist, and concluded with the anti-militarist statement:

> As I reflect on the enormous amount of good work that is left undone I cannot but say a word and look my disapproval when I hear that my country is spending millions upon millions of dollars for war and war engines – more, I have heard, than twice as much as the entire public school system of the United States costs us.[9]

In 1909 Helen Keller joined the American Socialist Party which its

[7] Helen Keller, *Journal*, Michael Joseph, 1938, entry for 21 Dec. 1936.
[8] Brooks, *Helen Keller*, ch. 6.
[9] Lash, *Helen and Teacher*, ch. 16.

leader, Eugene Debs, hoped would become the internationalist political arm of his international trade union movement – the Industrial Workers of the World (IWW). To Eugene Debs, as to Helen Keller, wars between nation states were nothing but 'Murder in Uniform' orchestrated by the conflicting, competitive interests of the élites in each country. The abolition of such wars could only come when the working people of the world recognized their supranational common cause and refused to kill one another for the rulers' sakes. In 1912 Helen Keller became more and more publicly committed to the increasingly militant IWW, sending money to their strike-fund and letters of support to their jailed leaders. But it was not just America's exploited working class she cared about – 'all suffering humanity is my affair', as she wrote to the socialist John Macy in January 1914. And, with the coming of August 1914, that meant all humanity.

> The world seemed one vast Gethesemane . . . I used to wake suddenly from a frightful dream of sweat and blood and multitudes shot, killed, and crazed, and go to sleep only to dream of it again. I was often asked why I did not write something new. How could I write with the thunder of machine guns and the clamour of hate-filled armies deafening my soul, and the conflagration of cities blinding my thoughts?
>
> I was in a state of spiritual destitution . . . It was extremely hard for me to keep my faith as I read how the mass of patriotic hatred swelled with ever wider and more barbaric violence. Explanations without end filled the pages under my scornful fingers, and they all amounted to the same frightful admission – the collapse of civilisation and the betrayal of the most beautiful religion ever preached upon earth.[10]

On 19 December 1915 – the same year that Eugene Debs declared: 'I have no country to fight for; my country is the earth; I am a citizen of the world.' – Helen Keller told an anti-war audience of two thousand people in New York: 'I look upon the whole world as my fatherland and every war has for me the horror of a family feud. I look upon true patriotism as the brotherhood of man and the

[10] Helen Keller, *Midstream: My Later Life*, Hodder & Stoughton, 1929, ch. 11.

service of all to all.'[11] Putting forward her alternative to military preparedness, she, like Kate and Leonard Courtney declared that 'the best preparedness is one that disarms the hostility of other nations and makes friends of them.'[12] She then endorsed the IWW's call for a general strike that would cross national frontiers in order to bring World War I to an end, in her speech at New York's Carnegie Hall on 5 January 1916 under the auspices of the Women's Peace Party and the Labour Forum:

> You are urged to add to the heavy burdens you already bear the burden of a larger army and to make additional warships. It is in your power to refuse to carry the artillery and the dreadnoughts . . . With the silence and dignity of creators you can end wars and the system of selfishness and exploitation that causes wars. All you need to do to bring about this stupendous revolution is to straighten up and fold your arms . . .
>
> Strike against the war, for without you no battles can be fought. Strike against manufacturing shrapnel and gas bombs and all other tools of murder. Strike against preparedness that means death and misery to millions of human beings. Be not dumb, obedient slaves in an army of destruction.[13]

The *New York Herald* said 'poor little Helen Keller', as though she were still a small girl and not a woman of 35; and *Life* magazine called her 'a blind leader of the blind'.

Undeterred, Helen Keller decided to participate in an 'Anti-War-Preparedness' lecture tour of the Mid-West, Nebraska, Kansas and Michigan. Already she had received thousands of letters from Europe asking for help, and now she was urged by American anti-militarists to give a moral lead with 'a lecture on Preparedness for Peace . . . Jane Addams isn't well enough to help steady the ship and she and Helen Keller are the only women the country will listen to'.[14] In the event, of course, the country did not listen, as Helen Keller herself acknowledged:

[11] Quoted in Philip Foner, *Helen Keller*.
[12] ibid.
[13] ibid.
[14] Lash, *Helen and Teacher*, ch. 23.

> [The] tour was far from successful . . . The group of which I was a part was doing all it could to keep America out of the war . . . What we desired was fair discussion and open debate. I wanted to have the whole matter put before the people so they could decide whether they wanted to go into the conflict or stay out. As it was, they had no choice in the matter . . . I believe war is the inevitable fruit of our economic system, but even if I am wrong I believe that truth can lose nothing by agitation but may gain all.
>
> I tried to make my audiences see what I saw, but the people who crowded the great tents were disappointed or indifferent . . . no words can express the frustration of those days.[15]

Even after the United States had entered the war, Helen Keller persisted in declaring her own absolute neutrality and her total opposition to this war for 'a place in the sun' between competing militarist powers. In September 1917, after her friend Giovannitti and other syndicalist leaders of the IWW were arrested as 'security risks', she made a public appeal in New York for a far more committed anti-militarist foreign policy than President Wilson's had now proved itself to be. She called for 'a people's peace – a peace without victory, a peace without conquests or indemnities'.[16]

In November 1917, Helen Keller shared the hopes of radicals the world over who welcomed the Bolshevik Revolution, not least because of the new Russian leaders' decision to stop fighting World War I, and she consistently protested against the Allied attempt to overthrow the Bolsheviks. When Debs was sentenced to ten years in prison under the Espionage Act for having denounced US participation in the war in June 1918, Helen Keller publicly championed him: 'You dear comrade! . . . I write because I want you to know that I should be proud if the Supreme Court convicted me of abhorring war, and doing all in my power to oppose it.'[17] There was, of course, almost

[15] Keller, *Midstream*, ch. 11.
[16] Lash, *Helen and Teacher*, ch. 25.
[17] cf. her letter at this time to Emma Goldman, then under sentence of imprisonment for her stand against conscription: 'Believe me, my very heart-pulse is in the revolution that is to inaugurate a freer, happier society.' Quoted by Emma Goldman in *Living My Life*.

nothing that was in her power. Nevertheless, throughout the early 1920s, a period of hysterical anti-communist reaction in the United States, Helen Keller never stopped testifying to her unpopular political convictions, including those on peace, war and 'national security', although she was dependent on public goodwill for her livelihood:

> Q: Do you think any government wants peace?
> Helen Keller: The Policy of governments is to seek peace and pursue war . . .
> Q: Do you think any nation really wants peace?
> Helen Keller: I think all the other nations would like to see Russia disarm . . .
> Q: What did America gain by the war?
> Helen Keller: The American Legion and a bunch of other troubles.
> Q: Who is your favourite hero in real life?
> Helen Keller: Eugene V. Debs. He dared to do what other men were afraid to do.
> Q: Who is your favourite heroine in real life?
> Helen Keller: Kate O'Hara because she was willing to go to jail for her ideal of world peace and brotherhood . . .
> Q: What do you think of war?
> Helen Keller: Read John Dos Passos's *The Three Soldiers*, and you will know what I think of war, the most atrocious of human follies.[18]

On 25 July 1925 Helen Keller defined the eradication of disease, poverty and exploitation as the only kind of war she believed in:

> More and more we should come to understand that we are our brothers' keepers, and that a state is great in proportion to the opportunities which it affords its citizens to become healthy, useful, happy human beings. A new will has come into the world, not a will to power, but a will to service. Everywhere I feel there is a growing desire to restore, to rehabilitate, to reclaim and promote better living for all men . . . We can, if

[18] Lash, *Helen and Teacher*, ch. 27.

> we are so minded, roll back the clouds of calamity which overshadow the world . . .
>
> Friendship and cooperation between nations are the most effective barriers to war . . . An international association for the prevention of disease and the conservation of health would be a long step towards creating the thing we hope for out of the travesty we call civilization.[19]

In 1932 Helen Keller joined Einstein's movement of War Resisters International and in 1933 her book *Out of the Dark* was burned by the Nazis in Berlin because it contained praise of Lenin. In 1936, she refused to have any of her books published in Germany as her protest against Nazism. The *Journal* that Helen Keller wrote in 1936–7 at the age of 56, as an attempt at self-therapy for her grief over the death of Teacher, constantly moves between her own private misery and her growing horror at public events in the increasingly fascist world outside:

> November 14 [1936]. Up early so that we could read *The Times*' comments on the alarming state of European affairs . . . It is devoutly to be wished that all statesmen should join Mr Baldwin in his warning that the world is moving towards war, but it is no news to me. For eighteen years I have tried to suppress a great fear of another world war and the yet worse misery it may entail . . . I cannot believe that the stronger Britain is in armaments, the greater will be 'the certainty of peace'. History teaches that fleets and armies are as provocative as weapons openly carried by private citizens, and that the innumerable treaties signed after wars have settled nothing.
>
> November 24. Sometimes my heart sinks when I hear that forty million gas-masks are being prepared for Britain alone, and that medical students in the University of Edinburgh are being trained to treat gas-poisoning. The situation looks indeed hopeless when war and its increasingly diabolical means of destruction are expected and prepared for . . .
>
> December 31. I have been wrapped in a tempest of grievous thoughts. What had this Old Year brought that was new? To

[19] Article in the *New Leader*, in Foner, *Helen Keller*.

me, only the illness of her for whom I lived, and sorrow old as mortality. To the world, black clouds threatening Europe's peace hopes, wicked anti-Semitic persecutions, and the sickening barbarities in Madrid.

January 16 [1937]. Hitler is Mephistopheles.

March 21 1937. Rozika Schwimmer and I spoke of the apparent triumph of militarism everywhere. She said we needed another Thomas Paine with irresistible eloquence to clear the way for a world federation of nations which would render it impossible for any state to call out its fighting forces without the consent of the rest. Alas, when shall we ever have such a desirable council of men?

March 27. Easter. How different my last Easter and this one are from all others! Besides its own blessed message for mankind, each Easter used to bring in a new way the thrilling sense of my own resurrection when Teacher awoke me with a word, a touch, from the only death I can imagine – dark silence without language or purpose or faith . . . Now there is no greeting from her on earth. But I do not forget the disheartening retrogression apparent in civilisation everywhere. Times have changed. Tyranny in its worst forms, denying human rights, has enslaved three peoples who are supposed to be progressive, and they are suffering themselves to be led into the accumulation of armaments which threaten mass murder in all lands.[20]

After Munich, September 1938, Helen Keller advocated and herself participated in an international boycott of goods from Germany, Italy and Japan. Finally, after Hitler had overrun France and the Netherlands, Helen Keller, like Simone Weil, Maude Royden and Virginia Woolf shortly before her, renounced her pacifism. She was 60 years old:

In the first World War I was a convinced pacifist, and I continued to hold that attitude until some months ago. Then, the atrocious happenings in Europe, the life-and-death quality of Nazi aggression and the uniqueness of this conflict as I saw it – a duel between human ideologies and a brutality deadly

[20] Helen Keller, *Journal*.

> with a false philosophy – tore me away, not from my ideal but from the joy of embodying it in the letter.[21]

Helen Keller's support for Roosevelt and for the United States' entry into World War II did not, however, convert her into a politically acceptable US citizen in the eyes of the FBI. They had kept a file on her ever since she had appealed for a lifting of the US arms embargo for Spain and they also noted all her eager expressions of solidarity with the Russian war-effort against Hitler. The Dies House Committee on Un-American Activities cited her 11 times before 1943. It was also in 1943 that Helen Keller began her tours of military and naval hospitals throughout the United States, as an offering of fellowship with the newly blinded and mutilated young casualties of the war. This literally 'first-hand' experience of other people's wounds forced her to experience the world war in her imagination – their burned, twisted hands in hers 'struck her somehow as trails crossing her palm'.[22] She was not totally reconciled to her decision to support the war – 'I still feel like a deserter, and I know that the conflict began as a rankly imperialistic one, but what could I do when it developed into a people's war of liberation?'[23]

Immediately World War II was over, all Helen Keller's political energy went into advocating a US foreign policy that would not be militaristic or rabidly anti-Russian and anti-Communist. She toured war-devastated Greece, Italy, France and Britain in 1946 on behalf of their blind, including all those combatants and civilians blinded not from birth but by war. And already she had to brood upon the next man-made threat to life on earth:

> The manufacture of bombs continues, and it dismays me to see how little the people are doing individually to prevent atomic warfare . . . I only hope they may be aroused to a sense of their danger before it is too late to assert their human dignity and put into office men who grasp the supreme issue – 'One world or none'.[24]

In 1947 Helen Keller appeared at a rally in support of civilian

[21] Letter from Helen Keller, in 1940, quoted by Lash, *Helen and Teacher*, ch. 37.
[22] Brooks, *Helen Keller*, ch. 11.
[23] Lash, *Helen and Teacher*, ch. 37.
[24] ibid., ch. 38.

control of atomic energy and in 1948, at the age of 68, she made a poignant return visit to Japan. There she found herself in the insupportable position of begging the victims of the US bombing of Hiroshima and Nagasaki for money for the blind – 'The bitter irony of it all gripped us overwhelmingly, and it cost me a supreme effort to speak.' But she did speak and the survivors of the two blasted cities still had the will to give to others. 'What can I say to such an invincible spirit of generosity?' She passed her worn fingers over the scarred face of one of the atomic victims and solemnly re-dedicated herself to the struggle against nuclear warfare and for the constructive uses of atomic energy. Ten years later, a friend reported that, now 78, Helen Keller was still a convinced nuclear pacifist:

> Peace is very much on Helen's mind . . . She has spoken of it every time I have seen her during the past couple of years. She feels that she betrayed a sacred thing when she laid aside her pacifism during the last war and is determined not to do it again. She says that Polly [her companion and interpreter after Teacher's death] will stand by her on this and I tell her that I hope I shall have the strength to do it.[25]

Helen Keller was thus much more than an unparalleled individual success-story in the history of the handicapped and much more than an unequalled publicist for the human rights of the world's blind. Despite her life-sentence of absolute darkness and silence – or perhaps in some way because of it – her intuitive moral sense penetrated to essentials, to 'simple truth mis-called simplicity!' No one could have had better reason to care exclusively about her own desperate predicament, and yet, 'far from being self-absorbed, [Helen Keller] proved herself capable of an all-embracing love for humanity and [a] profound feeling for its woe and despair' – as Emma Goldman, among others, testified.

'We live by each other and for each other.'

'I believe that happiness, attained, should be shared.'

'One world or none.'

[25] ibid., ch. 41, quoting Nella Braddy Henney.

Helen Keller's halting yet radiant, 'seeing' words deserve to penetrate our darkness also.

Poets and War

Helen Keller died in 1968 just at the time when the US assault on Vietnam was bringing a new generation of men and women peace-thinkers into existence in the United States. Some of the most eloquent and memorable responses, both to that war and to a future nuclear World War III, have been the words of women poets. In order to grapple morally with that Third war, the war that must never happen, we are dependent not, as we were in recent wars, on the unbearable eye-witness of the documentary photographs by a Don Cullin, or a Bert Hardy or Werner Bischof or Martha Gellhorn but on the visionary eye-witness of the imaginative artist and poet. For only a 'seer' can see – and communicate – what we must never allow to take place. But in attempting to be such 'seers', the poets have an almost impossible task; so desensitized have most of us in the developed world become in order to survive our twentieth-century history that it is difficult for anyone to feel very much for or about anyone else – outside, that is, our own immediate circle. And the precondition for a conscience, as Christa Wolf articulated in *A Model Childhood*, is precisely that capacity to have 'sensitivity to people who do not belong to one's own narrow circle'. As the American poet Denise Levertov has expressed it, the twentieth century's 'Life at War' has dirtied our imagination, blinding us inwardly:

> We have breathed the grits of it in, all our lives,
> our lungs are pocked with it,
> the mucous membrane of our dreams
> coated with it, the imagination
> filmed over with the gray filth of it.
> ('Life at War', from *The Sorrow Dance*, 1967)[26]

And the result is, as she says, moral and political paralysis:

[26] All Denise Levertov's poetry quoted in this chapter is published by New Directions, New York.

The poisoning
called 'getting used to'
has taken place: we are
the deads; . . .
Don't know
what to do: Do nothing.
('Biafra', from *Relearning
the Alphabet*, 1970)

So many images of unendurable mass suffering have become mere clichés of the cultural consciousness now. The very words 'holocaust', 'death-camp', 'genocide', 'bomb' have become dead words; they move us not, for 'Things thought too long can be no longer thought', as Yeats wrote as early as 1939 in 'The Gyres'. And all too often the horrors of our time have been not 'thought' but merely exploited – with ever-diminishing emotional returns – in films, in fiction, and even, unbelievably, in tourism.[27] And shock tactics that try to force us to feel only desensitize us still further. 'Insofar as poetry has a social function it is to awaken sleepers by other means than shock', as Denise Levertov wrote in *The Poet and the World*.[28] Thus the contemporary poet has to struggle, not, of course for the first time, but perhaps more urgently than ever before, to find unclichéd words that are not dead and thoughts that do not crudely bludgeon reader or hearer into a still worse insensibility. 'For,' as Wordsworth wrote, 'the human mind is capable of being excited without the application of gross and violent stimulants.' In his or her very effort to find words to express 'the essential passions of the heart', the poet is still – in the 1990s as in the 1790s – 'the rock of defence of human nature; an upholder and preserver'.[29]

[27] 'There are queues now to get into Auschwitz, Dachau, Mauthausen, Buchenwald and the rest and there is great demand for memorabilia and souvenirs of the holocaust.' Michael Simmons, *Guardian*, 16 July 1988.
[28] Denise Levertov, 'A Testament', in *The Poet and the World*, New Directions, 1973, pp. 3–5; 'By shock I meant the *invention* of sadistic images (as if competitively!) when life already presented so many real instances of pain and cruelty.'
[29] Wordsworth, Preface to *Lyrical Ballads*, 1802.

Muriel Rukeyser 1913–1982

One such upholder and preserver was Muriel Rukeyser. 'Born in 1913 on the eve of World War One, she . . . lived through the civil War in Spain [which she reported], the Second World War, the Korean War in the 1950s, and the war in Vietnam in the 1960s and against many of these wars Rukeyser . . . protested as citizen and as poet.'[30]

She also attempted to intervene on behalf of political prisoners in Greece, Chile, South Korea and Spain. Poetry, in Muriel Rukeyser's view, is an articulation of inner vision that can help the reader or hearer to engage with the world outside and even to change it. But such energizing, inner visioning is not easy nor even always possible. Already in 1944 Muriel Rukeyser had to diagnose her own twentieth-century shock and compassion-fatigue, writing of herself as one

> Who in one lifetime sees all causes lost,
> Herself dismayed and helpless, cities down,
> Love made monotonous fear and the sad-faced
> Inexorable armies and the falling plane,
> has sickness, sickness.
>
> ('Who in One Lifetime', from *The Beast in View*, 1944)

Nearly 20 years later, however, Muriel Rukeyser sloughed off her despair sufficiently to participate in political protest once more, becoming part of a group:

> [an] island of people who stayed out in the open in City Hall Park in April of 1961, while the rest of the city [New York] took shelter at the warning sound of the sirens. The protest against this nuclear-war practice drill was, in essence, a protest against war itself and an attempt to ask for some other way to deal with the emotions that make people make war.[31]

'An attempt to ask for some other way' – Muriel Rukeyser could hardly have put the need for an alternative politics more tentatively,

[30] Elaine Hedges and Ingrid Wendt (eds), *In Her Own Image: Women Working in the Arts*, Feminist Press, NY, 1980, Part IV, p. 240.

[31] Muriel Rukeyser, note to section 5 of her poem 'Waterlily Fire' in the volume of the same name, 1963. All Muriel Rukeyser's poems can be found in her *Collected Poems*, McGraw-Hill/Random House, 1982.

and her poem 'The Long Body' is correspondingly minimalist in its attempt to touch in, very gently, the simple, quiet insistence on going on living, despite official orders to prepare for death:

> Whatever can come to a woman can come to me . . .
> This moment in a city, in its dream of war,
> We chose to be,
> Becoming the only ones under the trees
> when the harsh sound
> Of the machine sirens spoke. There were these two men,
> And the bearded one, the boys, the Negro mother feeding
> Her baby. And threats, the ambulances with open doors.
> Now silence, Everyone else within the walls. We sang.
> We are the living island,
> We the flesh of this island, being lived,
> Whoever knows us is part of us today.
> Whatever can happen to anyone can happen to me.
> (from *Waterlily Fire*, 1963)

In 1968, Muriel Rukeyser wrote of herself in the past tense, as one already dead, destroyed in spirit by the compulsory mass hatreds of our time, living as she did in a phobically anti-communist, militaristic, commercial-enterprise United States:

> I lived in the first century of world wars.
> Most mornings I would be more or less insane,
> The newspapers would arrive with their careless stories,
> The news would pour out of various devices
> Interrupted by attempts to sell products to the unseen.

All that sustained her was the knowledge that she was not alone in her dissidence – other Americans were with her in the construction of an anti-war movement. Thus this same poem continues:

> I would call my friends on other devices;
> They would be more or less mad for similar reasons.
> Slowly I would get pen and paper,
> Make my poems for others unseen and unborn.
> In the day I would be reminded of those men and women
> Brave, setting up signals across vast distances,
> Considering a nameless way of living, of almost unimagined values.

As lights darkened, as the lights of night brightened,

We would try to imagine them, try to find each other.
To construct peace, to make love, to reconcile
Waking with sleeping, ourselves with each other,
Ourselves with ourselves. We would try by any means
To reach the limits of ourselves, to reach beyond ourselves,
To let go the means, to wake.

I lived in the first century of these wars.

('Poem', from *The Speed of Darkness*, 1968)

Five years later Muriel Rukeyser asked herself and us to identify our own black holes of inner blindness as being at the root of all war-waging. Although we, unlike Helen Keller, are able to see with our physical eyes, we do not seem able to see imaginatively that every human group is made up of feeling fellow humans. It is worth noting in the following poem that both the subject and the object of righteous hatred are always plural – it is in our group relationships and collective psychology that we are at our most pathological; always in need of someone to loathe or fear:

When they're decent about women, they're frightful about children,
When they're decent about children, they're rotten about artists,
When they're decent about artists, they're vicious about whores,
    What do we see?   What do we not see?

When they're kind to whores, they're death on communists,
When they respect communists, they're foul to bastards,
When they're human to bastards, they mock at hysterectomy –
    What do we see?   What do we not see?

When they're decent about surgery, they bomb the Vietnamese
When they're decent to Vietnamese, they're frightful to police,
When they're human to police, they rough up lesbians,
    What do we see?   What do we not see?

When they're decent to old women, they kick homosexuals,
When they're good to homosexuals, they can't stand drug people,

When they're calm about drug people, they hate all Germans,
    What do we see?   What do we not see?

Cadenza for the reader

When they're decent to Jews, they dread the blacks,
When they know blacks, there's always something: roaches
And the future and children and all potential. Can't stand themselves
Will we never see? Will we ever know?

('What Do We See?', from *Breaking Open*, 1973)

The poem 'St Roach' – 'For that I never knew you, I only learned to dread you' – takes this idea further. The analogy with that urban American *bête noire*, the cockroach, vividly expresses just how merciless we are to any form of life that we do not want to know, that we need to believe is an alien, undifferentiated enemy:

For that I never knew you, I only learned to dread you,
for that I never touched you, they told me you are filth,
they showed me by every action to despise your kind;
for that I saw my people making war on you,
I could not tell you apart, one from another,
for that in childhood I lived in places clear of you,
for that all the people I knew met you by
crushing you, stamping you to death, they poured boiling
water on you, they flushed you down,
for that I could not tell one from another,
only that you were dark, fast on your feet, and slender,
Not like me.

('St Roach', from *The Gates*, 1976)

Muriel Rukeyser decided to commit Civil Disobedience in protest against the American onslaught on Vietnam; she was arrested, tried, found guilty and imprisoned, staunchly insisting, 'We will help stop this war' ('Facing Sentencing', from *Breaking Open*, 1973). One of her very last poems, 'Looking', begins as a four-line threnody that is at once elegy, protest and prophecy, as she grieves over all the wars that have ever been and over all the wars to come:

Battles whose names I do not know
Weapons whose wish they dare not teach
Wars whose need they will not show
Tear us tear us each from each.

Denise Levertov 1923–

Muriel Rukeyser 'was a cathedral' to Denise Levertov – her friend and fellow poet – ('In memory of Muriel Rukeyser', from *Candles in Babylon*, 1982). Denise Levertov has been another passionately outspoken protester against the United States' atrocious war-crimes in Vietnam:

> Did the people of Vietnam
> use lanterns of stone? . . .
> Sir, their light hearts turned to stone.
> ('What were they like?' from *The Sorrow Dance*, 1963)

> She is weeping for her lost right arm.
> She cannot write the alphabet any more
> on the kindergarten blackboard . . .
>
> In the wide skies over the Delta
> her right hand that is not there
> writes indelibly,
> 'Cruel America,
> when you mutilate our land and bodies,
> it is your own soul you destroy,
> not ours.'
> ('Weeping Woman', from *The Freezing of the Dust*, 1972)

In 1967 Denise Levertov pleaded for the withdrawal of all US troops from Vietnam 'followed by the penitent presentation to the people of Vietnam, by the US, of huge quantities of food and supplies' ('Writers Take Sides on Vietnam', in *The Poet in the World*, 1973). Her freedom to express her dissidence was limited, however, to publication of little-read poetry and prose; Denise Levertov was not allowed to make the following statement on NBC television, although originally asked to speak:

> We are living at war: the shame and horror of being citizens of the country which, in its ruthless imperialism, is not only ravaging Southeast Asia, but, with its military bases, its Polaris submarines, the machinations of its CIA, and the tentacles of its giant corporations, is everywhere the prime force of antilife

> and oppression – this shame and horror cast their shadow over all we say, feel, and do. ('Statement for a Television Program', 1972, in *The Poet in the World*)

Today Denise Levertov is still a front-line political protester, warning Americans against the material and psychological preparations for World War III. Her 'Speech for an Antidraft Rally, DC, 22 March 1980', sobs with the fierceness of her outrage and irony as she insists on telling her listeners what she knows the majority of Americans simply do not want to see:

> 'Bomb Tehran' – 'Bomb Moscow' I heard them say.
> Ach! They're the same ones, male and female, who ask,
> Which came first, Vietnam or Korea?
> What was My Lai? The same kids who think
> Ayatollah Khomeini's a, quote, 'Commie'. Who think
> World War Two was fought against, quote, 'Reds', namely
> Hitler and some Japs.
>
> No violence they've seen
> on the flickering living-room screen familiar since infancy
> or the movies of adolescent dates . . .
> None of that spoon-fed violence
> prepares them. The disgusting horror of war
> eludes them. They think
> they would die for something they call America
> vague, as true dreams are not; something they call
> *freedom*, the *Free World* . . .
> Great. They don't know
> that's not enough, they don't know
> ass from elbow, blood from ketchup, that knowledge
> is kept from them, they've been taught to assume
> if there's a way there's
> also a future, they know,
> not only nothing,
> in their criminally neglected imaginations, about
> the way war always meant
> not only dying but killing
> not only killing but seeing
> not only your buddy dying but

your buddy in the act of killing, not nice,
not only
your buddy killing but the dying
of those you
killed yourself, not always
quick, and
not always soldiers.
Yes, not only do draft-age people mostly
not know how that kind of war's become almost a pastoral
compared to new war, the kind
in which they may find themselves . . .
. . . but also
they know nothing at all about radiation
nothing at all about lasers
nothing at all about the bombs
the Pentagon sits on like some grotesque
chicken caged in its nest and fed
cancerous hormones, exceed and exceed and exceed
Hiroshima, over and over and over, in weight
in power
in horror
of genocide.

When they say
'If there's a war,
I'll go,' they don't know
they would be going to kill
themselves
their mamas and papas
brothers and sisters
lovers.
When they say, 'If there's a war, I'll get pregnant,'
they don't seem to know
that war could destroy that baby.
When they say, 'I'd like to fight,'
for quote, 'freedom',
for quote, the 'Free World,'
for quote, 'America' . . .
. . . they don't know they'd be fighting
very briefly, very

successfully,
quite conclusively,
for the destruction of this small
lurching planet, this confused
lump of
rock and soil, ocean and air,
on which our songs, cathedrals, gestures
of faith and splendour
have grown like delicate moss, and now
may or may not survive
the heavy footsteps of our inexcusable ignorance
the chemical sprays of our rapacious idiocy,
our minds that are big enough
to imagine love, imagine peace, imagine
community – but may not
be big enough to learn in time
how to say no.

(from *Candles in Babylon*, 1982)

What Denise Levertov dreads is going to happen to our world because of our 'criminally neglected imaginations', visually spoonfed since birth on unreal, televisual violence, she has expressed, 'seer-like' in the form of a prophetic fable:

Once a woman went into the woods,
The birds were silent. Why? she said.
Thunder's coming.
She walked on, and the trees were dark
and rustled their leaves. Why? she said.
The great storm, they told her,
the great storm is coming.
She came to the river, it rushed by
without reply, she crossed the bridge,
she began to climb
up to the ridge where grey rocks
bleach themselves, waiting
for crack of doom,
and the hermit
had his hut, the wise man
who had lived since time began.

When she came to the hut
there was no one.
But she heard his axe.
She heard the listening forest.
She dared not follow the sound
of the axe. Was it
the world-tree he was felling?
Was this the day?
('Sound of the Axe', from *Candles in Babylon* 1982)

The 'wise man' is, one assumes, an ironic reference to all the all-too clever men now alive who have rationalized mega-death, making it both technically feasible and politically legitimate. Why 'hermit'? Does the word invoke connotations of 'hermetically sealed off' from the ordinary and human? In an earlier poem, Denise Levertov had already expressed her horror (which she shares with the East European Christa Wolf among others) at the diabolic misuse of 'masculine' intelligence by a few brilliant men:

Smart bombs replace
dumb bombs . . .
the smartest boys, obedient to all the rules, who never
aimed any flying objects across the classroom,
now are busy with finely calibrated equipment
fashioning spit-balls with needles in them,
that fly at the speed of light multiplied
around corners and into tunnels to arrive
directly at the dumb perfection of living targets,
icily into warm wholeness to fragment it.
('May our Right Hands Lose their Cunning', from *The Freezing of the Dust*, 1975)

Traditionally in folk-tales the hermit or wise man has gnomic answers to life's problems and directs the troubled hero or heroine on to the true moral path; but *our* imaginatively blind smartest boys-turned-hermit will, unless stopped in time, take their axes to our whole world-tree. Denise Levertov does not, it should be stressed, single out men as being the sole source of the world's war-evil. In her

Antidraft Rally speech, she indicts all those young Americans, whether male or female, who are high on mindless patriotism, and, like Muriel Rukeyser, she reaches out to men as well as to women in the struggle before us.

Sharon Olds 1942–

More recently, the poet Sharon Olds has also imagined 'it' – only in her case not if it happens but when, in the poem she calls 'When':

> I wonder now only when it will happen,
> when the young mother will hear the
> noise like somebody's pressure cooker
> down the block, going off. She'll go out into the yard,
> and there, above the end of the street, in the
> air above the line of the trees,
> she will see it rising, lifting up
> over our horizon, the upper rim of the
> gold ball, large as a giant
> planet, starting to lift up over ours.
> She will stand there in the yard holding her daughter,
> looking at it rise and glow and blossom and rise,
> and the child will open her arms to it,
> it will look so beautiful.[32]

Sharon Olds's collections of poetry (*Satan Says*, *The Dead and the Living*, *The Gold Cell*) have two areas of near-obsession – the war to the death within the family and the wars to the death in the world outside. War between parents, between children, between parents and children – in poem after poem Sharon Olds breaks through the taboo concealing these shameful facts of family life and gradually the reader makes connections between one kind of war and another. The almost unbearably painful poems in Part I of *The Dead and the Living*, for example, are divided into two sections 'Public' and 'Private'. The public poems make us see, really see, some loathsome twentieth-century photographs – condemned prisoners in China in 1905, suspended on made-to-measure wooden crosses as they await execution; Russian and Armenian children either dying or just dead of starvation in 1921; political prisoners in the Iran and Chile of the

[32] From Sharon Olds, *The Gold Cell*, Knopf, 1987.

1980s to whom 'things that are worse than death' have just been done; a mother of a (bayoneted) newborn baby in Rhodesia in 1978, the mother's face:

> beaten and
> beaten into the shape of a plant,
> a cactus with grey spines and broad
> dark maroon blooms . . .
> Don't speak to me about
> politics, I've got eyes, man.
>
> ('The Issues')[33]

For those with eyes, 'politics' cannot even begin to legitimate atrocity, ever. But you've got to have eyes.

The private world, however, was no compensatory haven for Sharon Olds. 'What went on at home / I couldn't bear to see' ('The Indispensability of Eyes', from *Satan Says*). Cruelty had a human face in the form of her sadistic, boozing father and a mother who

> had to put herself
> first.
> She had to do whatever he
> told her to do to the children; she had to
> protect herself.
>
> ('The Forms')[34]

Sharon Olds was therefore conscripted as a 'student of war' when very young. She quickly learned that real dictatorship and real torture can exist inside the home. She learned to hate, and she also learned how cruelty can corrupt people, through fear, in private just as it does in public. Indeed she came to see that this very cruelty in the family is one root cause of the mega-cruelty in the world outside. Family life of one sort or another produces all the damaged people on earth – both those able to inflict the horrors and those who, cowed, acquiesce in that infliction. The unjustly punished son:

> When he cools off and comes out of that door
> will not be the same child who ran in
> and slammed it . . .

[33] From Sharon Olds, *The Dead and the Living*, Knopf, 1984.
[34] ibid.

The long impurification
has begun this morning.
('The Unjustly Punished Child')[35]

If the times are right, the brutalized son of a bullying parent may even grow up to be a Camp Guard ('That Year', from *Satan Says*). For 'the child hit in the face over and over [presages] the end of the world' ('Geography', from *The Gold Cell*). Sharon Olds agrees with the psychotherapist Alice Miller that 'the need to commit murder' – even on a world scale – 'is the outcome of a tragic childhood . . . every persecutor was once a victim.'[36] As for Sharon Olds herself, she confesses painfully:

I have never thought I could take it, not even
for the children. It is all I have wanted to do,
to stand between them and pain. But I come from a
long line
of women
who put themselves
first.
('The Fear of Oneself')[37]

Thus this poet is someone for whom the worst will happen – 'I wonder now only when it will happen' – because it already has happened, has been done to her over and over again and has infected her in her turn.

One reason why Sharon Olds is so certain at times that there is no hope for us is suggested in the poem 'Rite of Passage' about her six-year-old son's birthday party. All the little boys there have already been successfully socialized by family life, television and the school playground into accepting the age-old virility test for males. Readiness to kill is their 'Rite of Passage'.

As the guests arrive at my son's party
they gather in the living room,
short men, men in first grade
with smooth jaws and chins

[35] From Sharon Olds, *Satan Says*, University of Pittsburgh Press, 1980.
[36] Alice Miller, *For Your Own Good: The Roots of Violence in Childrearing*, first published 1980, republished Virago, 1987, pp. 195 and 249.
[37] From Olds, *The Dead and the Living*.

Hands in pockets, they stand around
jostling, jockeying for place, small fights
breaking out and calming. One says to another
How old are you? Six. I'm seven. So?
They eye each other, seeing themselves
tiny in the other's pupils. They clear their
throats a lot, a room of small bankers,
they fold their arms and frown. I could beat you
up, a seven says to a six,
the dark cake, round and heavy as a
turret, behind them on the table. My son,
freckles like specks of nutmeg on his cheeks,
chest narrow as the balsa keel of a
model boat, long hands
cool and thin as the day they guided him
out of me, speaks up as a host
for the sake of the group.
We could easily kill a two-year-old,
he says in his clear voice. The other
men agree, they clear their throats
like Generals, they relax and get down to
playing war, celebrating my son's life.[38]

We would seem to have come full circle – right back to 'Saki' in 1914! – 'Nearly every red-blooded human boy has had war . . . for his first love.'

But Sharon Olds despaired too soon. The distorted masculinity of readiness to kill is not the whole truth about Gabriel Olds. He is also a compassionate would-be life preserver, able to put himself into another's shoes and feel an urgent wish to feed the hungry other – as his mother herself testifies:

Every time we take the bus
my son sees the picture of the missing boy.
He looks at it like a mirror – the dark
blond hair, the pale skin,
the blue eyes, the electric-blue sneakers with

[38] ibid.

slashes of jagged gold. But of course that
kid is little, only six and a half,
an age when things can happen to you,
when you're not really safe, and Gabriel is seven,
practically fully grown – why, he would
tower over that kid if they could find him
and bring him right here on this bus and
stand them together. He sways in the silence
wishing for that, the tape on the picture
gleaming over his head, beginning to
melt at the centre and curl at the edges as it
ages. At night when I put him to bed
my son holds my hand tight
and says he's sure that kid's all right,
nothing to worry about, he just
hopes he's getting the food he likes,
not just any old food, but the food
he likes most, the food he is used to.
('The Missing Boy')[39]

So recovery is possible – not just survival but resurrection. Hurting and killing do not have to have the last word, there are also love, birth, desire, and the rebirth of the capacity for pity with each new generation.

It seems a very long way from the purity of idealistic vision that streamed from blind Helen Keller to the unblinking focus on deliberate torture, so often found in Sharon Olds. Both women abhor cruelty but perhaps there was an unquenchable optimism still possible to someone born in 1880 unattainable to someone born in 1942. Sharon Olds does not finally leave us with no hope at all, however. She, like Muriel Rukeyser and Denise Levertov, feels a Helen Keller-like outrush of pity for all victims and she insists that there are still two paths for us to choose between:

All I can do is
tell about it, say *This is the human, the*
clippers, the iron – and This is the human, the
hand, the milk, all I can do is
point out the two paths, we can go down either.
('The Paths')[40]

[39] ibid.
[40] Published in Jim Schley (ed.), *Writing in a Nuclear Age*, University Press of New England, 1984.

9

Living Voices from Europe

> How dare the government presume the right to kill others in our names?
>
> Women at Newbury Magistrates Court, 14 April 1982

Women anti-militarists are all agreed that our planet and every species on it are now in desperate danger. Where they disagree is in their diagnosis of the ultimate cause of total-war-preparedness, and in their prescriptions of a possible cure. Some, the 'essentialist' or fundamentalist feminists, see the threat of nuclear war as being the predictable, logical outcome of the characteristic defects of one sex – men. Others, the humanist feminists, insist that it is a 'slovenly syllogism . . . to conclude that all men are fascists'.[1] All men must not be scapegoated just because so many have succumbed to a brutalizing ideology of masculinism over the years – an ideology constructed both consciously and unconsciously by men and women since time out of mind.

This argument between women is not new. Feminists have disagreed about the causes and cure of militarism repeatedly throughout this century. Before World War I there was a dominant, sanguine consensus among feminists that as soon as the world-wide woman's movement triumphed, permanent world peace would become a reality. (Socialists, of course, believed that there would be

[1] Barbara Ehrenreich, Foreword to Klaus Theweleit, *Male Fantasies*, Polity Press, Minnesota, 1987.

a similar happy ending after world-wide revolution.) Catherine Marshall declared as late as April 1915 in her speech to the Conference of the Independent Labour Party in Bradford: 'The sense of the common motherhood of women which the Women's Movement is awakening will, when fully realized, make it impossible for one nation to shoot down the sons of another.' The Dutch feminist Dr Aletta Jacobs asserted: 'Women Suffrage and Permanent Peace will go together.'[2] And C. K. Ogden and Mary Sargant Florence wrote: 'Woman has neither part nor share in the slaughter of humanity . . . woman the sympathetic, the unanimist, the creator.'[3]

But the actual behaviour of most women throughout Europe immediately after August 1914 and during the years that followed revealed to many pacifist feminists that women as a sex are *not* essentially the force for peace and against war that they had so recently believed. 'Men couldn't have made [the war], if the mass of women had not been admiringly, even adoringly with them,' admitted Helena Swanwick.[4] It was a woman who nearly assaulted the pacifist Kate Courtney at an outdoor meeting in July 1915,[5] and it was women who tried to lynch the pacifist Maude Royden and her Peace Caravan.[6] 'The souls of women were as much possessed by [war] passion as the souls of men. It often appeared as though their case were worse.'[7] In 1918, Emmeline Pethick Lawrence, the veteran feminist and pacifist, discovered that it was women who attacked her for her Peace Platform when she stood as a Parliamentary candidate: 'the women . . . were all for "going over the top" to avenge their husbands and their sons. *My Supporters were the soldiers themselves* . . . It was a strange experience to watch working class mothers, with their babies and small children, eagerly going to the poll to record their votes against me.'[8] Maude Royden summed up

[2] Quoted in Jill Liddington, 'The Women's Peace Crusade', in Dorothy Thompson (ed.), *Over Our Dead Bodies*, Virago, 1983.
[3] Florence, Marshall and Ogden, *Militarism versus Feminism*, 1915, reprinted by Virago, London, 1987. See also Olive Schreiner's chapter, 'Women and war' in her *Woman and Labour*, Fisher Unwin 1911, and Charlotte Perkins Gilman's *Herland*, 1915 repr. Women's Press, London 1973.
[4] Helena Swanwick, *I Have Been Young*, Gollancz, 1935, ch. 4.
[5] See above, ch. 2, p. 34.
[6] See above, ch. 3, p. 55.
[7] Caroline Playne, *Society at War 1914–16*, Allen & Unwin, 1931, ch. 4.
[8] E. Pethwick Lawrence, *My Part in a Changing World*, Gollancz, 1938.

Inga Thorsson, UN expert on disarmament for development.

the hard lesson that the women's movement had had to learn – and was later once again to forget:

> the belief that women are innately more pacific than men has been severely shaken, if not altogether destroyed. It is now very evident that they can be as virulently militarist, as blindly partisan, not as the soldier, for in him such qualities are generally absent, but as the male non-combatant, for whom the same cannot always be said. Among women, as among men, there are extremists for war and for peace; pacifists and militarists; women who are as passionately convinced as Bernhardi that war is a good thing, women who accept it as a terrible necessity, women who repudiate it altogether. All these views they share with men. There appears to be no cleavage of opinion along sex lines.[9]

Between the two world wars, Simone Weil never appealed either as a woman or to women alone to perceive the lethality of blood-filled abstract nouns with a capital letter, although she did identify the fear 'of seeming unmanly' as a prime motive for ruthlessness in war and she did want to protect little boys in the future from being taught that a military dictator could possibly be a great man to be emulated. Virginia Woolf, who came very near at times to indicting men as a sex for the institution of war, for instance in her long essay *Three Guineas*, nevertheless concluded that same essay by insisting that the fascist Führer is a *human* figure from which we cannot dissociate ourselves and which we ourselves can change, and by 'we' she meant anti-fascist men as well as anti-fascist women. She ended by stressing that 'A common interest unites us; it is one world, one life.' In her later essay 'Thoughts on peace in an air-raid' she instanced slavish, sexually stereotyped women as her example of a subconscious Hitlerism, out to enslave. Women are not necessarily

[9] 'War and the women's movement', in C. R. Buxton and G. L. Dickinson, *Towards a Lasting Settlement*, Allen & Unwin, 1915. Cf. Bertha von Suttner, the first Nobel Laureate for Peace, writing to the German Women's Peace Movement, (just before her death in 1914): 'Some people think that women are by nature hostile to war. They are mistaken. Only women of progressive views, those who have been able to educate themselves in social thinking, who have had the strength to remain unfascinated by thousand-year-old institutions, have also found the energy to oppose these institutions.'

liberators, but men do need liberating from their 'manliness', just as much as women need liberating from their 'womanliness'. And it never once occurred either to Sophie Scholl or to Helen Keller to see the militarism versus anti-militarism issue as a matter of gender.

Shortly after World War II a little-known collection of essays was published on the subject of the special role of women in the prevention of war – *Der Ruf der Mütter* (The call of the mothers).[10] Many contributors, including Dorothy Thompson of the United States and Karin Michaelis of Denmark, still maintained that there is a special contribution that women must make, *qua* women, to the prevention of World War III. Once again, as before World War I, they postulated that women, as mothers, *must* be a force for peace not war, life not death. However the book also included a few dissentient, sceptical voices. Clara Ragaz, for example, who was a lifelong worker for both the Swiss and the International sections of the Women's International League for Peace and Freedom, called her essay 'Ist die Frau Pazifistin?' (Is woman a pacifist?) She declared right at the outset that she did not believe that women *qua* women have a decisive role to play in the struggle against war and injustice. She did not think that if women were to gain greater influence in public life then that alone would mean a strengthening of the will towards peace and reconciliation. On the contrary, precisely because of her maternal role, a woman could fall into the temptation of putting her *own* children, and therefore her *own* country, first at all times. It was all too easy for a woman to be convinced that love of one's neighbour simply meant looking after her own nearest and dearest. And precisely because Clara Ragaz believed that women are not naturally public-spirited or naturally capable of transcending their passionate narrow nationalist loyalties she felt that women badly needed to form their own organizations to help them to focus on the world's problems, including war. Then they could eventually combine effectively with similar movements organized by men.

The Dutch sociologist Dr Hilde Verwey-Jonker refused to contribute to *Der Ruf der Mütter* at all, her reasons being printed in the book's Appendix. She wrote, in June 1948, that it was a dangerous and all-too German mistake to accept the assumption that

[10] Barbara Nordhaus-Lüdecke (ed.), *Der Ruf der Mütter*, Verlag Kurt Desch, Munich, 1949.

war was man's business, peace woman's. German women were as responsible as were German men for the last war, given their willingness to vote for Hitler in the election of 1932. Hedwig Rohde accepted that German women shared responsibility for the last war, above all for having remained silent as they saw it approach, and therefore she held it to be all the more necessary for German women to realize their true nature and counter the militaristic world-view of men. Dr Verwey-Jonker answered that she herself had been forced to renounce her pacifism on account of the hideous brutality of the Nazis and that her own and other women's participation in the Dutch resistance had had to rely, in the last resort, on taking up arms together with men. Now that World War II was over she put her faith in the slow, piecemeal establishment of an agreed system of international law as the best guarantor against world-wide, war-waging anarchy. She was in fundamental disagreement with Hedwig Rohde's view that our species is divided between a male drive towards destruction and a female drive towards life-preservation: 'I know men as comrades in peace and in war in the struggle for freedom and for peace. I know that precisely in Germany, of all places, intelligent and upright men have struggled against the war right to the last.'[11] But Hedwig Rohde held to her biological view of the basic opposition between male and female drives.

Given the long history of this controversy within the women's peace movement during the first half of our century, it is perhaps surprising as well as dispiriting to find that many of the same assumptions and counter-arguments are still being thrown back and forth at the end of the second half of the century – only generating more heat and less light.[12] For the most notorious, the most extreme, and yet the most logically conclusive statement of the fundamentalist feminist position on male responsibility for war, it is necessary to go to the United States. Valerie Solanas's *Scum Manifesto* was written in 1967 and first published in 1968. It was reprinted in 1970

[11] ibid., p. 207. Dr Verwey-Jonker, 1908–, socialist and feminist, former Labour Party member of Dutch parliament, member of Dutch delegation to 1st Assembly of UN in 1946, co-founder of International Refugee Organization.
[12] e.g. see Herrad Schenk's lucid analysis of the controversy in her *Frauen Kommen ohne Waffen: Feminismus und Pazifismus*, Verlag C.H. Beck, Munich, 1983, *passim*.

in New York and in 1984 in London.[13] It begins by announcing the necessity for the destruction of the male sex, asserting that:

> To be male is to be deficient, emotionally limited; maleness is a deficiency disease and males are emotional cripples . . .
>
> The male, because of his obsession to compensate for not being female combined with his inability to relate and to feel compassion, has made of the world a shitpile. He is responsible for *War*: the male's normal method of compensation for not being female, namely getting his Big Gun off, is grossly inadequate, as he can get it off only a very limited number of times; so he gets it off on a really massive scale, and proves to the entire world that he's a 'Man'.

Having asserted that the emotionally and morally deficient male sex *is* the problem and responsible for all war, Valerie Solanas proceeds to her (final) solution:

> Just as humans have a prior right to existence over dogs by virtue of being more highly evolved and having a superior consciousness, so women have a prior right to existence over men. The elimination of any male, is therefore, a righteous and good act . . .
>
> As for the issue of whether or not to continue to reproduce males, it doesn't follow that because the male, like disease, has always existed among us that he should continue to exist. When genetic control is possible – and it soon will be – it goes without saying that we should produce only whole, complete beings, not physical defects or deficiencies, including emotional deficiencies, such as maleness . . .
>
> Women are improvable; men are not . . .
>
> Both destruction and killing will be selective and discriminate . . .
>
> The few remaining men can exist out their puny days dropped out on drugs or strutting around in drag . . . or they can go off to the nearest friendly suicide center where they will be quietly, quickly and painlessly gassed to death.

Even without those last ten words the fascism of Valerie Solanas

[13] Matriarchy Study Group, London 1984.

is quite blatant. Beginning with her crudely reductive allegation that there exists a huge, undifferentiated degenerate class of humans – not Negro, Slav or Jew this time, but simply male, she proceeds to allege that this low form of subhuman life is both parasitic and endangering to the higher, female form, and above all that it endangers the world through its compulsive drive to make war. The inescapable logical consequence of Solanas's biological diagnosis is her prescription of genetic control and extermination in order to eliminate the war-waging sex. Then, in her version of the thousand year Reich, there will be 'total female control of the world . . . A completely automated society . . . and a fantastic new era' can begin. Like all fascist propagandists Solanas is fundamentally self-contradictory – legitimating her own mercilessness by alleging emotional and moral 'deficiency' in those she is out to kill, blind to the fact that she herself embodies the very absence of compassion for which she indicts – and dreams of gassing – men. There could not be a better concise object lesson that when we dehumanize others we make monsters of ourselves. 'Attempting to be more than Man we become less.'[14]

'But she cannot be serious!' is a natural reader-response. Valerie Solanas, however, was sufficiently serious to shoot and wound Andy Warhol – an act for which she was sent to Elmhurst Hospital in New York for psychiatric observation. But if she was mentally deranged, then her manifesto can be disregarded, surely. Unfortunately for the contemporary women's peace movement, it is not so simple. Valerie Solanas's views, very selectively quoted, have in fact been endorsed and echoed by several influential radical feminists.[15]

[14] William Blake, 'The Four Zoas'.

[15] e.g. the American feminist theologian Mary Daly praises Valerie Solanas for her 'blaze of insight' connecting the male and war, in *Gyn/Ecology*, Women's Press, London, 1979, ch. 9; Andrea Dworkin writes: 'violence is male and the male is the penis', *Pornography*, Women's Press, London, 1981. Laurel Holliday claims that 'the relation between the male sex organs and aggression has been obvious to animal breeders for centuries; castration has been used to tame aggressive bulls for at least 5,000 years', *The Violent Sex: Male Psychobiology and the Evolution of Consciousness*, Bluestocking Books, 1978. Robin Morgan holds men responsible for 'the evils of sexism, racism, hunger, war and ecological disaster', *Going Too Far*, Random House, 1978. Helen Caldicott maintains that 'if a male has normally functioning androgens . . . he is typically more psychologically aggressive than women . . . the hideous weapons of killing and mass genocide may be a symptom of several *male* emotions', *Missile Envy*, William Morrow, 1984, pp. 295 and 297; my emphasis.

In Europe, recent examples of women who endorse the premises of Valerie Solanas though *not* her logical conclusion include the London-based Matriarchy Study Group, the French biologist Odette Thiabault,[16] Anne-Marie de Vilaine in *Sorcières*,[17] and the Norwegian Birgit Brock-Utne.[18] It is disturbing that Solanas's premises have been accepted by so many feminists in the West who, unlike Solanas herself, have failed to perceive where the logic of those same shared premises must lead them. For not only did Valerie Solanas say what other women had only dared to think, she also dared to say what they had *not* dared to think but what was in fact the inescapable conclusion of what they had begun to think. For if men are genetically programmed to perpetrate violence and war, and women alone can relate and love, then it must follow that for life on earth to survive, we shall have to have a woman-only world. The male must die. If he is not willing to die, he must be exterminated. Working backwards, if we are not willing even to fantasize about the extermination of men, then we must believe that men are not irredeemable, that they do not have to have recourse to war-waging until the whole world is destroyed, and that war is not a biologically determined gender issue.

The best-known British women's peace protest in recent years, based at Greenham, was not separatist feminist at the outset but began as a humanist protest against World War III-readiness. In August 1981, 36 women, four men and a few children responded to Ann Pettitt's call to march from Cardiff in Wales to the American Cruise Missile base at Greenham in order to bring pressure on the British government to permit a parliamentary debate about the

Herrad Schenk, *Frauen Kommen ohne Waffen*, pp. 194–5, cites a European admirer of Valerie Solanas, the French radical feminist Francoise d'Eaubonne, who published 'Eine Rose für Valerie' in her *Feminismus oder Tod*, Frauenoffensive, Munich, 1975.

[16] See 'Les inquiétudes d'une biologiste, féministe et pacifiste', in Le Bricquir and Thiabault (eds), *Féminisme et pacifisme même combat*, Les Lettres Libres, Paris, 1975: 'The compulsion to kill is deep-rooted in the heart of man – by which I mean the human male . . . The [biological] links between virility and aggression are well known. One can say that [war] is the most important festival for men . . . the great Carnival where everything is permitted – theft, rape, pillage, torture.'

[17] See the February 1980 number of *Sorcières* devoted to 'Murdered nature'.

[18] e.g. 'We should help men to think and feel like women' – Birgit Brock-Utne in *Education for Peace: A Feminist Perspective*, Pergamon Press, 1985.

projected deployment of the missiles. The British government ignored them and some of the women then decided to remain at Greenham, 'entrenching' themselves in a woman-only peace camp, believing that neither the British government nor the people could simply continue to ignore the issue. Scores of these 'Greenham women' and those who joined them have suffered much harassment and even violence, hundreds have been arrested for 'obstruction' and fined or jailed. The humanism that inspired them was expressed in statements like that of Sarah: 'A woman in Russia is the same as myself, the same emotions, leading the same sort of life. In no way will I be part of anything that will murder her.'[19] Or the women's statement at Newbury Magistrates Court, 14 April 1982: 'We are concerned with the preservation of all life. How dare the government presume the right to kill others in our names?'[20] Or Stephanie Bowgett: 'Blowing up or threatening to blow up innocent people is wrong, and I, for one, will not let anyone do such a thing in my name without protest.'[21] Or Alice Cook and Gwynne Kirk in their Conclusion to *Greenham Women Everywhere*: 'People have a wealth of skill, intelligence, creativity and wisdom. We could be . . . making a society which is life-affirming in all its aspects.'

The Greenham women's peace camp found such an echo among other women in the British peace movement as a whole at first, that in December 1982, over 35,000 women of all ages and all occupations went to Greenham to respond to the call: 'Embrace the base!' We went there (this writer included), in order to try to make ourselves audible and visible in our protest against the inhumanity and senselessness of nuclear war preparations. We simply could not believe that preparing for nuclear war would prevent nuclear war any more permanently than preparing for non-nuclear war had prevented any of the non-nuclear wars of the past. Up on the nine-mile perimeter wire fence went our children's drawings, our family snaps, a headmistress's class photo of her last sixth form, nappies, bootees, the covers of our favourite records, pictures of the children of our putative 'enemy' in Eastern Europe, quotations from our most revered writers and thinkers, prints of our best loved paintings – an

[19] Sarah, quoted in *The Greenham Factor*, Greenham Print Prop, London, 1983.
[20] Alice Cook and Gwynne Kirk, *Greenham Women Everywhere*, Pluto Press, 1983.
[21] ibid.

Open Letter to the World. Around the perimeter fence we planted seeds, bulbs, shoots and saplings as a symbolic counter-statement to nuclear missiles being patrolled by military police, helicopters, guards in watch-towers and Alsatian dogs on short leads. Not only did we renounce the material preparations for World War III, we repudiated our rulers' psychological war-preparedness also. We yearned for an end to the Cold War.

It is significant, in retrospect, that our symbolic offerings on that fence in 1982 were not exclusively female – pictures of fathers, husbands, lovers, brothers and sons were also tied on the wire; the music and painting and literature quoted included the creative and humane work of men as well as of women. Without consciously making a 'humanity comes in two sexes' statement, I remember sewing a photograph of Käthe Kollwitz on to my 'Greenham banner' beside the picture of a vulnerable man's hand that had been carved by Tilman Riemenschneider 500 years before; I took a photo of cheeky small boys I had recently seen outside an East German kindergarten as well as photos of my own children of both sexes. As the candles were lit around the base at nightfall we played Kathleen Ferrier singing, from Bach's St Matthew Passion, the protest 'Ihr Henker, haltet ein!' (You executioners, stop!) after Pilate has washed his hands. Absurd, perhaps, to have hoped that such emotion-laden icons might help to make peace-makers of the powerful. But for a little while we did hope and possibly there was a slight shift in British public opinion.

Now, six years later, that early bonding between the Greenham peace camp and the tens of thousands of women active in the British anti-war movement has largely broken down. The sheer logistics of maintaining a continuous camp at the base without any co-ordinating organization has meant that the 'Greenham women' had to become a self-selected and unusual group of volunteers without dependants. Gradually, increasing emphasis came to be placed upon the *feminist* significance of the camp as a 'woman's space' surviving through all weathers and despite the brutal efforts of men – police, bailiffs and army – ranged to destroy it every day. The embattled *camp* became the focus of attention rather than the military base against which it was protesting, and the threat of nuclear world war itself became subsumed under the 'real' enemy – 'male violence'. Understandably many of these women campers became more and more psychologically entrenched in their female separatism.[22] My own unease at the direction that Greenham was taking came a year or so after December 1982, when, once again, I went to a mass gathering of women there and wanted to play a tape of Paul Robeson singing, in Harlem, 'We are climbing Jacob's Ladder' – only to realize that a man's voice, any man's voice, was now unacceptable. And where Robeson was unacceptable I could no longer wish to be.

Separatist feminism is a totally understandable response to abhorrent, crude masculinism – as instanced in the deplorable and despicable vilification of the Greenham women in the popular press,[23] or in the sexually contemptuous, sadistic and death-centred training of an American marine. But one fascism cannot be defeated by another. And the delusion that war is, at bottom, the biologically determined product of the violent male *can* only lead either to fascist fantasies of the extermination of men as a sex, as in Solanas, or else to day-dreams of miraculous conversion on the part of men who recognize at last that they will be saved by faith in women alone. But, as Jean Bethke Elshtain has commented tartly: 'despite the paeans to the day when the beautiful [female] souls all get together to curb the primitive [male] beasts and usher in the reign of harmony and peace, no sane person really believes in this outcome.'[24] A separatist feminist *peace* movement is a contradiction in terms: we are hardly overcoming our lethal propensity for enmity when we insist that no less than half our species should be perceived as the 'real' enemy.

Most women in the contemporary West European anti-war movement are not fundamentalist, separatist feminists however, but humanist feminists. In West Germany, the feminist theologian Dr Dorothee Sölle, author of *Armaments Kill Even Without a War*[25] and *In the House of the Man-eater: Texts on Peace*[26] has said in a recent interview that feminism must not become another form of racism, preaching the necessary exclusion of the male from the

[22] See Caroline Blackwood, *On the Perimeter*, Heinemann, 1984.
[23] See Ulrike Meinhof, '"Revolting women": subversion and its media representation in West Germany and Britain', in S. Reynolds (ed.), *Women, State and Revolution*, Wheatsheaf/Harvester, 1986, and University of Massachusetts Press, 1987.
[24] J. Steinhem (ed.), *Women and Men's Wars*, Pergamon, Oxford, 1983.
[25] D. Sölle, *Aufrüstung tötet auch ohne Krieg*, Kreuz Verlag, Stuttgart, 1982.
[26] D. Sölle, *Im Hause de Menschenfressers*, Rowohlt, 1986.

creation of a peaceful 'new order' on account of an alleged irredeemably aggressive chromosome: 'By the word feminism, I understand 'humanity-movement' [*Menschheitsbewegung*] . . . Feminism is the awareness that one cannot leave out half of humanity, including that female half in men themselves.'[27]

The Dutch feminist theologian Professor Dr Catharina Halkes, in her recent address 'Women's Work for Peace in a Patriarchal Society', agrees:

> We should not speak about women as a homogeneous group or caste who have everything in common. Women live in very different contexts, cultures, economic classes, races. The only thing that we have in common is that we have the same type of bodies . . .
>
> I reject the biologically-determinist view that men are inherently aggressive, while women are naturally nurturing . . . My own thesis is that differences between the sexes stem from social conditioning, i.e. learned behaviours . . .
>
> As a theologian I believe that all human beings are created after God's image and likeness. This means that we are called to live in a creative liberating way by transcending all these man-made social roles and norms imposed on us.
>
> . . . women are not better than men or, as Letty Russell, a well-known American theologian would say: women are also sinners.[28]

Catharina Halkes agrees with Dorothee Sölle and Christa Wolf (and with Virginia Woolf 50 years earlier) that men have been educated 'not only to kill others as enemies, but also to kill the enemy of tenderness, love and care within themselves. The linking of male sexuality to aggression is the root both of patriarchy and of war.'[29]

[27] Heike Mundzeck, *Als Frau ist es wohl leichter, Mensch zu werden*: *Gespräche mit Dorothee Sölle, etc.*, Rowohlt, 1985, p. 45.

[28] Keynote speech to the 23rd congress of the Women's International League for Peace and Freedom, held in the Netherlands, 1986, published in *Women Unite for Justice and Peace*, WILPF Int. HQ, Geneva, Switzerland. Dr Catharina J. M. Halkes is emeritus professor in Feminism and Christianity at the Catholic University of Nijmegen, Netherlands. In 1977 she started the project 'Feminism and Christianity', an initiative which was recognized in 1983 with the first and only chair in the field of feminist theology in Europe.

[29] ibid.

The male is made to fear that he will become a castrated male if he surrenders to the 'weakness' of sensitivity to vulnerable others; thus he is moulded into 'hardness', conditioned into becoming a dominating and aggressive fighting-male. 'I do not hate men,' says Catharina Halkes, 'I hate the patriarchal system which dehumanizes many men.' And we women are far from totally innocent in this system; in so far as we continue to acquiesce in it we are colluding with it. 'It is not in violence but in the passive acceptance of authority that I perceive the present war-danger today.'[30] The alternative to the dominance/acquiescence system of patriarchy is, according to Catharina Halkes:

> a different way to understand power, viz. as derived from 'posse', that which we can do; power as our inner strength, our capacities. Feminists talk of power as a *means to empower others* and of the possibility of sharing power instead of concentrating it at the top. Empowering others implies that we need power ourselves, not to dominate or to keep it for ourselves, but on the understanding that if I am to have room to live, I have to enable others to have their own room to live . . . Empowering instead of dominating over is the first task for the male on behalf of the female sex. Then we all of us women and men could become powerful human beings, by enabling men to accept the caring and loving aspects within themselves and, together, to refuse violent competition and destruction of humanity and cosmos.[31]

The French academic Dr Theresia Sauter-Bailliet agrees:

> A world in which women are just as culturally creative as men and men just as close to the body and to nature as women would correct our sexual, political and ecological imbalance . . . For such a transformation of the world, the good will of women and of men is necessary.[32]

In Britain, the most sustained critique of separatist, self-adulatory feminism and its claims to save the world has been made by Lynne

[30] ibid.
[31] ibid.; my emphasis.
[32] T. Sauter-Bailliet, 'Le lien entre feminisme et pacifisme en Allemagne', in Le Bricquir and Thiabault, *Féminisme et pacifisme*.

Segal in *Is the Future Female*? Like Clara Ragaz 40 years earlier, Lynne Segal points out: 'The weight of responsibility for one's own children can mean a contraction of social vision, an envy and resentment of the welfare of others . . . women are not necessarily . . . any less nationalistic, racist or committed to class privilege than men.'[33] As a socialist, Lynne Segal argues for joint engagement by women and men

> in a whole variety of political campaigns against militarism and arms production. [This] means facing the difficulties of economic planning to convert military industries to other forms of production (when cutbacks in defence spending would cause major dislocation of much of British industry) and formulating a programme for major restructuring of the economy away from military production.[34]

One outstanding example of a woman who has engaged in precisely this radical peace-centred economic thinking about the need for conversion from military production is the Swedish United Nations expert Inga Thorsson. Inspired by her friend and fellow economist the late Dame Barbara Ward,[35] Inga Thorsson has never tired of insisting that our world's resources must and *can be* redistributed 'so that the fundamental necessities of human life, such as clean water, food, elementary health care and schooling, are available to all people throughout the world'.[36]

[33] Lynne Segal, *Is the Future Female*, Virago, 1987, ch. 6, p. 6.

[34] ibid., ch. 5, 'Men, women and war', pp. 201–2. One outstanding example of such work in Britain is Mary Kaldor's study of the economic disadvantages (and military uselessness), of our perpetually innovating modern military technology, in her *The Baroque Arsenal*, Deutsch, 1982. See especially her conclusion on the urgent need to evolve institutional, including industrial, alternatives to this arsenal.

[35] Barbara Ward was the author of *The Decade of Development: A Study in Frustration*? Overseas Development Institute, 1965, and *Progress for a Small Planet*, T. Smith, London, 1979.

[36] From the fourth question (based on the UN Charter) now being put to all UN member states by the Great Peace Journey. The other questions now being put to all the governments of the world by the Swedish women who initiated the Great Peace Journey (chaired by Inga Thorsson), are: (1) Are you willing to forbid your country's defence forces from leaving your own country's territory – if all other UN countries do the same? (2) Are you willing to forbid nuclear weapons and other weapons of mass destruction in your country – if all other UN countries do the same? (3) Are you willing to forbid the export of weapons from your country – if all other UN countries do the same? (4) Are you willing to solve future conflicts

Between 1978 and 1981 Inga Thorsson chaired the United Nations study on the positive potential links between disarmament and development. That study concluded that: 'The world finds itself today at a crossroad. It can either pursue the present course of intensified arms race or it can change direction, choose another road, which leads to a more sustainable economic and political order. It cannot do both.' Inga Thorsson alerted the world's governments to the need to plan in advance for any national economic problems entailed in future disarmament measures and to work out beforehand ways of *converting* the resources used for weapons and weapon systems to useful civilian purposes. None of the governments have made any attempt to do this, with the exception of Sweden, which, in 1984, commissioned Inga Thorsson to report on the economic and manpower viability of conversion from military to civil production in Sweden. She concluded that:

> If Nato and the Warsaw Treaty Organisation were to cut their total military forces by half including a sharper reduction of their clearly offensive units, Sweden could also reduce its defence effort by 50% without renouncing its security-policy of maintaining independence and security.
>
> This disarmament [would] involve a progressive reduction in military efforts over a 25 year period (1990–2015) . . . There is reason to believe that the effects of disarmament would be manageable . . . [If] well planned and carried out gradually, [they] would not lead to increased unemployment. The Swedish economy as a whole would undoubtedly benefit from disarmament. Moreover resources released from the defence sector could be used not only to improve economic and social conditions in Sweden but also to increase international development cooperation with the Third World above and beyond the present Swedish goal of devoting 1% of the GNP to development assistance.[37]

In July 1986, Inga Thorsson submitted a paper to the 23rd

with other nations through peaceful means, and not through military actions or threats?

[37] *In Pursuit of Disarmament: Report by the Special Expert, Inga Thorsson*, vol. 1B: *Summary, Appraisals, Recommendations*, Stockholm, 1984. See also *In Pursuit of Disarmament*, vol. 1A: *Background and Analyses*.

International Congress of the Women's International League for Peace and Freedom, meeting in the Netherlands, in which she outlined an alternative definition of 'security' which may be seen as analogous to Catharina Halkes' alternative definition of 'power'. Inga Thorsson began by pointing out that in 1978 the United Nations General Assembly published a Final Document summarizing the findings of its First Special Session on Disarmament. 'The word security in that document was used twenty-five times and in every place the term was used in its old and still prevalent sense of military security against military attacks.' She went on to assert our crucial and urgent need for 'a redefinition of the [very] concept of security' which would include the idea of security from the *non*-military threats of degrading poverty, hunger, disease, unemployment, homelessness and illiteracy. From this point of view 'security purposes' for the use of world resources would mean *not* 'military purpose' at all, but 'peaceful development purposes'. She quoted the statistics which we are in such danger of not registering in our imagination:

> There are 500 million undernourished in the developing world, 800 million illiterate adults, 1.5 billion without medical services and as many unemployed . . . There is one soldier per 43 people but only one doctor for 1,030 people. Every minute thirty children die from hunger . . . and disease and every minute the world spends two million US dollars for military purposes.

In a speech on 'Militarization and Underdevelopment' given at an International Convention of the European Campaign for Nuclear Disarmament held at Coventry in July 1987, Inga Thorsson hammered home more of these facts of life:

> Arms imports are responsible for 24% of the Third World Debt Burden . . .
>
> In Africa, the country with the highest military budget has the lowest life expectancy, and that with the lowest military budget the highest life expectancy.

Thus in the 1980s Inga Thorsson is reiterating the call once made by Kate Courtney in 1919 'to save the lives of the children of Europe' (see above, ch. 2), but today Inga Thorsson is having to enlarge the scope of that cry to include *all* the world's children. Like Kate Courtney, Inga Thorsson believes that the conservation of life could also serve us as our antidote to war: she too believes in Peace Through Bread – Bread that is redistributed fairly according to a mature, just, international economic system.[38]

One important difference between Inga Thorsson and earlier women anti-militarists is her new realization of the ecological issues in our global future and of the links between such issues and modern war preparations. It was the birth of the nuclear energy industry developed purportedly for peaceful uses, but in fact 'incidentally' for the manufacture of weapons-grade plutonium, with all that same industry's latent dangers – which first alerted people to possible links between our endangered ecology and contemporary weapons production. We now know we have gone too far too fast in our reliance on developing nuclear reactors, both because we have produced toxic and virtually indestructible radioactive waste which we still do not know how or where to store, and because of the immense hazards of nuclear reactor technology, and the decommissioning of spent reactors.

Some of the first people in Europe to articulate the world's new reasons for fear were the German Greens, among them a great many women.[39] In March 1983, in the Preamble to their *Bundesprogramm*, they warned that the established political parties in Germany

> are leading us to the hopeless alternative of nuclear state or nuclear war, Harrisburg or Hiroshima . . . Our foremost principle is that human goals cannot be achieved by inhumane means . . . Worldwide disarmament is a must. Nuclear, biological and chemical weapons must be destroyed on a world scale, and troops must be withdrawn from foreign territories. Humanity can only survive if right takes the place of might.[40]

To the Greens, the only real defence in the twenty-first century

[38] cf. 'The more sophisticated questions of national grouping and territorial control would gradually adjust themselves if the paramount human question of food for the hungry were fearlessly and drastically treated upon an international basis.' Jane Addams, *Peace and Bread*, 1924 (reprinted G.K. Hall, Boston, Mass. 1960).

[39] e.g. Petra Kelly, Eva Quistorp, Christa Nichels, Antje Voltmer, Beck Oberdorf, Halo Saibold and also a great many less prominent women at the grass roots.

[40] *Programme of the German Green Party*, tr. Jonathan Porritt, Heretic Books, London, 1983, p. 6.

must mean evolving new forms of 'social defence' by means of 'civil courage, resistance, alternative and decentralised structures [so] as to make immediately clear to an aggressive foreign power that attempted occupation and domination would entail more difficulties and a greater burden than the increase in power and profit it might bring'.[41] The women in the German Green Party are inspired by a humanist, non-separatist vision of women's political responsibility in the contemporary world:

> The aim of the Greens is a humane society built on complete equality of the sexes in the context of an overall ecological policy. Carrying through this survival policy will require the utmost participation of women in the political arena in safeguarding the life of the next generation together with men.[42]

The immense contribution that women have made to ecological thinking during the 1980s, not just in West Germany but throughout the whole world – one has only to remember the Chipko forest-protecting women in India and their spokeswoman Vandana Shiva,[43] or the women for a Nuclear-Free and Independent Pacific, or the many women ecologists in Scandinavia, Italy, Australia and Brazil – testifies to the value of a non-separatist approach. Women contribute most, it would seem, when they are least conscious of being women as opposed to being men, and are most conscious of being fellow humans facing, together with men, a common peril.

The Greens have influenced priorities, policies and actual government measures far beyond Western Europe. Confirmed by recent near-catastrophes such as that at Harrisburg and the appalling human and environmental catastrophes of Bhopal and Chernobyl, the Green ecological perspective on global thinking has become increasingly influential in almost every part of the world. As evidence of this, in December 1983 the General Assembly of the United Nations called into being a World Commission on Environment and Development in order to formulate 'a global agenda for change'. The Commission consisted of environmental experts from all the major countries of the world, both communist and anti-communist. The person called

[41] ibid., p. 9.
[42] ibid.; my emphasis.
[43] See 'Ecology Movements in India', *Alternatives*, 11, (1986), pp. 255–73.

on to establish and chair this special commission was a woman, Gro Brundtland, the leader of the Norwegian Labour Party, a former Minister for the Environment and now the Prime Minister of Norway. Gro Brundtland had already served both on the Brandt Commission on North–South issues and on Olaf Palme's Commission on Security and Disarmament; she was supremely well-placed, therefore, to see the causal interconnections between our short-sighted exploitation of the environment, both North and South, and our equally short-sighted East/West reliance upon 'nuclear deterrence': '[As] part of our "development", we have amassed weapons arsenals capable of diverting the paths that evolution has followed for millions of years and of creating a planet our ancestors would not recognize.'[44]

The findings of the World Commission – which were unanimous – were not as gloom-laden, however, as one might have expected:

> This Commission believes that people can build a future that is more prosperous, more just, and more secure. Our report, *Our Common Future*, is not a prediction of ever increasing environmental decay, poverty and hardship in an ever more polluted world among ever decreasing resources. We see instead the possibility for a new era of economic growth, one that must be based on policies that sustain and expand the environmental resource base . . . But the Commission's hope for the future is conditional.[45]

One condition that must be met is that the deepening and widening global environmental crisis should be halted before it becomes a source of political unrest and international tension. A second condition is the curtailment of military spending that is now damaging so many societies' development efforts – as Inga Thorsson had pointed out. The third and most fundamental condition for our creation of a more prosperous and a more just world, is, it goes without saying, that we avert nuclear war:

> Studies suggest that the cold and dark nuclear winter following even a limited nuclear war could destroy plant and animal ecosystems and leave any human survivors occupying a devas-

[44] *Our Common Future*, Report of The World Commission on Environment and Development, OUP, 1987, Foreword, pp. 1–23.
[45] ibid., 'From one earth to one world – an overview'.

> tated planet very different from the one they inherited. Among the dangers facing the environment, the possibility of nuclear war is undoubtedly the gravest.[46]

Gro Brundtland's Commission concluded that 'a comprehensive approach to international and national security must transcend the traditional emphasis on military power and armed competition.'[47] In other words, for the world's very survival, the nations' rulers must now grow up and discard their outdated Bismarckian assumption that *Machtpolitik* is the only realistic mode of politics. As the Commission points out, 'There are no military solutions to environmental insecurity.' The Commission continues:

> The world spent well over 900 billion US dollars on military purposes in 1985 . . . The real cost is what the same resources might otherwise be used for: an Action Plan for Tropical Forests would cost . . . the equivalent of half a day of military expenditure world-wide each year for 5 years.
>
> Implementing the UN Action Plan against Desertification would cost the equivalent of less than two days of military spending every year for twenty years.
>
> Clean water could have been provided for all at the approximate equivalent of ten days of military spending.[48]

The choices before us are clear indeed. The Brundtland Commission concluded with three 'musts' for us all:

> Nations must not become prisoners of their own arms race. They must face the common danger inherent in the weapons of the nuclear age. They must face the common challenge of providing for sustainable development and act in concert to remove the growing environmental sources of conflict.[49]

The report of the Brundtland Commission brings every argument available to reason and every relevant fact at our disposal to bear upon our current global predicaments in order to suggest a positive approach to their solution. But reason and facts alone, however

46 ibid.
47 ibid., ch. 11.
48 ibid.
49 ibid. See the Commission's twelfth chapter: 'Towards common action: proposals for institutional and legal change'.

telling, will not succeed in triggering an enlightened, humane collective determination to construct a sane, just world. For, as the poet Shelley perceived more than one hundred and fifty years ago:

> There is no want of knowledge respecting what is wisest and best in morals, government, and political economy, or at least what is wiser and better than what men now practise and endure. But we let *I dare not* wait upon *I would*, like the poor cat in the adage. We want the creative faculty to imagine that which we know; we want the generous impulse to act that which we imagine; we want the poetry of life.[50]

In other words, we need to 'see it feelingly', as Gloucester said in *King Lear*; and it is imagination, rooted in experience, that best enables us to do so. There have, of course, been many attempts to make us see just where our irrational rulers, our righteous enmities, our militaristic reflexes and nuclear mega-technology could now be taking us – poems like those by the American women writers quoted in the previous chapter; films such as *The War Game*, *Threads*, or *Letters from a Dead Man*; apocalyptic painting and music and novels such as Christa Wolf's *Cassandra*.

But will anything short of a nuclear weapons accident upon our own soil teach us to 'see feelingly' in time?

[50] P. B. Shelley, *The Defence of Poetry*, written 1824.

10

Conclusion

> We cannot be made better except by the influence upon us of what is better than we are . . . We can find something better than ourselves . . . in the past.
>
> Simone Weil, 'The Romanesque Renaissance' (1942), in *Selected Essays*

Every informed adult now alive acknowledges that we have the potential to wipe ourselves out. The adherents of iron-fisted *Realpolitik*, however, among them notably and vociferously Margaret Thatcher, Jeanne Kirkpatrick and Olga Maitland, regard this potential for self-destruction not as a problem, rightly understood, but as a blessing. Our rulers no longer try to affirm, as von Treitschke did between 1870 and 1890, that war is really a good thing. Nevertheless they persist in maintaining that even a nuclear war would be less terrible than domination by an enemy power, and they try to reassure us that our computerized, hair-trigger readiness to initiate or retaliate in a nuclear war is precisely what will prevent such a war from ever breaking out. But 'forever' is a long time, and contemporary anti-militarists, both men and women, are not so sanguine about our prospects – for reasons that are philosophical, historical, technical and psychological.

Philosophers point out that since existence is a continuous succession of changes, the only constants being conflict, instability and unpredictable conjunctures of events not wholly within human control, it is inconceivable that any status quo could possibly last forever. Historians remind us of past examples of wars which were not prevented by armed 'deterrence' but rather in part caused by the very momentum, the tension and the delusions of strength inherent in every arms race – particularly when master-minded by hubristic leaders.[1] Contemporary historians and scientists cite the many technical and/or human errors that have already caused catastrophic disasters in our century – for instance Bhopal and Chernobyl – and that have more than once only just missed causing the global horror of an accidental nuclear war.[2] Meanwhile the terrible secret weapons systems continue to 'advance' and proliferate until, in the twenty-first century, who knows what mega-destroyer will go out of control, who knows where? 'Why ask to know what date, what clime? . . .[3] For the psychologists, in their turn, tell us that we only do to other people what we have been conditioned to believe it possible to do; the reason that we no longer commit such abominations as ritual human sacrifice, witch-burning, slave-auctioning or the gassing of children is that we have now been conditioned to deem such acts unthinkable. Culturally they are not on our agenda. It is our very 'preparedness' to risk incinerating alive all 'enemy' children via a remote controlled, multiple missile or laser strike that far from preventing such an atrocity, may well enable it one day to happen.

But how on earth could we ever have come to such a pass as this preparedness to torture other people's children to death? Do we not believe that every human being is a human being and in our individual relationships do we not usually try to act on that

[1] See George Kennan on the causes of World War I in 'Cease this madness!', *UN Disarmament Times*, vol. 2, no. 11; and J. G. Stoessinger, *Why Nations Go to War*, St Martin's Press, 1974, ch. 7.

[2] See Gwyn Prins (ed.), *Defended to Death: A Study of the Nuclear Arms Race from the Cambridge University Disarmament Seminar*, Penguin, 1983. chs 4 and 8.

[3] The last lines Emily Brontë wrote:
Why ask to know what date, what clime?
There dwelt our own humanity,
Power worshippers from earliest time,
Foot-kissers of triumphant crime
Crushers of helpless misery,
Shedders of blood, shedders of tears,
Self-cursers avid of distress;
Yet mocking heaven with senseless prayers,
For mercy on the merciless.

Gro Brundtland, Prime Minister of Norway.

assumption? But our collective interaction is a different matter. There, neither in theory nor in practice, do we start from the premise that all humans are human. And the consequence is the iron-fistedness of most of our rulers and of all too many of the ruled – including, in particular, every militant political group. It is not only Israel and White South Africa that pursue an open and unapologetic policy of the iron fist. Righteous collective hatreds rooted in collective fears, rooted in their turn in the traumatic memories of collective suffering, produce a collective, abstract 'enemy' – and in this way countless people become 'the disappeared ones' of our day. It is this undiagnosed, schizoid split between our pseudo-moral collective psychology, driven on by what we fear may be done to us, and our authentically ethical personal psychology, animated by how we feel we ought to behave towards others, that makes possible our paranoid preparedness to commit collective mass murder.

The women thinkers discussed in this book, however, did diagnose our condition. Their political philosophy, grounded in authentic personal ethics, offers us not only an alternative but also an antidote to the cynical, paranoid equation of all the Bismarcks: '*Realpolitik* = *Machtpolitik*'. They have worked out alternative, constructive definitions of such terms as 'reality', 'realism', 'security' and 'power', their most important and subversive contribution being, in my opinion, the deconstruction and rejection of the very concept of 'the enemy'. For if there is no 'enemy' there is no need for an iron fist – and consequently no need for iron leaders equipped with that essential member.

It was Kate Courtney, the most unassuming of all these thinkers, who first pointed out the wickedness and folly of extending our revulsion at the acts of people in power to all those *not* in power under them. Kate Courtney insisted on taking apart the construct of 'the enemy', in order to reveal the manifold, pitiable, human realities beneath. To her 'the enemy' was no more, and never less, than 'the most unfortunate because most hated people',[4] whether such people were Boer women and children dying in British concentration camps in South Africa, or German prisoners and internees in World War I Britain, or Austrian and German women starving in Europe because of the Allied food-blockade after that war was officially over.

[4] Kate Courtney's letter to *The Times*, 26 March 1915.

Our so-called 'enemy', in Kate Courtney's view, are in reality not villains but victims – the victims both of their own brutal rulers' oppression and indoctrination and, simultaneously, of others' righteous enmity towards them. 'The enemy' are those people whom we are most in danger of hurting or wiping out; enmity itself is our real 'enemy within'.

The idea that millions of people somewhere 'over there' constitute an ever-present threat to us was also rejected, a priori, by Maude Royden. Her Utopian advocacy of unarmed intervention between the very ranks of the embattled, and of lying down in front of the troop-trains that take men to war, was intended as a testimony that love for the victims of both sides can be a greater force for good than any righteous hatred towards an assailant. Like Kate Courtney, Maude Royden believed that we need to tackle the 'Prussianism' first of all within ourselves and on our own side, rather than allow our own country to become ever more authoritarian, militaristic and ruthless – under cover of a vaunted detestation of all 'Prussianism'.

Simone Weil went still further than did Kate Courtney and Maude Royden in the intellectual and linguistic analysis of enmity, alerting us to the inflated abstractions so often invoked by those in power – verbal fig-leaves that conceal their own compulsive need to prepare to wage yet another war for war and power's sake:

> What a country calls its vital economic interests are not the things which enable its citizens to live, but the things which enable it to make war; petrol is much more likely than wheat to be a cause of international conflict. Thus when war is waged it is for the purpose of safeguarding or increasing one's capacity to make war.[5]

But that, of course, is what we are never told. Instead we are told that we must defend such abstractions as 'national security', 'democracy', or 'socialism' and be ready to destroy other abstractions such as 'imperialism', or 'communism'. Precisely because these over-simplified abstractions are not quite real it is impossible ever to prove their non-existence and yet countless real, complex, irreplaceable people are destroyed in their name.

[5] Simone Weil, 'The Power of Words', (March 1937) in Rees, (ed.) *Simone Weil: Selected Essays, 1934–43*, OUP, 1962.

> For our contemporaries the role of Helen is played by words with a capital letter. If we grasp one of these words, all swollen with blood and tears, and squeeze it, we find it is empty . . . it is a characteristic of these words that each of them has its complementary antagonist. [And tragically], corresponding to each empty abstraction there is an actual human group.[6]

Virginia Woolf also considered national enmity to be totally irrational and unreal. 'Why should charity cease as the Channel boat starts?'[7] Even the German pilot flying above her head in 1941 ready to drop a bomb on her was simply a young man who, when brought down in a nearby field, could tell his captors how glad he was his war was over. What really mattered to Virginia Woolf at the end of her life – just as it did to Maude Royden and Simone Weil – was that we should all bring the 'unconscious Hitlerism' within ourselves up to the level of our consciousness,[8] so that we might be enabled in time to confront those twin destroyers – our drive for domination and our need for acquiescent subservience.

For Sophie Scholl, it was even more blatantly obvious that the real enemy was not some inhuman abstraction such as 'Jewish finance' or 'Russian Bolshevism', but the grotesque actual inhumanity of her own side towards millions of Jews and Slavs dehumanized in the Nazi slogans of hate and fear. Therefore she chose, even at the cost of her life, 'treasonable' solidarity with the so-called 'enemies of Germany' who were in fact the tortured victims of a mass enmity-psychosis.

More recently, the East German communist writer Christa Wolf has caused her Trojan heroine Cassandra to discover, when captive in Mycenae, that Troy's hated Other, the Greeks, were really the Trojans' Greek selves: 'They are like us! . . . we are all alike. The difference lies in whether we know it.'[9] And that difference in knowing exists *within* each armed camp; it is not the difference between them.

[6] ibid.
[7] Virginia Woolf, First scrapbook for *Three Guineas*, 1935, Monks House Papers, B16f, p. 38.
[8] Virginia Woolf, 'Thoughts on peace in an air-raid' (Sept. 1940), in *The Death of the Moth*, Hogarth Press, 1942.
[9] Christa Wolf, *Cassandra*, Virago, 1984, pp. 12–13.

Similarly that incorrigible idealist, Helen Keller, insisted that our best real 'preparedness' is a politics that disarms enmity, and that in reality, for life to go on at all, we must live by each other and for each other, not each against the rest. After Helen Keller's death Muriel Rukeyser and Denise Levertov have persisted in prodding their fellow Americans to question the ideas of an alien 'enemy', an 'evil empire':

> For that I never knew you, I only learned to dread you,
> for that I never touched you, they told me you are filth,
> they showed me by every action to despise your kind;
> for that I saw my people making war on you, . . .
> crushing you, stamping you to death, they poured boiling
> water on you, they flushed you down,
> for that I could not tell one from another,
> only that you were dark, fast on your feet, and slender,
> Not like me.
>
> (Muriel Rukeyser, 'St Roach', from *The Gates*, 1976)

As for the humanist feminists now active in the anti-World War III movement throughout contemporary Europe, it is axiomatic for all of them that the apart-hate of Cold War has been our real enemy within for years, serving the rulers, not the ruled, and that East and West must now come together in a *dis*armament race whose by-product will be sustainable development for the whole world.

But, it will be said, so many of these women – all those who were adult witnesses to Nazism – eventually renounced their absolute rejection of enmity and war because of Hitler. Does that not invalidate them now as witnesses against the notion of a possible 'Just War' in our own nuclear age? To such a question I would reply that although these women did want Hitler to be resisted, they most emphatically did not want him to be out-Hitlered.[10] Furthermore, the war against Hitler did not entail the possible destruction of all life on earth. Faced by another Hitler figure, in the twenty-first century, this time threatening the whole world with weapons of global extermination and to fight against whom would also risk global extermination, I

[10] See Simone Weil's advocacy of de-colonization as a touchstone for genuine anti-fascism and her insistence that the Allies never imitate Hitler either during the war or after his defeat.

believe that these women would advise us to surrender rather than destroy the planet. If a new Judgement of Solomon should ever have to be made, the true parents of the earth would give up their own claims rather than ensure that all other living creatures be tortured to death. Simone Weil spelt it out:

> We owe our respect to a collectivity: First because it is food for a certain number of human souls – each of which is unique and if destroyed cannot be replaced. Secondly, because . . . [it] contains food . . . for the souls of beings yet unborn. Thirdly . . . It constitutes the sole agency for preserving the spiritual treasures accumulated by the dead.[11]

All these women, were they alive today, would, I think, be nuclear pacifists for the very same reason they renounced their 'conventional' pacifism in 1939 – namely their humane, life-reverencing, anti-fascist definition of 'reality'.

To a woman like Helen Keller, the 'real' world is not, as the Bismarckians would always have it, a world of power-relations, but rather a world of vulnerable people, all of whom have the same basic needs and almost all of whom would, in normal circumstances, wish other people's basic needs to be answered as well as their own. A helping human hand, as she of all people had cause to know, is our real daily alternative to the iron fist. A city is not, in reality, nothing more than a numbered, code-named military target on a computer screen; it is also always, as Christa Wolf puts it: 'a place [where] people grew up, the place where they had been humiliated or first fallen in love'.[12] As for the circumambient, fragile beauty of creation both natural and human, that too constituted 'reality' for these women. We have only to remember Kate Courtney's joy over a 'tender evening sky' or Helen Keller's delight in the worlds of scent and touch, or Sophie Scholl's rapture over wind and leaves, or Virginia Woolf's evocation of the mystery and power of music in *Between the Acts* – not to mention the life-nourishing concern for ecology in the work of contemporaries like Inga Thorsson, Gro Brundtland and the Greens.

But 'reality' of course also includes real, terrible, collective conflicts

[11] Simone Weil, *The Need for Roots*, Routledge, 1952, Part I.
[12] Christa Wolf, 'Citadel of reason', 1980 lecture, in *Socialist Register*, 1982.

both of interest and of needs all the time. However, the sane way to the lasting resolution of such conflicts is by negotiation, arbitration and international law, all these women believed, not by stupid, self-defeating and ultimately all-destroying competitions in massacre.

Accompanying their positive, life-centred definitions of 'reality' – definitions that emphasized human kindness and creativity – went an alternative definition of 'realism'. The two novelists, Virginia Woolf and Christa Wolf, and the two poets, Muriel Rukeyser and Denise Levertov, have all challenged the vaunted realism of the military strategists. Military 'realism', they say, is pseudo-realism masking a black-hole nihilism. True realism, in the writers' view, is an imaginative realism that can put other people's emotional experience of life on to the map of the world. Thus when Virginia Woolf forced herself in *Mrs Dalloway* to create the agonized inner life of Septimus Smith, she did so for the sake of 'true reality'.[13] All her writing life she set herself to imagine the 'succession of days which are furled' in others.[14] For Christa Wolf:

> Every place and landscape, everything about human relationships which literature had described minutely, exactly, and partisanly, painfully, critically, devotedly, fearfully and joyfully, ironically, rebelliously and lovingly, should be erased from the [nuclear] strategists' map of death.[15]

To Muriel Rukeyser, poetry has the power 'to equip our imaginations to deal with our lives',[16] and Denise Levertov indicts the whole pernicious *un*realism about 'the disgusting horror of war in the criminally neglected imagination' of the TV-fed American young.[17]

Did it make any significant difference to the thinking of these women that they were women? Their independent-mindedness was most probably strengthened by the fact that they were all to some degree political outsiders – either unenfranchised like Kate Courtney and Simone Weil or else only very recently admitted into political citizenship. Moreover it should always be easier for women than for men to detach themselves from the ideology of war, since war does

[13] Virginia Woolf, *Diary*, 24 Feb. 1926.
[14] ibid., 27 Aug. 1918.
[15] Wolf, 'Citadel of Reason'.
[16] Muriel Rukeyser, *The Life of Poetry* (1949) Kraus reprint, NY, 1968.
[17] Denise Levertov, speech for an antidraft rally, 1980.

not challenge women to prove that they are women, whereas, of course, war has been accepted as the great touchstone of 'manliness' since time immemorial. Virginia Woolf was the only one of these thinkers to find the alleged 'manliness' of war merely contemptible – 'We are all paying now for the manly diversion. Naturally they will have another.'[18] The other women who perceived war's lethal 'masculinity' – most notably Maude Royden, Simone Weil, Denise Levertov and Sharon Olds – felt rather the pity of the distortion of men's spirit by this accursed militarist/masculinist acculturation. They would all have endorsed Catharina Halkes's statement in 1986: 'I do not hate men, I hate the patriarchal system which dehumanizes many men.'[19] However, although they saw war as a human institution, and not an exclusively male one, they did believe that women could bring some profoundly relevant, traditionally female experience and attitudes to bear upon our common problem.

Maude Royden invoked the psychological sensitivity that so many women have had to learn in order to keep even a minimum of peace within each family.

Simone Weil singled out women's work as nurses to symbolize practical, life-sustaining compassion that summed up for her the very essence of *anti*-fascism, and *anti*-militarism.

Virginia Woolf advocated extending the traditionally non-competitive, non-hierarchical and non-acquisitive social work of many women 'Outsiders' to be a model of future practice in the professions – in the hope that the less like jungle animals we were within our own societies, then the less of a jungle we would make our whole world. We might even be able to do some fresh, iconoclastic thinking on what is really meant by 'Defence'.

Most recently, Inga Thorsson has asked for the very concept of 'security' to be redefined by international agreement so as to include, henceforth, the *non*-military life-needs familiar to countless women the world over – security from poverty, security from hunger, security from disease, security from unemployment, security from illiteracy, security from homelessness.

Reinforcing these values, Dr Catharina Halkes has articulated a humanist feminist redefinition of what can be meant by the term

[18] Woolf, Scrapbook for *Three Guineas*.
[19] See above, ch. 9, n. 28.

'power': Power does not have to mean 'power to destroy' or 'power to kill' – it can also mean the power to enable others to have life and to have it more abundantly. 'Feminists talk of power as a means to empower others . . . All of us, women and men, could become powerful human beings, by enabling each other to develop our full potentialities.'[20]

Finally, one shared 'female' aspect of these women's thinking was their lack of embarrassment when writing about children. Childless themselves for the most part, they were, nevertheless, acutely conscious that it is the world's babies who are always the most pitiful sacrifices to the world's weapons and not one of these women was paralysed by a fear of being thought 'sentimental' or 'soft-minded' in saying so. 'Penalising has meant death to the little ones', wrote Kate Courtney as early as 1901.

Nevertheless, despite such unapologetically women-identified perspectives, these women never claimed that women alone can save the world. The antidote to war-validating masculinism is not a holier-than-thou, collectively self-idealizing feminism, they believed, but rather that much-battered and at present unfashionable -ism, humanism. Humanism calls on us 'not to admire force, not to hate the enemy, nor to scorn the unfortunate', as Simone Weil wrote in her essay on *The Iliad*. It advocates compassion for all suffering that cannot be prevented and energetic intervention whenever prevention or remedy is possible – 'for the sense of human misery is a pre-condition of justice and love'.[21] Humanists also maintain that 'Each one of us carries within us the seeds of all possible actions.'[22] Women are precisely as human as men – both for better and for worse. While it is true that women have not been primarily responsible for creating the socio-political, economic, technological and military lunacies of the twentieth century, that is not because women are better than men, it is because women have not, hitherto, had the same opportunities to wield power. It is the nature of political and economic power – the morally dubious routes to its attainment and retention, its crudely simplistic, reductive, adversarial ideologies and

[20] ibid.

[21] Simone Weil, '*The Iliad*, the poem of force' (1940) (see ch. 4 n. 53).

[22] Dr Adelaide Hautval, former slave-doctor at Auschwitz and Ravensbrück, who refused to obey orders to carry out Nazi medical experiments on people, interviewed in *The Listener*, 21 Oct. 1971.

its over-centralized, ever-growing gigantism that constitute our real political problem, these women believed, not simply the sex of the powerful.[23]

None of these women saw herself as proclaiming an exclusively Female Gospel, however. Each was simply testifying in her turn to a humane ethic that had been advocated, as she well knew, by many others, mostly men, long before her. The concept of righteous enmity had been rejected by Sophocles in *Antigone*, by Asoka, by Mencius and by Christ. The conviction that we must feed the destitute and turn our swords into ploughshares to that end – the 'internationalism of the deed' – had been voiced by the Old Testament prophet Micah. The idea that humane law must replace retributive violence is found in the *Eumenides* of Aeschylus' *Oresteia* as well as in Erasmus, in Grotius, in Kant – and in the conclusion to Peter Calvocoressi's recent *A Time for Peace*. Even the insight, so modern and feminist, that the males of the world have been psychologically deformed by war-validating warrior-masculinism was already clearly present in Shakespeare's *Macbeth* and *Coriolanus*. And the ecological principles of the Gro Brundtland Commission and the contemporary world's Greens were familiar to all those Stone-Age cultures in every continent that have reverenced air and water, earth and trees.

But the women in this book were not claiming to have discovered brand-new truths, only to have found their own way and their own words for some age-old ones. And it is not the least of their achievements that when they did at last begin to take their place in the long mental fight against war, they should have done so in a spirit of fellowship with all like-minded people, including men, before them. The crosses on the Munich grave of Hans and Sophie Scholl are joined together as one double cross and that legacy also should not be forgotten. For if ever in the world's history there were a crucial task addressing us all it must surely be the task of averting our own destruction of our species and our planet. Neither sex can

[23] The best analysis I know of the anti-social psychology of the powerful is that by Alastair Mant, in *Leaders we Deserve?*, Martin Robertson, 1983: 'Inadequate leaders do not rise by accident – it is what they have to do to realize their ambitions that renders them unfit, in the end, to bear authority.' See especially ch. 6 on 'the military-industrial idiot'. cf. E. M. Forster to Sassoon: 'Give a man power over the other men and he deteriorates at once' – *Selected Letters of E. M. Forster*, vol. 1, 1879–1920, Collins, 1985.

possibly fulfil this task alone, yet together, side by side, we may still enable one another to uphold the Law against the laws and so parent our world. But it will demand strong minds and stout hearts if we are to succeed in resisting the authoritarian militarism of the iron-fisted ones still in power today.[24] 'Un esprit dur, du coeur tendre', as Sophie Scholl reminded Hartnagel in 1943: 'A tough spirit and a tender heart.' And we also need, in our extremity, all the inspiration that we can summon up from our most humane dead. Hence this book.

[24] Not all those in power now are intransigent in their iron-fistedness. But Gorbachev cannot be left to be Atlas by himself indefinitely.

Index of Names